4808749

THE MANAGEMENT STYLE OF THE CHIEF ACCOUNTANT

To Nora

The management style of the Chief Accountant

A situational perspective

EUGENE F. McKENNA

SAXON HOUSE

© Eugene F. McKenna 1978

 British Library Cataloguing in Publication Data

McKenna, Eugene F
    The management style of the chief accountant.
    1. Accountants 2. Leadership
    I. Title
    658.4'2   HF5657

    ISBN 0-566-00216-7

Published by
Saxon House, Teakfield Limited,
Westmead, Farnborough, Hants., England

ISBN 0 566 00216 7

Printed in Great Britain

Contents

TABLES

FIGURES

Acknowledgements

The research programme on which the monograph is based was financed by the City of Birmingham Polytechnic. I would like to thank the Research Committee and in particular David Burns for providing the facilities and conditions which allowed me to undertake the project.

I am grateful to Russell Wicks of the Department of Psychology, University of Surrey, for his advice and encouragement and to George O'Sullivan of the City of Birmingham Polytechnic for his advice on statistical analysis. My thanks also to Mildred Jelfs who prepared the typescript speedily and efficiently. A project of this type required an enormous amount of co-operation and patience from respondents and interviewees. To the numerous accountants who participated in the study I would like to acknowledge their invaluable assistance.

1 Background to the research

INTRODUCTION

This is a study concerned with the development of
situational leadership theory in relation to the role
and immediate work environment of the Chief Accountant
or Financial Controller in industry. The author's
interest in leadership springs from a research study
for a master's degree when leadership styles were
analysed in relation to a number of individual, managerial and organisational variables. The rationale
for embarking on the present study can be gleaned from
a concluding remark contained in the master's thesis:
'.... future research might begin by constructing a
typology of typical decisions taken by managers within
a work organisation. Each type of decision would then
be related to the leadership continuum, and finally,
within this framework the identification and measurement of situational variables.... could be pursued.
It is felt that such an approach.... would enlarge and
enhance our understanding of leadership styles in
industry' (McKenna, 1972).

Ever since the arrival on the scene of the contingency model of leadership (Fiedler, 1967) the situational approach to leadership has assumed a new importance, though a very minor situational concern has been
expressed by influential participative management
theorists (Likert, 1961; McGregor, 1967). A perusal of
the recent literature on leadership shows clearly the
growing importance attached to the need to consider
situational variables (e.g., Kavanagh, 1972; Bass et
al., 1975; Vroom, 1976). Proponents of the Ohio State
school of leadership felt it necessary to postulate
situational propositions, which they consider more
closely reflect the concern of the school, in the face
of criticism relegating Initiating Structure and Consideration - dimensions of leadership behaviour - to a
position of historical importance (Kerr et al., 1974).

1

They concede, quite rightly, that we have not yet arrived at a point of theoretical adequacy in our quest for a leadership theory. This viewpoint is reinforced by Yukl (1971), who maintains that leadership research has often failed to include intermediate and situational variables which one should consider in order to understand how a leader's actions can affect his subordinate's productivity.

It is both conceptually and physically impossible to define and study the numerous important variables which comprise the situational environment. It is consequently necessary to select environmental elements which are measurable and exert a significant effect on leadership style. The situational and structural variables chosen for the present study reflect the judgement of the author as to what constitutes important immediate environmental variables. They consist of typical decisions facing the Chief Accountant; the extent of specialisation and specialism within the finance function; the status, power and influence attached to the Chief Accountant's position; the qualities and skills deemed important and the extent to which they are possessed by his subordinate; the psychological distance between the Chief Accountant and his least preferred subordinate; the nature of his role within the organisation; his level within the organisational hierarchy; his span of control; the length of time spent in his present position; and the size of the finance function and the organisation. These would then be related to a measure of leadership style; the latter would also be related to dimensions of leadership behaviour. Some, but not all, of the situational or structural variables mentioned have been considered previously in connection with leadership (Heller, 1971; Ritchie and Miles, 1970; Blankenship and Miles, 1968). This then seems to be a concrete and positive approach to leadership theory since it endeavours to incorporate the UK structural tradition (Woodward, 1965; Pugh et al., 1969) and the USA interpersonal tradition (McGregor, 1960; Likert, 1961) in a single framework. Evidence related to the leadership styles of accountants as an occupational group is rather scant and tends to emphasise style without any acknowledgement of the impact of situational or structural variables. McKenna (1972) reports that accountants more than non-financial managers experienced a restrictive leadership style. Heller (1971), for example, suggests that finance and production managers are prone to a centralised style, which is less likely to be the case with personnel and general managers, and attributes this phenomenon to constraints on the degree of freedom suffered by the former group of managers. These constraints are not however made explicit, save reference to different leadership patterns in production and non-production departments (Fleishman et al., 1955), and differentiation in style and productivity between foremen in assembly line production departments as opposed to other departments (Argyle et al., 1958). Perhaps nearer the mark is Heller's reference to a directive style being complementary to highly structured tasks (Shaw and Blum, 1966).

There is, therefore, good justification for undertaking a leadership study of a key manager in the finance function - the Chief Accountant - so as to assess in a more methodical and rigorous fashion 'constraints' on his degree of freedom.

ACCOUNTANTS AS A DISTINCTIVE OCCUPATIONAL GROUP

Initial interest in the social and technical dimensions of the Accountant's role in both a professional and industrial environment was activated and nurtured whilst the author was pursuing a programme of training in the offices of accountants in the early 1960's. Subsequently endowed with a little more wisdom and experience one felt compelled to penetrate the sober and sometimes dull exterior of the accountant and unearth some of the attributes or qualities often the subject of a satirical representation of his personality. This was facilitated by two research programmes which afforded me the opportunity to gain a deeper insight into the influences shaping the attitudes and

3

work orientations of accountants.

As a professional group accountants are an influential body of people engaged in the collection, processing and interpretation of accounting and financial data, and offering a service to management both on an internal and external basis. It has become almost commonplace in recent times for educators and others interested in the academic maturation of the profession of accountancy to level criticisms, in many cases justified, at the standards of education prior and post entry to professional training. Vatter (1963) recognises that accountancy has a right to claim professional status and asserts that with the growth of sophisticated techniques and the development of mature ways of looking at things, more exacting educational standards for entrants to the profession are required. A similar perspective is taken by Lowe (1964) who stresses that there are signs of accounting information systems being no longer self-sufficient. This is also a view shared by Trueblood (1963) with the added comment that accounting will become an integral part of a complex of disciplines or methodologies. The computer will relieve the accountant of the task of processing routine data, opening up the way for a new breed of people with analytical and scientific minds, less inclined to rely on hunches based on historical data with more emphasis given to quantification of variables and recognising the importance of a multidisciplinary approach (Lowe, 1964). This has obvious importance in pointing the way to the development of exacting education standards, with a shift to teaching the individual to be adaptive, to be receptive to new ideas and at the same time have the mental faculties to sift through ideas and assess their relevance.

Over a decade ago in the USA Trueblood (1963) advocated a better balance between business and liberal arts subjects on degree programmes with a bias in favour of accountancy and deprecated programmes emphasising descriptive material. In this country there is a growing recognition that, given the movement of

4

the abler students from the grammar and comprehensive
schools to higher education, the professional educational process must acknowledge the particular needs,
abilities and problems of the graduate. Perrin (1971)
rightly states: 'in recent years the leading spirits
in the profession have recognised that the recruitment
of graduates is essential to prevent the profession
sliding backwards in terms of both the absolute and
relative intelligence and abilities of its entrants,
and also in terms of the profession's perceived status
and authority in the world at large.' He also maintains that the accountancy profession prided itself in
the fruits of craft training which led to the mastery
of relevant techniques together with the acquisition
of the conventional wisdom of the profession. The
drawback in educational terms of this outlook is the
absence of the opportunity 'to learn to conceptualise,
to search out and evaluate alternatives and perhaps
above all to challenge convention with reasoned arguments.' This type of observation appears to have a
firm historical factual basis to it and is substantiated by an earlier experience of two chartered
accountants who pursued a graduate programme of study
in business administration at an American University.
Extolling the challenges and benefits of the courses
offered and favourably commenting on the calibre of
staff they were exposed to, Hughes and Barclay (1967)
went on to say: 'To someone who received his main
theoretical training by dull correspondence course at
the sterile hands of a firm of accounting tutors, the
difference is striking. The constant interaction of
wits in discussion with fellow students, the clarifi-
cation of ideas through the necessity of defending
them before one's peers: all this makes the articled
clerk's formal education emasculated by comparison.'
Perhaps it is fair to say that this view is not now
fully representative of the quality of the educational
process as a one year full time foundation course with
a tendency towards academic rigour is widespread and
obligatory for those proposing to qualify as chartered
accountants. Proposals put forward in the Solomons'
report - Prospectus for a Profession - highlight an
urgency and perhaps determination to raise standards

in both spheres of education and training with the recommendation that non-graduates proposing to enter the profession should first pursue a full time course of at least two years duration leading to a Diploma of Higher Education (Solomons and Berridge, 1974). Apparently the latter proposal is considered by one of the accounting bodies as unsatisfactory on the grounds of the maintenance of standards; other proposals are also contentious for a number of practical reasons, for example, the proposal that students of all accountancy bodies should spend a mandatory period of time in both a practising office and in industry or commerce or the public service.

A typical accusation directed at the type of training received is that the training tends to promote conservative practice rather than an innovative mentality (Tricker, 1967). There is little doubt that preoccupation with educational and training standards is generating serious attempts to upgrade standards of education and training. This momentum is welcome in a period of rapidly developing technology and its application in a number of areas including accounting. In due course, perhaps future events will in some way dilute the substance of a justifiable assertion by Perrin (1971): 'Indeed the profession has sometimes been accused of a distinctly anti-intellectual bias - and at least a few of its members have seemed to glory in accepting the accusation as a compliment.'

Various speculations centre on the question of whether certain personality types choose accountancy as a career or alternatively whether certain socialisation processes mould individuals of different personality patterns to produce certain identifiable behaviour characteristics of the accountant. Accountants as a group are likely to be practical, realistic, resolute, make decisions and take action on their own, responsible, direct a group on a practical and realistic no-nonsense basis, but are uncultured, sometimes phlegmatic, hard, cynical and smug (Barden, 1970). One might venture to suggest that the process of training, of which more will be said later, requiring

6

the accountant to place excessive attention to detail, patience, much concentration, a good memory and an ability to handle figures accurately, is anything but an experience designed to inspire and develop a humanistic perspective and a flexible mode of operation.

It is felt that entrants to well defined professional occupations, such as chartered accountancy and law, display some interest in or attachment to the idea of pursuing a professional career prior to entry. Super (1953) has argued that in choosing an occupation an individual is in effect choosing something which will realise his self-concept; this view has received support in a number of empirical studies. Of particular relevance is the work of Lancashire and Cohen (1970) who conducted follow-up studies on groups of people who had earlier undergone vocational guidance at the NIIP. The selected sample - chartered accountants and solicitors - unlike a random sample, representing people who had followed a diverse range of occupations, had shown a stronger interest in the idea of an office professional career prior to their consultation and there was a slightly greater tendency for their father to have the same profession as that recommended to the son. This could be attributable to childhood and adolescent identification with an adult who acted as a role model for the prospective accountant (Super, 1953). Alternatively, the accountant may have perceived his family and friends as having favourable attitudes towards the profession (Englander, 1960). In an exploratory study conducted by the author it was found that the promise of job satisfaction was ranked as the most important determinant of career choice; this could be a function of early socialisation, and the answers to the open-ended questions firmly endorsed the influence of parents, family or friends (McKenna, 1972).

The influence of socialisation processes during training in a professional office warrants examination, because these processes initiate and cultivate a professional perspective, total adherence to which can lead to dysfunctional consequences in certain areas of industrial accountancy. Hastings (1968) maintains that

7

the professional socialisation process which the articled clerk in training is exposed to is likely to contribute to the development of an attachment to the following values: caution; exactitude; anti-theoretical pragmatism; professional exclusiveness; quantification and rationality. Though Hastings' study is specific to the value system of chartered accountants, it is reasonable to suppose that other professional account-ants are similarly endowed with at least some of the values. After all, many generations of chartered accountants have contributed to the moulding and shap-ing of the work and social environment within the finance function in industry, either internally as executive accountants or externally through the advice offered supplementary to their role as auditors. The latter influence may be felt in the form of procedural determination or modification.

The professional attitudes will invariably have to be tempered to suit the demands of roles in industrial or-ganisations (Scott, 1966), or alternatively the pro-fessional accountant may experience conflict and strain (Millerson, 1964). Attachment to the professional values by the chartered accountant was found to be affected in varying degrees by subsequent socialisation in organisations outside the professional office (Hastings, 1968). But in any assessment of the extent to which the industrial work role affects professional values one would have to be cognizant of the degree of harmony or conflict between both the individual's con-ception and demands of his adopted role and the adjust-ment needed to fulfil the demands of the role.

Those engaged in financial accounting and internal audit work are expected to show a strong attachment to exactitude and anti-theoretical pragmatism, though the extent to which the accountant is attached to this set of values is dependent upon the demands made on him to shift his attitudinal position on acquiring his first industrial experience. A firm challenge to the rele-vance of professional values at this stage could have the effect of significantly modifying them. Those engaged on all work activities are likely to have caution firmly ingrained in their outlook, unless they are dependent upon non-accountants for promotion. A lesser attachment to professional exclusiveness is likely to materialise if the organisation considers other professional accountants to be on par with chartered accountants, or where the chartered account- ant has little contact with his institute's affairs. Quantification may be considered functional but exact- itude and anti-theoretical pragmatism are on balance dysfunctional in the practice of industrial account- ancy. However, there is a danger in overstating the functional nature of quantification.

The substance of the above research evidence is reinforced by the observations of those who are or have been close to the practical scene. Because of his un- preparedness to grapple with situations exposed to risk and uncertainty the accountant in management tends to maintain the cautious attitudes he had at the lower levels when dealing with problems nearer the top of the organisation (Tricker, 1967). Exacti- tude is evident in the willingness of the accountant to be precise about detail and Wilson (1965) states that the accountant's mind tends towards complete accuracy in contrast with the techniques of the stat- istician which consider how an acceptable level of accuracy can be achieved. Anti-theoretical pragmatism is symbolised in a convention-based approach rather than a flexible analytical approach to problem solving. Elgin (1965) reports the comments of the then Assistant Controller of the Ford Motor Company to the effect that a costing variance analysis exercise calls for high analytical ability in determining the true causes and the detection of ominous trends, but that 'often the pure accountant was too immersed in the technicalities of his work and that young graduate economists are often better at tracking down the real cause.' By over stressing the desirability of quantification of data one may all too easily ignore that which cannot be quantified. This does not appear to silence voices calling for strict adherence to the quantification process. For example, Lee (1968) in his exhortations to the accountant to accept future challenges advises him to preserve his objectivity and apply impartial numerical expressions to historical and predictive data. In fact, this advice is unlikely to fall on deaf ears as the accountant is more adept at quantifying than verbalising.

It will be noted that more than a fair share of comment in the discussion focuses on the chartered accountant rather than on the other recognised professional accountants. This appears to be inevitable as a preponderance of emphasis in the literature is firmly balanced in favour of chartered accountants, probably due to their historical and present status and the easily identifiable and structured nature of the articled clerk's training. Finally, one may deduce from the discussion so far that the accountant's education and training could be instrumental in engendering a basic conservatism in outlook with a leaning towards the practice of a restrictive style of leadership. The latter sentiment is succinctly expressed by Hastings (1968) when commenting on the accountant's attachment to the value of caution. He states that the accountant who supervises the processes involved in the operation of accounting systems 'shows a particular tendency to check the work of subordinates and in particular to limit the discretion of subordinates who are not qualified accountants.'

We are now beginning to appreciate more than ever before the behavioural assumptions underlying the conception and design of accounting systems and the human reactions they are likely to promote. These will be reflected in the appropriate sections of the text, but at this stage before examining the work activities of the Chief Accountant, a brief reflection on the concept of cost seems opportune. A Professor of Accounting - McRae (1971) - adopting a viewpoint of Likert argues that conventional accounting measures of performance ignore the value of the current psychological state of the human organisation, and that, for example, the damage perpetrated by the short term profit go-getter is not reflected in the accounting records in circumstances where the quality of human

resources are severely dented after his departure.
Somewhat idealistically Argyris (1964) maintains that
a proper management accounting system ought to measure
gold bricking, rate setting, apathy and non-involvement,
lack of openness, conformity, mutual distrust, extreme
commitment and interdepartmental rivalries. Closely
allied to these alleged shortcomings are that accounting systems do not adequately reflect the value of the
human resource to the organisation in terms of the
expenditure incurred on it, its opportunity cost and
the benefits accruing from its deployment (Brummet et
al., 1968). An innovative suggestion, if not at
present practicable, is one encouraging departments
to bid against each other for the service of organisational personnel and in the process place values on
the individual's worth; the accepted bid would then
form the asset value base (Hekimian and Jones, 1967).
No doubt Likert (1967) would disagree fundamentally
with this position on the grounds that certain key
psychological variables - e.g., loyalty, mutual trust,
co-operation - developed in working group relationships, on which the efficient operation of the enterprise rests, have not been considered. Either approach
is a tentative move to clear the way for a more realistic assessment of the real value of human resources in
organisations. Measurement of human resources still
remains problematic (Rhode et al., 1976), though Craft
and Birnberg (1976) are of the belief that human
resource accounting may prove useful internally rather
than externally as a means of evaluating the effectiveness of personnel and managerial programmes.

WORK ACTIVITIES OF CHIEF ACCOUNTANTS

One immediately encounters a difficulty when attempting to identify and describe areas of work typically
considered to constitute the job description of the
Chief Accountant. The role of the Chief Accountant
in different industrial environments may not always
show the similarities one might expect to find because
of a tendency nowadays in some companies to elevate
the status of the traditional Chief Accountant by

giving him authority for certain functions previously carried out by a person of the status of Financial Director. It would probably then be the practice to give the position the classification of Financial Controller. Weston (1954) in his analysis of the Finance Function states that no one title typified the role of executive with responsibilities for the finance function. The chief financial executive was frequently referred to as, for example, Controller, Treasurer, or a combination of the two, or Vice-President Finance. Dauten (1955) cites a paper analysing the duties of the major executive in the financial area. This is a global description and reads as follows: 'In general most companies' concepts of the treasurer's job involve financial planning, cash management, banking relations, handling credit and collections and the custody of company assets. The controllership function encompasses accounting, control, auditing, tax management and financial interpretation. And where there is a vice-president of finance or a finance committee, they are usually responsible for financial planning, the establishment of financial policy, the assignment of functions to the financial staff and overall control.'

Respondents in a survey of the duties of one hundred and fifty Chief Financial Officers employed in Canadian corporations performed duties similar to the ones referred to above, but ranked cash management-relationship with financial institutions, investment policy, insurance and pension fund management and debt collection management – as the most important duty (Levesque, 1976). No doubt this preference highlights the importance of cash flow in conditions of economic recession. However, many of the respondents felt that many so-called minor duties might well become major responsibilities in the future. Weston (1954) shares this view to some extent when he maintains that job areas, often referred to as subsidiary activities, connected with stimulating sales, salary administration and personnel management activities in general, could be legitimately considered to be within the province of the chief financial executive. It hardly needs

12

stating that the work area of the major financial executive is not clearly defined.

The lack of clarity in definitions of the role of the major financial executive, below the level of Finance Director, is mentioned by implication by Tricker (1967) in a British context when he admits that this level of responsibility can be divided between the Financial Controller and the Finance Manager. The Financial Controller participates in corporate strategic planning, engages in a continuous appraisal and interpretation of influences external to the business, and co-ordinates market forecasts, sales objectives and resource allocations into profit plans. As a member of the top management he also participates in the setting of objectives and development of policies; in the organisation of planning and control systems; in establishing, administering and developing procedures for resource and expense budgeting; in the setting of operating standards and levels of performance; and the appraisal of capital projects and subsequent control of performance. He would also be actively involved in the final interpretation of information for management purposes and with the aid of management accounting control techniques he provides assistance in the processes of organisational planning, control and co-ordination. He assesses managerial performance using budgetary performance standards, evaluates performance in key results areas and relies on appropriate feedback from the control mechanisms he manages. Acquisitions management is an area likely to occupy a fair share of his time if the company is expanding by merger strategy.

The functions of the Finance Manager, on the other hand, are - often in conjunction with the Financial Controller - to schedule and programme the monetary requirements of the company as specified in its plans; to provide the company with finance by helping to raise capital and other forms of long term finance, and arranging customers' credit facilities and collection of debts; to provide the necessary organisation for money-handling facilities - the receipt, custody, banking and payment of company monies; and finally, to recommend the investment fund policy to be pursued by the company. The role of the Chief Accountant is likely to incorporate aspects of both the role of the Financial Controller and Finance Manager in some companies.

In eighteen of the thirty-two companies visited by the author, in the course of the research study, the person in charge of the finance function at the operational level, traditionally classified as a Chief Accountant, performed duties which were a cross between the stereotype duties of both the Chief Accountant and Financial Controller. This was found to be the case to a greater extent in small companies, slightly less in larger companies and to a lesser extent in medium sized companies. The normal expectation is that the Chief Accountant assumes responsibility for the recording of historical happenings, preparation of periodic accounts and the performance of predictive and interpretive duties within guidelines set by a Financial Controller or Financial Director. On the other hand, the role of the Financial Controller, as commented on earlier, is very much concerned with planning and controlling the financial element of business operations and influencing company policy. A respondent from a medium sized company maintained that the roles of Chief Accountant and Financial Controller could be merged in a small company. Another respondent from a medium sized company, who acted the role of Financial Controller but bore the title of Financial Director, felt that Chief Accountants in large companies often perform the typical duties of a Financial Controller. In another situation, a Financial Director in a small company acted in the capacity of a Chief Accountant. It is then not surprising for some respondents to express views such as: 'titles mean little: they are just internal labels; titles are often created for political reasons: a Financial Controller is brought in to compensate for an inefficient Chief Accountant.' The manner in which titles are distributed among the sample is shown in Table 7, Appendix 'B'. The title of Chief Accountant will be used fre-

14

quently in the body of the text as a generic term to denote respondents.

Whatever his title, the person endowed with operational responsibility for day to day management of the finance function oversees the working of a number of accountancy sub-systems. Hastings (1968) identifies a number of industrial accountancy sub-systems as: wages calculation and payment; staff salary preparation; customer accounts and creditor settlement; expenditure records and control; departmental operations reporting; sales analysis; inventory recording and valuation; financial accounts preparation; product, job or process costing; pricing; long range economic forecasting; internal credit; organisation and methods; systems and procedures; data processing (ADP and punch cards); investment appraisal; short term investing; fund raising; cashier work. Though this may appear to be an exhaustive list, certain basic functions (e.g., debtors control) may not form part of the structure of the finance function, as is the case with companies trading as retail establishments. Hastings believes one can find different types of accounting operators in the finance function and they can be classified as follows: Data Analyst; Systems Designers; Accounting Systems Manager; Auditor.

Industrial accountants acting with the delegated authority of the Chief Accountant are likely to have the greatest degree of involvement in the roles of both data analyst and accounting systems manager, though it is not unusual to find accountants playing the role of internal auditor, checking the operation of various systems to verify established rules and procedures. Design of accounting systems or modification is sometimes within the province of the Chief Accountant but not always.

The type of activity associated with data analysis consists of: inspecting and passing suppliers' accounts for payment; preparing departmental budgets and operating statements; calculating the effect of a variation in product mix on profitability; examining a capital

15

expenditure proposal to see whether it yields a return on investment which would justify its approval; calculating the relative advantages of buying or leasing certain capital equipment; consolidating the financial accounts of subsidiary companies to produce the annual accounts; and preparing a tax computation. Management of accounting systems finds expression in, for example, the supervision of a cost office and controlling staff who are responsible for invoicing, keeping sales ledgers, analysis of sales and despatching invoices and statements of account.

Finally, as if to confuse matters one stage further, but fortunately from the point of view of the study, only in a few instances did one find the structure of the finance function varying quite dramatically from conventional practice by the fragmentation of accounting activities. This can be best expressed in diagramatical form - see Figure 1.3 - to depict the situation in one company.

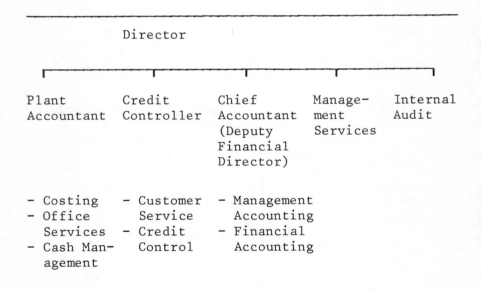

Director

| Plant Accountant | Credit Controller | Chief Accountant (Deputy Financial Director) | Management Services | Internal Audit |

- Costing
- Office Services
- Cash Management

- Customer Service
- Credit Control

- Management Accounting
- Financial Accounting

Figure 1.3 Pharmaceutical and cosmetics company finance function

Though the Chief Accountant may frequently act in an advisory capacity to other functional managers within an organisation his role within his own function is very much a managerial one. Numerous attempts have been made to identify and describe managerial functions. The management theorists considered forecasting, planning, commanding and controlling as the main avtivities of managers. More recently managerial functions have been analysed in an explicit fashion embracing planning; co-ordination; evaluation; supervision; representation; negotiation. The two most important activities were found to be supervision and planning, in that order (Mahoney et al., 1965). The entrepreneurial type - the manager - is actively involved in the setting of goals and shaping the structure of the organisation, whereas the administrator handles routine decisions (Litzinger, 1963). Though according to another source most managers cannot be classified as entrepreneurs because they are not the source of all formal authority in present day organisations, something which rests only in the entrepreneur (Hartman, 1959).

Identifying managerial functions in which managers or administrators are engaged in activities internal and external to the organisation captured the attention of Hemphill (1959) but rather discouragingly, or as one might expect from the discussion a short while ago, he claims that numerous jobs with the same title often show wide variation in requirements. In this country Horne and Lupton (1965) conducted an empirical investigation of the work activities of middle managers and conclude that every activity of a manager could be recorded by referring to four elements: formulating, organising, unifying and regulating. Formulating involves a definition of objectives on a short and long term basis with the added activity of specifying the human and technical resources necessary for their attainment. Organising is concerned with the development and maintenance of the means and conditions necessary for the implementation of plans and policies which arise from the explicit statement of objectives. Unifying activities embrace the numerous

17

procedures and practices designed to facilitate co-ordination and harmonisation of diverse activities with the aim of bringing about smooth working, adaptation and efficient operation of the enterprise. Regulating is the activity connected with the arrangement and shaping of human and material resources. This was the activity which managers from all functional areas spent the greater proportion of their time. But in fact managers engaged in finance and administration were ahead of the rest in devoting more time to regulating. The management process, as one might expect, consisted of considerable time devoted to talking and listening; so the adage of management getting things done through people was endorsed. By labelling the managerial activities described as task orientation we come close to defining the style of leadership 'Initiating Structure' (Fleishman and Harris, 1962). So implicit in the managerial role is the exercise of leadership and the next chapter will be devoted to an analysis of leadership or decision-making behaviour. This constitutes the dependent variable and being the major variable in the research study it warrants examination from a number of angles.

2 Decision-making behaviour and situational factors

Sometimes a distinction is drawn between supervision and leadership. The role of the supervisor, endowed with formal authority to direct and control the activities of his group, may be referred to as that of 'head' (Weissenberg, 1971). Leadership is then said to differ from supervision in that the person who is a leader, unlike the supervisor who may not be a member of the actual group which he supervises, has received acceptance and membership in a specific social group. Most research concerned with managerial decision-making behaviour would have as an underlying assumption the equation of the formally appointed supervisor with that of leader. It would appear difficult to exercise the responsibilities of supervision in many organisations in our culture without some degree of group centredness. However we define the leadership role the base of a leader's power lies in all the resources he can exploit in order to affect the behaviour of another. These resources according to Dahl (1957) include wealth, capability, prestige, skill, information, physical strength and personal rewards like recognition or affection. In addition the motivation to lead is enhanced by large rewards promised by accomplishing the group's task, reasonable expectancy that by working on the task it can be accomplished, a task which requires a high rate of group decisions, a situation which leads to acceptance by other members of the group for attempting to exercise leadership, the possession of superior knowledge or competence relevant to the accomplishment of the task, and finally, previously acquired status as the group's leader (Hemphill, 1961). Obviously many organisational situations fail to satisfy all of these conditions.

TRAIT APPROACH TO LEADERSHIP

Early attempts to define leadership centred on the tendency to stress the possession of a constellation of desirable qualities by the leader. This amounted to imputing to the leader special powers and perceptive abilities unlikely to be found in a person who was not born to be a leader (Bavelas, 1960). The modern traitest approach is less ambitious in creating the supremo image, but it would seem that popular traits such as quickness of decision, the courage to take risks, coolness under stress, intuition and even luck could be valuable attributes to possess as a leader. Stogdill (1948) drawing on an extensive review of the literature at the time, felt that the personal characteristics or qualities of the leader could be classified in accordance with the following criteria: capacity, achievement, responsibility, participation and status. A re-awakening of some interest in the traitest approach in the last couple of years appears to have been triggered off by the presence of economic crisis or the prospect of an accelerating crisis situation. In popular journalism one has noted some reference of late to the absent qualities of leadership. In a prominent feature article – In quest of Leadership – which appeared in 'Time Magazine' (1974) we are told that most definitions of leadership emphasise honesty, candour and vision combined with sheer physical stamina and courage, but leaders with these qualities are in short supply. It is then concluded that social and communication media changes have removed the myth of leadership as if to suggest that perhaps the qualities of leadership were a rare phenomenon anyway. Younger (1974) writing in the capacity of Managing Director of Hay-Msl, Management Consultants, echoes some nostalgic yearnings for the characteristics found in the immediate post war management leaders. These characteristics are said to be 'integrity and moral courage, team spirit, loyalty and will power; persuasiveness by example and by physical presence at the scene of action.' He maintains that technocrats have proliferated with the noticeable absence of the capacity to inspire, to foster co-

operation, to develop goodwill and secure the following of the men on the shop floor. It is the trade
union officials - union leaders - not the managers
who appeal to 'the admirable emotive qualities of
loyalty, solidarity, sense of comradeship and common
purpose and communicate in the language of their
members.' Younger is not far from the truth when he
observes the neutralisation of the foreman's role as
a result of the growth of functional specialisms and
the increasing sophistication of high speed information systems. This leaves a gap at first-line
supervision level and opens the way to intervention
by a new generation of managers - often highly edu-
cated with many whose fathers may be members of a
blue-collar union - who are not fully conversant with
the language, values and folklore of the shop floor.
It is now generally accepted that leadership is not a
question of passive and undynamic status in an organisation or the mere possession of some combination of
traits. Rather it is a phenomenon in which a leader
acquires status through active involvement and participation in a task, normally in a group situation,
where the leader demonstrates his capacity for carry-
ing co-operative tasks through to completion. In order
to successfully achieve this objective it is likely for
him to be intelligent, alert to the needs and motives
of others, and possess insight, initiative, persistence,
self-confidence and the ability to assume responsibility
(Stogdill, 1948). In this way we recognise the importance of the interaction between personality, task and
group factors as influences contributing to the determination of leadership styles. One tends to be inclined to the view expressed by Yukl (1971) that -

> there is a great deal of semantic confusion
> regarding the conceptual and operational
> definition of leadership. Terms defining leader-
> ship behaviour have proliferated over the years
> and the same term is often used differently from
> one study to the next.

Nevertheless this must not deter us from our endeavours
to identify the significant strands of thought per-

meating this area of study.

LEADERSHIP STYLE AND PERSONALITY

The first major study of leadership styles took place in a non-industrial setting where aspects of group functioning under different types of group atmosphere and different types of leadership were investigated (Lippit and White, 1958; 1968). Differentiation in leadership style - autocratic, democratic, laissez faire - was associated with different behavioural reactions among group members. The groups appeared to react very favourably to the imposition of democratic leadership practice. There appeared to be greater group purpose, harmonious interaction, less aggression and hostility and group unity in the democratic groups than in the autocratic groups. The reaction of group members to the laissez faire style was marked with a lower degree of efficiency, organisation and satisfaction.

More relevant are the observations of Lowin (1968) on leadership style, since they apply to the work organisational setting. He postulates the ideal autocratic and democratic leadership style. In the autocratic model there is a noticeable absence of credit for suggestions emanating from subordinates and lack of formal recognition of subordinates' efforts. A learning experience and frequent reinforcement is denied the subordinate because he has no feedback to rely on due to the lack of institutionalisation of his contribution to decision making. Neither does the subordinate develop an insight into the factors which must be considered in choosing among alternatives in a decision situation. Should he make a contribution he probably gets no credit for it. The subordinate, as a result, has little motivation to contribute beyond what is minimally expected of him. Under an ideal democratic or participative system, participation by subordinates is more frequent and more constructive. Managers are more prepared to discuss relevant issues with subordinates and to respect their suggestions. When suggestions are received and evaluated the reaction is transmitted to the subordinate in the form of feedback. This contributes to a desirable level of motivation and promotes the quality of future suggestions. It also leads to greater involvement and contributes to high performance standards. This is a theme which will be taken up and expanded later, but first we shall analyse the influence of personality as an intervening variable in the determination of leadership style.

In any examination of the applicability of a particular style of leadership cognizance of factors residing in the personalities of both the superior and subordinate is welcome. Drawing on empirical observations or insightful perception one shall, in the first instance, examine personality from the stance of the subordinate.

It is suggested that the hostile individual does better under the autocratic leader; his latent hostility must be controlled so as to confine his work to constructive ends. The aggressive co-operative type of individual will work better under democracy and laissez faire. His self-assertiveness will take constructive paths and he will head in the right direction when on his own. The individualist who is very familiar with his job is better of under laissez faire (Uris, 1963). A participative style appears to be appropriate if the subordinate's need for independence is high (Tannenbaum and Schmidt, 1958). If leadership practices result in a superior monopolising official communication with the attendant consequence of denying the subordinate pertinent information, this creates certain disadvantages. A cognitive structure of the work situation is denied the subordinate and this results in emotionalism, lack of direction and alienation. 'Furthermore, the denial of information by concealing the relation between activities and the larger group objectives denies the satisfaction of knowing one is part of a larger, important, co-operative effort' (Thompson, 1961). Likewise the subordinate could feel frustrated in situations where

23

the superior can interfere with his freedom of action and the realisation of his ambitions. Any hostility released by the subordinate as a result is not compatible with acts of submission to the superior because of the likelihood of creating guilt. In psychoanalytical terms, a reaction formation sets in when hostilities are repressed and replaced by admiration. Autocratic leadership behaviour is also said to interfere adversely with spontaneity, creativity and attacks co-operativeness (Coch and French, 1948).

According to Argyris (1973) authoritarianism appeals to the infancy dimensions of the subordinate's personality and promotes dependency and submissiveness. So if the subordinate is fixated at the infancy end of the personality continuum then perhaps he is more likely to appreciate autocratic behaviour.
Tannenbaum (1962) cites evidence suggesting that one group of female clerks did not wish to avail of the opportunity to participate more in decisions affecting their work, instead they preferred to be submissive, dependent on others, obeying the rules and following the instructions. Apparently, any motivational benefit springing from subordinate participation is likely to be offset by anxiety (Hickson, 1966). But surely this must depend on the proneness to suffer from anxiety in the first instance. Wispe and Lloyd (1955) produce evidence suggesting that low productivity insurance salesmen were prone to suffer some anxiety, they indicated a desire for interpersonal interaction through the vertical hierarchical structure where decisions were made by the district manager, and they preferred people in authority to act aloof but with a certain friendly disposition and not to be too intimate. The more successful, less threatened, salesmen preferred more permissive authority relations with an absence of communication barriers due to status, and the emphasis they gave to reporting through the chain of command was that much less evident. Those of a personality type which manifests itself as authoritarian or having a strong need for independence respond less favourably to the opportunity to participate in decisions (Vroom, 1960). This is a view not shared by

Tosi (1970) who was unable to replicate the results of Vroom's study, and the assertion that a strong need for independence is not compatible with a participative style is in direct opposition to the proposition of Tannenbaum and Schmidt (1958). One might also take issue with Argyris (1973) on the question of the implied association between conformity and authoritarianism. In fact the generality of the relationship between conformity and authoritarianism has been challenged (Bass, 1955; Steiner and Johnson, 1963).

The reaction of group members to different leadership styles in the White and Lippit experimental study is quite illuminating in terms of subordinate response. Autocracy was found to promote much hostility and aggression, and led to the harbouring of latent discontent. This was found not to be so in the democratic groups. But equally the autocratic leader by not disclosing at the outset the sequence of steps in the work process, having decided instead to reveal them in a piecemeal fashion, had the effect of reducing anxiety and promoting dependence because of the presence of a partial rather than global picture of the work cycle. Perhaps anxiety prone subordinates are those who have become accustomed to expressing behaviour closer to the infant end of the personality continuum (Argyris, 1959) or have a history of low productivity (Wispe and Lloyd, 1955).

We have so far discussed the relationship between the personality of the subordinate and leadership style. It is now time to shed some light on the nature of personality of the superior in the context of leadership style. However, it is well to remember that often the individual who in one capacity acts as a subordinate in another acts the role of a superior. The right to exercise control - authority - has a number of psychological meanings. It relates to superiority, dominance, submission, guidance, help, criticism and reprimand. It also conjures up images of manliness and virility (Tannenbaum, 1962). A superior whose feelings of insecurity in an uncertain situation does not allow him to release control over

25

the decision-making process may be unable to involve subordinates to the extent required by participative leadership (Tannenbaum and Schmidt, 1958). If he has a strong need for predictability and stability, he may consider the act of releasing control as something that reduces the predictability of the outcome. Frequently one hears mentioned the difficult supervisory role inherent in the role of the foreman (the man in the middle). He suffers from a lot of pressure further up the hierarchy and this may have the effect of creating dependent, subordinate and submissive individuals. According to Argyris (1959) the nature of their managerial role does not permit them to voice undue criticism or display apathy or indifference.

There appears to be some evidence to associate authoritarian behaviour with authoritarianism, and the latter with a lower level of intelligence (McGee, 1955) but since this evidence is derived from a laboratory experiment one ought to exercise extreme caution in any extrapolation to the industrial scene. Sales (1966) seems to equate efficiency with high intelligence in a work situation but does so rather superficially. He indicates that the more intelligent supervisor is likely to diagnose production difficulties more quickly, takes remedial action more effectively and is more proficient at the exercise of skill related to day to day production problems. For these reasons the highly intelligent supervisor is believed to be the most efficient. Support for this viewpoint comes from French and Synder (1959) who found that airforce officers who exerted the greatest influence over subordinates' judgements were rated the highest on general intelligence by subordinates. Apparently an executive new to his job and feeling uncertain about situations confronting him is likely to seek elaborate counsel, but the self-contained manager prefers to deliberate alone (Litchfield, 1956) obviously involving his subordinates to a minimum extent in the decision-making process. One frequently comes round to asking why someone seeks the role of the manager or supervisor in the first instance and then subsequently adopts one style rather than another?

26

This is a rather difficult question to answer and the answers that are available are speculative. For example, Thompson (1961) feels that people with great dominance and status needs evolve within the hierarchy, though some satisfy their dominance needs by identifying with their superiors; this in turn reinforces the superior's dominance and status drives. A superior may impose autocratic rule as an outlet for aggressions repressed because of his own exposure to autocratic rule as a subordinate (Fromm, 1942). Still on the theme of the characteristics of the autocrat, McMurry (1958) goes to some length in distinguishing between the strong (benevolent) and weak autocrat. His greatest admiration is reserved for the strong or benevolent autocrat who he believes is aggressive, hard-driving, self-reliant, task-centred but apparently is in no way a tyrant or exploiter. As a contrast, the weak autocrat is the one that causes a bad image for autocracy. Though often intelligent, loyal, conscientious and technically well qualified, he places an overwhelming emphasis on security, tends to be dependent, fearful and anxious and compensates for his insecurities by assuming an arbitrary authoritarian exterior, often punctuated by a great emphasis on status and symbols. He tends to abide religiously by the rules and regulations and his lust for power is only matched by his tyrannical manner which acts as a mask for his inner doubts or uncertainties and eliminates the likelihood of he having to defend his position. He tends to be a strict disciplinarian with subordinates and obsequious to superiors. Perhaps Tannenbaum and Massarik (1963) had the weak autocrat in mind when they suggested that a leader may resort to discipline of a harsh nature in order to express a deep-seated hostility need. We appear now to enter the realm of unconscious motivations in leadership behaviour and this obviously poses acute problems from the standpoint of their identification and measurement, though Litzinger (1963) - using the Gordon Survey of Interpersonal Values, Questionnaire - made a brave attempt. Selected personality variables were found to differ when the roles of centralised and decentralised bank managers were examined. It could now be argued

that the personality disposition of both the superior
and subordinate is influential in determining the
appropriateness of a particular style of leadership,
just as situational variables, to be discussed later,
are also likely to have an impact. It is for this
reason that the research instrument accommodates
measures of a semi-personality nature.

LEADERSHIP EFFECTIVENESS

It is commonplace to find all-round leadership effectiveness associated with a democratic or permissive
leadership style. In this section it is proposed to
examine the claims made by the proponents of democratic leadership. In doing so one will attempt to pin-
point instances where this style may be inappropriate
and a more directive style appropriate.

   Likert (1961) at the Institute for Social Research,
University of Michigan, has identified differences in
leadership styles that appear to influence managerial
effectiveness. According to Likert the supervisors
and managers who are credited with the highest productivity, lowest costs, least turnover and absence
rates, and the highest level of employee motivation
and satisfaction are employee-centred rather than
job-centred. The employee-centred manager is perceived by his subordinates as supportive, friendly
and helpful rather than hostile. 'He is kind but firm,
never threatening, genuinely interested in the well-
being of subordinates and endeavours to treat people
in a sensitive considerate way.' He is also capable
at such activities as planning and scheduling, training
subordinates, supplying them with the necessary methods
and materials and initiating work activity. Bowers
and Seashore (1966) have done an excellent job in comparing and integrating a number of established schools
of thought in leadership and come up with a scheme not
far removed from that of Likert. The four concepts of
leadership - support, interaction facilitation, goal
emphasis and work facilitation - draw our attention to
the leadership role as one designed to enhance one's

self-esteem, fosters close mutually satisfying relationships, stimulating enthusiasm to meet group goals
with the emphasis on high performance, and finally,
scheduling, planning, co-ordinating and providing the
facilities and knowledge to enable subordinates to
achieve their targets. These leadership roles need
not necessarily be provided by a formally designated
leader but by any member of the group. Bowers and
Seashore conclude from an analysis of their field
study that different aspects of performance are associated with different leadership characteristics.

The employee-centred manager, as defined by Likert,
would appear to rank high on Consideration and Initiating Structure. It was a group of researchers at the
Ohio State University who isolated and identified
Initiating Structure and Consideration as basic dimensions of leadership behaviour. Before finally
settling on these two dimensions Halpin and Winer
(1957) devised the 'Leader Behaviour Description
Questionnaire' (LBDQ) which incorporated Consideration,
Initiating Structure, Production Emphasis and Sensitivity. A consideration orientation indicates friend-
ship, mutual trust, respect and warmth. Initiating
Structure is the type of behaviour that defines and
organises organisational relationships or roles,
establishes well defined patterns of organisation,
channels of communication and ways of getting jobs
done. A production emphasis and sensitivity orientation are respectively concerned with pointing the fin-
ger at goals to motivate subordinates, and developing
awareness to interrelationships and internal and external group pressures. In recent times a new scale,
Tolerance of Member Freedom, was introduced and this
could be regarded as a measure of degree of participation.

The job-centred manager would appear to rank high on
Initiating Structure and low on Consideration.
Although there are certain similarities between the
Ohio and Michigan questionnaires, nevertheless, their
empirical equivalency is in question (Yunker and Hunt,
1976). Fleishman et al. (1955) when examining the

leadership scores and the behavioural outcome measures conclude that foremen who scored high in Initiating Structure and low in Consideration had more accidents, unexcused absences, formal grievances and turnover. However, Greenwood and McNamara (1969) claim that both Initiating Structure and Consideration are un-correlated with various behavioural measures of super-visory performance, attitudes or abilities. Implied in Fleishman's (1953) comments on attitudinal and behavioural dimensions of Initiating Structure and Consideration are a recognition that these two factors are mutually exclusive. Weissenberg and Kavanagh (1972) maintain that the orthogonality of the dimen-sions Initiating Structure and Consideration is to a large extent dependent on the type of leadership be-haviour questionnaire used. The greatest independence is attributable to the Leadership Opinion Question-naire. This means that one can be directive in manag-ing subordinates towards achieving organisational goals and at the same time establishing highly sup-portive relations with them. When subordinates des-cribe their leader's behaviour under the LBDQ they perceive Consideration and Initiating Structure as having lesser independence than that prevailing under the Leadership Opinion Questionnaire. In addition, Kavanagh (1972) maintains that task complexity and subordinate competence - situational variables - mediate the independence of Consideration and Initiat-ing Structure, with subordinate competence being the more important. In a later publication Kavanagh (1975) concludes from his empirical data that the role of the leader does, and is expected to, integrate the approaches of Initiating Structure and Considera-tion.

In Likert's advocacy of permissive leadership we witness the promulgation of a set of ideas which form the foundation base of the school of participative leadership. Bennis (1966) conceives this type of leadership largely in terms of a 'system of values' governing behaviour with a commitment to full and free communication, a reliance on consensus rather than on the more customary forms of coercion or compromise to

tackle and manage conflict, and an atmosphere that
permits and encourages emotional expression as well
as being task-oriented. This would be supplemented
by the suggestion that influence rests on technical
competence and knowledge rather than the vagaries of
personal whims or prerogatives of power, and is considered the ideal recipe for knowledge-oriented and
scientific-based industries (Slater and Bennis, 1964).
Argyris (1973) argues that as the individual moves from
the infant end of a personality continuum where he is
basically dependent and submissive, with few and
shallow abilities and a short time perspective, to
the adult end where he is endowed with relative independence, autonomy, self-control, many abilities
and a few in depth, and a long-time perspective, then
we have to design or redesign jobs to permit increased
self-regulation, self-evaluation, self-adjustment and
participation in the setting of goals. By doing so it
is alleged we bring about a betterment of productivity
and attitudes. McGregor (1960) views the position of
man in organisations in a similar vein. He contends
that, contrary to general misconceptions, man has
within himself the capacity to exercise self-direction
and self-control in the achievement of objectives to
which he is committed. He is likely to assume responsibility rather than to shed it and if he is lazy,
indolent or passive it is not due to inherent human
weaknesses but attributable to previous organisational
experience. There is also a recognition that the full
potential of human resources is not realised in organisations. This is a theme very much in evidence in the
Human Resources model postulated by Miles (1965).
Heavily influenced by the writings of theorists such
as Likert, McGregor and Haire, he maintains that there
exists in organisations reservoirs of untapped resources and that 'these resources include not only
physical skills and energy but also creative ability
and the capacity for responsible, self-directed, self-
controlled behaviour.' The model has also something
to say about the improvement of the quality of decisions and company performance through effective delegation, and that involvement in decisions applies to
non-routine as well as to routine matters. Also, the

opportunity for the exercise of self-direction and self-control should be a progressive thing in line with the growth in ability and experience of the individual. The dual-factor theory - motivator/hygiene - of Herzberg (1966) would accommodate this perspective when it expounds the view that it is the motivator factors, centring on the job itself, which bring about job satisfaction and increased commitment to the task in hand. On the other hand, hygiene factors if improved can alleviate job dissatisfaction. In the spirit of participative management the practical implementation of the dual-factor theory is a job enrichment scheme.

Sales (1966) rationalises the relationship between high performance and democratic supervision by appealing to a basic tenet of experimental psychology. This states that high levels of performance will prevail in situations in which the reinforcement is large. So it follows that the more reinforcement an employee receives for production the higher the level of production. He also invokes the view of the self-actualisation and ego-esteem school of thought - based on the work of Maslow (1954) - which maintains that democratic supervision provides the means for satisfying the higher level human needs. This is achieved by allowing subordinates freedom in determining the specific form and content of their work, and as a result implicating their personalities in the tasks they perform. This can be contrasted with the behaviour of the authoritarian supervisor who puts the subordinate in a situation where he carries things out at the will of the supervisor, at the same time reducing the opportunity to express certain important needs on the job; all this, of course, rests on the assumption that workers wish to satisfy higher level human needs. Because work is less satisfying under autocracy it is concluded that productivity would suffer.

The Survey Research Centre, University of Michigan, relying primarily on ratings by self, superior, subordinate or observer seems to extol the virtues of general supervision, as we found earlier in connection

with the work of Likert. Drawing on their studies of
a variety of industrial situations - e.g., railway
maintenance crews, insurance office staff, production
lines in heavy industry - Katz and Kahn (1960) conclude that general supervision together with employee-
oriented attitudes in the supervisor were associated
with the highest productivity. Though a note of caution should be added. Katz et al. (1951) failed to
replicate findings supporting participative management. In this country Argyle et al. (1958) undertook
a replication of these investigations and found that
foremen of high producing work groups tended to use
general rather than close supervision and were relatively more employee-oriented in their behaviour than
were foremen of less productive groups. An employee-
orientation is present when a leader acknowledges the
importance of the human relations aspects of his job,
he has a healthy respect for human beings, takes an
interest in them and accepts their individuality and
personal needs. Argyle et al. make the point that
certain conditions had to be fulfilled before democratic supervision was effective. These were abandonment
of piece rates and the existence of operator-controlled
tasks. The beneficial aspects of a participative
leadership style in terms of managerial success are
reported by Blake and Mouten (1964), and Bavelas and
Strauss (1961) draw our attention to the problems
created by management arbitrarily revoking, without
consultation in face of opposition, the productivity
bonuses female workers had come to expect as a result
of been given the opportunity to determine their work
rate by controlling their own conveyor belt.

   Moving on to professional groups, Baumgartel (1957)
found that participative patterns of behaviour, as
opposed to directive or laissez faire patterns, were
associated with higher task motivation and a greater
sense of progress among scientists. Pelz and Andrews
(1966) report that scientists were more effective when
they were able to influence key decision makers. The
scientists experienced a combination of both autonomy
and moderate levels of co-ordination by their supervisors; having too much or too loose co-ordination was

counterproductive. But it would seem that a moderate amount of autonomy, where the scientist experiences a certain amount of direction, is also necessary, in order to achieve an impressive publications output. Having too much or too little autonomy was associated with lower productivity (Cotgrove and Box, 1970).

Other evidence blurs this picture somewhat by either being less clearcut or contradictory. Weschler et al. (1952) studied the relationship between job satisfaction, level of morale and productivity to restrictive and permissive supervisory styles in two comparable divisions of a naval laboratory. When the subordinate scientific personnel rated themselves on the dimensions mentioned, job satisfaction, morale in general and productivity were higher in the permissive leadership groups. The picture changed in one significant respect when superiors, supported by specialists, did the rating. Although the highest level of job satisfaction and morale was still attributable to the permissive-oriented groups, productivity was considered to be higher in the restrictive-oriented group. The important thing to remember here is not necessarily the relationship between satisfaction and morale on the one side and productivity on the other, which in any case is not necessarily a positive correlation, but the superiority of autocracy on the basis of efficiency as seen through the eyes of the superior and objective bystanders. The best researcher was found working under restrictive supervision. But age may somehow be an important variable likely to have influenced the result because invariably those subjected to restrictive supervision were much younger, and perhaps more eager. In a study of scientists working in a research centre, Andrews and Farris (1967) felt the quality of supervision and a good human relations approach had not much of a relationship with innovation. It was also found that a lacking in job related, human relations and supervisory skills could be compensated by granting freedom to subordinates, consulting them, with the superior still taking some decisions on his own. This was found to promote positively the level of innovation.

34

An interesting view of leadership in a research environment has been put forward recently by Barnowe (1975) when he reported that leadership tended to assume greater overall importance when scientists were in some way disadvantaged, that is when they were unable to consult with colleagues in their field and when they had relatively less research experience. He concludes with a view of leadership which is essentially non-interventionist. The research and development supervisor serves primarily in a helping role, providing assistance to subordinate scientists as needed, but he is not necessarily relied upon or considered influential when not needed.

A general level of support for democratic leadership emerges from the findings of survey investigations conducted in organisations. In the survey investigation one must be prepared to err on the side of caution when drawing causal inferences from the data. Therefore it would seem worthwhile to establish whether the above patterns or trends are sustained by the evidence derived from experimental studies conducted in organisations. Coch and French (1948) conducted an experimental study at a plant of the Harwood Corporation. It was prompted by the presence of acute employee resistance to work methods and job changes which resulted in a high grievance and turn-over rate, very low efficiency and restriction of output. The researchers decided to create an experimental and control group, the experimental group participating in the evaluation and redesign of their jobs. The latter group surpassed their previous performance, unlike the control group, but only after experiencing an unsatisfactory contribution for a transitional period. During this period sixty two per cent of employees whose jobs were modified suffered a chronic substandard performance or left the job during the retraining stage. An encouraging note to these experiments was the impressive performance of control groups when exposed to the same conditions as experienced by the experimental groups. In a very ambitious and penetrating investigation Morse and Reimer (1956) created groups exposed to either demo-

35

cratic or autocratic styles of supervision by altering
the styles used in an ongoing industrial setting.
Four divisions within a company were subject to investigation. In two divisions a participative style was
used, decision making was deliberately pushed down
the hierarchy, supervisors were trained to use supervisory methods of a democratic nature and there was
an appreciable increase in their freedom of action.
In the other two divisions greater hierarchical control was introduced by an increase in the closeness
of supervision and there was a noticeable shift upwards in the level at which decisions were made.
These conditions prevailed for a year and approximately 500 employees were involved. It was found
that both programmes contributed to a significant
increase in productivity, surprisingly with a slight
advantage accruing to the authoritarian system. A
similar result was reported by French et al. (1960)
when they replicated the earlier study of Coch and
French. Both on productivity and attitudinal dimensions the results were discouraging for the participation group, though one should point out that members
of the experimental (participative) group were faster
learners. In trying to rationalise the failure of the
experimental group, Lowin (1968) maintains that the
contributory factor responsible was management's
failure to include central issues such as production
level and rate-setting in the participative decision-
making process; also it is alleged that only minor
matters were discussed. Perhaps a better rationalisation would be in terms of cultural variation. The
study conducted by French and his colleagues took
place in a Norwegian factory. Similarly, a study by
Whyte (1971) challenges the universal applicability
of the USA participative management school by showing
that in Peru it was the close supervisor who exercised
definite pressure for production and was as a consequence the most highly regarded. Obviously the findings from the experimental studies quoted above are
somewhat discouraging when it comes to the endorsement of participative leadership.

When we turn our attention to the findings from

36

experimental studies outside work organisations we are still not convinced of the alleged superiority of participative leadership. Shaw (1955) created three communication networks to engage in problem-solving exercises and nominated the person who received the highest independence score in each network to behave in either an autocratic or democratic manner. He found that the subjects exposed to autocracy, rather than democracy, required less time to solve problems and made fewer errors regardless of the communication networks in which they were placed. In a similar experimental situation McCurdy and Eber (1953) reached an indecisive result. They exposed groups, engaged in a task which consisted of the proper setting of three switches, to autocratic and democratic conditions. In the autocratic climate one person was the absolute supervisor with power to order the others. In the democratic climate the instructions from the experimenters emphasised equalitarianism, stating that each person could offer suggestions and that nobody could issue orders to other members of the group. It was found that neither the autocratic or democratic style of supervision was superior on a productivity criterion. However, an unequivocal movement in the direction of democratic leadership can be discerned from a finding of Day and Hamblin (1964). They trained a female student to employ close and general supervisory styles and to lead groups of female students engaged in an assembly-line task in a laboratory setting. The most effective productivity record was found among subjects who worked with the leader practising general supervision. The group method of decision making, in which members are allowed to discuss their feelings, raise objections and request information on judgemental matters, appears to be very effective indeed (Lewin 1968). This can be explained in terms of 'owning' a decision in which one participated in determining coupled with the influence of group pressure, in some cases leading to a reduction in cognitive dissonance where a private view is at variance with a publicly stated one.

What is surprising, and contrary to one's expectations, is that the nature of the task does not appear to be an important consideration, generally speaking, in the laboratory experiments. Because we find problem-solving exercises lending themselves to autocratic supervision or to both types of supervision. Routine tasks, which one might consider amenable to autocratic or restrictive leadership behaviour, are performed better under democratic practices. It is then not surprising for Lowin (1968) to voice an opinion that participative decision-making models are simplistic ones in a laboratory setting because 'they fail to reflect just those issues which form the very heart of the organisational phenomenon.'

The findings of the survey investigations - rather than the experimental findings - come down firmly on the side of democracy and its benefits. Sales (1966) offers an explanation to account for the failure of the experimental method to replicate the survey findings. Generally the brevity of the experimental session would rank as a serious explanation if it was not for the fact that the experiment lasted for a year in one situation. Perhaps the nature of the task is not given enough serious consideration. Sales maintains that the exercises in the experimental studies whereby the subject suggests possible solutions to simple problems is not enough to implicate the unique personalities of the subjects in their tasks, and he cites Morse and Reimer (1956) who report that 'both groups of clerks indicated that their jobs throughout the course of the experiment did not give them a very high degree of self-actualisation.' Sales also feels that intervening variables - e.g., turnover, absenteeism - which mediate the relationship between leadership style and performance are crucial factors and should receive more of our attention. His solution as a starter would be to eliminate the influence of turnover and absenteeism from the relationship between leadership style and performance in the survey studies and create more opportunities in the experimental studies for self-actualisation. Then we would be favourably disposed to comparing the effectiveness of each style. Lowin (1968) also

38

stresses the point that we should consider the influence of the mediating variables he believes to be
important - personality, culture, work expectations
and environment and leadership patterns set at the
higher organisational levels. Influenced by Lowin,
Ritchie and Miles (1970) empirically established that
the degree of trust and confidence the immediate superior had in his subordinate and the frequency with
which he consulted him were the important mediating
variables between leadership style and satisfaction
with immediate supervision. We have already considered personality as a mediating influence, and situational factors will receive more emphasis later. But
first, a return to participative or democratic leadership. A point worthy of note is the extent to which
it has influenced thought processes and prescription
as a panacea for corporate ills in the area of management education and training but particularly, since we
are concerned with the behaviour of accountants, in
the area of behavioural accounting.

We are only too aware of the impact of varying
applications of control techniques by those occupying
leadership positions in organisations. The impact is
felt in terms of individual satisfactions, frustration, tension, euphoria and self-actualisation. One
such important control technique operated by accountants within organisations is budgetary control. The
relationship the accountant has with the appropriate
functional manager is not normally a vertical relationship but a lateral one. Nevertheless, it is
maintained that conventional budgeting practice based
on planning and control relies on pressure, coercion
and close supervision (Gibson, 1970). Commenting on
the value of conventional cost control systems, such
as budgetary control, designed to monitor employee
performance where information on variances is passed
up, across and down the organisational hierarchy,
Argyris (1953) favours a movement towards self-control
and self-discipline as a motivating force. The individual at the lowest level of the organisation is then
given the opportunity to draw from the control system
the information needed to evaluate his own performance

39

and communicate upwards at his discretion matters requiring attention and action. For this to take root it would require a truly participative leadership climate in which mutual acceptance and trust between organisational participants exists as to the design and use of managerial control systems. Hofstede (1968) in his influential study of budgeting practice states the belief that supervisors or managers strive for the gratification of higher level human needs – self-esteem, esteem from others and self-actualisation – in the cycle of events leading to the achievement of the budget. Also they are likely to seek challenge from the setting of budget standards. It is usual when using the budget as a motivational device to build on the lower psychological needs for these people, which may prove ineffective or possibly have a negative effect. Relating formal budget goals to the individual's aspiration level is considered important in terms of challenge or withdrawal, leading to feelings of success or failure (Stedry and Kay, 1966; Child and Whiting, 1954).

Implicit in a number of the above remarks is an acknowledgement that the system of control is based on an authoritarian model of human behaviour (Caplan, 1971). Those who share this view are eager and ready to recommend participation as essential in the process of setting budget standards and find it easy to amass supporting evidence, for example: the more participation there is in the process of setting budgets, the greater the commitment of personal motivation towards the achievement of budgets (Coch and French, 1948); a higher level of participation leads to a higher level of motivation (Hofstede, 1968); employees participating in setting standards performed better than those who did not (Bass and Leavitt, 1963); active participation in the budgetary control system aims to get the participants ego-involved not just task-involved (Wallace, 1966). In addition Dunbar (1971) would argue that discussion regarding goals is not enough; it must be backed up with goal getting. Lest the unsuspecting accountant is complacent he is admonished to be on his guard in case pseudo-

40

participation and biasing creep into the pragmatism of participants. Argyris (1953) emphasises the pseudo-participative tactics of the controller who at one and the same time encourages an exchange of opinions and, believing that line supervisors have not much to contribute anyway, is very keen to get their approval - just in case of comeback. On the other hand, budget biasing, which is probably easier to perpetrate in a participatory system, amounts to managers inflating costs or reducing revenue at the budget stage (Schiff and Lewin, 1970). According to Lowe and Shaw (1968) managers felt it to be in their interest to agree lower rather than higher budget standards, striking a balance between present job security and increasing future income. They highlight the subtlety of the individual manager, whose track record may be either impressive or wanting, in influencing forecasts to win short or long term approval or personal benefits.

Doubts have been cast on the substance of ideas emanating from the participative leadership school. Katz and Kahn (1966) commenting on the group discussion method refer to two assumptions underpinning it which are apparent but not always explicit and certainly not always met in practice. First, that the groups are peer groups, with each person being equal in terms of formal authority; in many reality situations however an authority or status figure is present at the discussions. Second, the participants come to the group representing their own beliefs about cause/effect and preferred outcomes, rather than as formal representatives of other groups. Bobbitt et al. (1974) argue that we need a clearer understanding of what we mean by democratic group discussion. Target setting, for example, is considered highly influential (Locke, 1968), and perhaps in the total effects attributable to interpersonal participation in reaching decisions a sizeable proportion is due to target setting. Social interaction, a natural concomitant of participation, may have the effects of impairing performance in problem-solving exercises (Vroom et al., 1969). Perhaps this is one reason why

autocratic supervision was found effective in a laboratory experiment on problem solving mentioned
earlier in the discussion. Is it necessary to consider commitment in addition to interaction when we
speak of participation? It would appear that should
the individual identify with a decision he helped to
make, then he would become motivated to ensure successful adoption of that decision, if only to maintain a favourable self-concept. Increased commitment
to carry out decisions is, however, not the same thing
conceptually as increased task motivation. A subordinate could succumb to group pressure and commit himself to a decision which has the effect of restricting
output or resisting change (Yukl, 1971). Does it
really matter if somebody does not participate in
actuality but perceives that he does (March and Simon,
1958)? Our pseudo-participative controller referred
to by Argyris would no doubt consider perceived but
unreal or deceptive participation to have beneficial
psychological effects, just like real participation.
But Heller (1971) believes this discounts the percep-
tiveness of the highly intelligent subordinate, so
the psychological reaction to deceptive participation
is unlikely to be the same as it is to real participation. Earlier it was considered that subordinate participation helps to reduce resistance to change (Coch
and French, 1948). The subordinate is given the chance
to air his doubts and fears about the proposed change.
If the change is to the subordinate's advantage all is
well, but if the proposals are clearly detrimental to
the subordinate, problems in eliciting support are an
inevitable consequence. Leavitt (1965) doubts whether
the 'total participation' condition was fulfilled in
the Coch and French experiment. He feels that the
objective of the discussions appears to have been to
gain acceptance of a preconceived desired change and
asks what would happen if the change being urged by
management was not attractive to the groups. Therefore he concludes that the approach adopted amounted
to manipulation. A similar accusation is levelled at
participative management in the same context by
Gomberg (1966). He feels that participative management at the Harwood Corporation amounted to involun-

tary manipulation. The way the groups subsequently embraced the union seemed to confirm this observation. Experimental secret groups developed, normally as a precaution against speeding up activities by the organisation. Gomberg asks a number of pertinent questions: 'Was this a cleverly contrived managerial device to break the solidarity of the group? Were the workers free to decline the management invitation to increase production? Was there real participation in defining mutual objectives, or did management define the objectives and then democratically manipulate the workers as a means to achieve them? Did the workers feel threatened by this kind of manipulative democracy?'

Challenging the legitimacy of the assertions made by the proponents of group decision making that acceptance, consensus, stimulation and growth, improvement in communication and seriousness of work contribution have desirable consequences, McMurry (1958) feels they suffer a number of shortcomings. For example, group decision making could be very suitable only where groups are small, socially well integrated and homogenous. It also fosters group dependency, breeds conformity, because one dare not oppose, and as a result discourages the able non-conformist. There could also be a reluctance to disagree on the side of the subordinate because of status differentiations. It could also be argued that group decision making does not lend itself to quick action, decisions may fall on the side of conservatism as opposed to innovation and where unanimity is required consensus may be an illusion and amount to some members suppressing their views or feelings. Commenting on the limitations in the use of group decision making, Bobbitt et al. (1974) maintain that –

..... all of the studies have primarily dealt with the employment of group decision-making under conditions of change. What happens under conditions of stability remains problematic at this point?

43

Questioning the basic philosophy of the participative management or leadership school, Strauss (1968) believes there is a tendency to place an overwhelming emphasis on personal co-ordination and control to the detriment of impersonal control techniques. The neo-human relations school or participative management school is also accused of overlooking the important role played by bargaining and the use of power in interpersonal relationships. Democracy is conceived largely in non-structural terms by some writers and the emphasis on group harmony, expressing itself in individual/organisational goal congruity, is perhaps oversimplified because it is doubtful whether this exists in any organisation other than an organisation where normative power and moral compliance (e.g., church) exist. In an earlier publication Strauss (1963) maintains, contrary to the above impression, that engaging in consultation or joint decision making (participative management) provides the opportunity for bargaining and agreement on a compromise proposal which the subordinate can support. It would appear that his 1968 comment reflects more accurately the thinking of the participative management school.

One can argue that the main theoretical base of the participative management school is the 'force for growth' theory of personality. This basically states that man contains within himself the urge to grow and he will express the highest qualities of thought, creativity, altruism, humanitarianism, of which he is capable, if given the opportunity to do so. This view, reflected in the writings of neo-Freudians – Jung, Adler, Fromm, Rank – is perhaps best represented by Rogers (1951) and Maslow (1954). It is well to remember that this theory is but one of at least three main theories of personality. Lazarus (1971) makes the point that 'the force-for-growth concept has been criticised as mystical and value laden, since it flirts so continuously with the evaluation of man in terms of normative judgements of high and low, advanced and primitive, good and bad.' Maslow (1965) expresses a word of caution about the indiscriminate acceptance of his own conclusions –

After all, if we take the whole thing from McGregor's point of view of a contrast between a Theory X view of human nature, a good deal of the evidence upon which he bases his conclusions comes from my researches and my papers on motivations, self-actualisation et cetera. But I, of all people, should know just how shaky this foundation is as a final foundation. My work on motivations came from the clinic, from a study of neurotic people. The carry-over of this theory to the industrial situation has some support from industrial studies, but certainly I would like to see more studies of this kind before feeling finally convinced that this carry-over from the study of neurosis to the study of labour in factories is legitimate. The same thing is true of my studies of self-actualizing people - there is only this one study of mine available. There were many things wrong with the sampling, so many in fact that it must be considered to be, in the classical sense anyway, a bad or poor or inadequate experiment. I am willing to concede this - as a matter of fact, I am eager to concede it - because I'm a little worried about this stuff which I consider to be tentative being swallowed whole by all sorts of enthusiastic people, who really should be a little more tentative in the way that I am.

Whether or not we recognise the theoretical base as tentative, one has become accustomed to reading accounts of the successful implementation of participative management at the macro level. At one time it was exemplified in the experiences of the Yugoslav work councils, a vivid manifestation of the benefits of industrial democracy. It is interesting, therefore, to note the comments of Mulder (1971) on the reality surrounding the operation of these councils. For example, ninety per cent of the talkers in the council were experts who had received higher education, the workers were inadequately motivated, in evidence was the growth of a power elite and also the growth of a small circle of competent and responsible people.

From an empirical study of self-management in Yugoslavia, Obradovic (1975) endorses this view but adds that the rank and file workers participate more actively when discussion shifts from technical issues to human relations problems at the individual and group level; to standard of living and social welfare issues; and to hiring and placement problems. Warner (1975) on reviewing some critical evidence of self-management in Yugoslavia feels the 'problems of alienation in the workplace cannot be magically solved by simply installing workers' councils' but is himself inclined to the view that much less might be achieved in terms of industrial democracy 'if an even weaker system of worker participation had been arrived at, or in future is set-up.'

Having expressed the view that permissive supervision is likely to promote acceptance and quality of decisions and private commitment, Bass (1967) then draws our attention to the view that permissive supervision may be impossible, unwarranted and less likely to succeed or be difficult to introduce in many circumstances. It is to an examination of these circumstances that we now turn to in order to justify the relevance of an alternative to the democratic style in specified situations.

Where group norms are not supportive of participation or there is a legitimate organisational structure for decision making, group decision making will most likely have limited effects (Bobbitt et al., 1974). Democratic management could be functionally impaired by uniformity of policy and practices designed to ensure co-ordination, and by a history of bureaucratic traditions (McMurry, 1958). With the growing importance of technological and economic constraints in the use of limited resources someone has to assume responsibility for the ultimate decision. Given the movement in large-sized organisations towards decentralisation of functions, democratisation is not a logical development because control still resides at the centre or apex of the organisation (Gomberg, 1966).

A directive style is more appropriate 'when the subordinate group is large, when communications are poor, when superiors and subordinates are physically or socially distant from each other, or when inter-action potential is low among superior and subordinates' (Bass, 1960). If the subordinate suffers a deficiency in knowledge or skill relevant to a particular decision, and the superior possesses the appropriate talents, a centralised style is justified (Yukl, 1971). Participation is also likely to be negatively related to group performance when rapid decision making is required. The prevailing leadership environment at the higher levels of organisation may encourage anything but the exercise of a permissive style by the superior (Tannenbaum and Massarik, 1963). Also because of prevailing or past culture subordinates may expect and demand strong directive leadership from superiors. McMurry (1958) believes that management tries to push decisions down the hierarchy but this is invariably resented from below. To support this point of view he presents an observation the embodiment of Theory X: 'at least three quarters of those whom I have encountered in business have shown a pathetically small desire or capacity either for genuine self-improvement or for self-direction. They don't really want to improve themselves if this requires effort. They do not want responsibility. They simply want a safe, secure job and someone to tell them what to do.' In the discussion justifying an alternative to the democratic style in certain circumstances it was inevitable to consider the influence of situational factors. The next section will pursue a study of situational factors in greater depth.

SITUATIONAL FACTORS

According to Uris (1963), in considering the applicability of a particular leadership style one has to consider the status attached to a job, the relevance of the subordinate's experience, his qualifications, training and intelligence. A stable group that works

47

well together and has the skill and experience to take decisions would probably find a democratic style most suitable. An untrained and undisciplined group or a group operating in a novel situation may call for a more autocratic style. The motivational disposition of a group may also be of importance. Groups with a high level of motivation and the highest level of productivity were associated with a performance and human relations-oriented leadership style. Groups with a low level of motivation and the highest level of productivity were associated with a performance-oriented supervision. The greatest level of group cohesion seemed to be promoted by performance-oriented supervision at the cost of a lower degree of satisfaction and a greater degree of hostility levelled at the supervisor. The supervisor who emphasised the performance and human relations aspects of the job had the effect of promoting the highest degree of satisfaction and the weakest level of hostility (Misnmi and Seki, 1971).

The importance of the decision to the subordinate could be a major determinant of preferences for participative leadership (Maier, 1965). If therefore a decision is considered very important by the subordinate, he is likely to prefer to exert as much influence as possible. Where decisions are considered not to involve matters of importance, subordinates are unlikely to object to the imposition of a directive style, particularly a benevolent one. In circumstances where subordinates place trust in the leader to make a decision favourable to them, the less they will feel it necessary to participate in order to protect their interests.

Likewise the bureaucratic orientation of subordinates may dictate their preferences for leadership style. Kavanagh (1975) found that 'persons higher in their preferences for an organisational climate characteristic of the classical bureaucratic model want an ideal supervisor higher in Initiating Structure and Production Emphasis behaviours but lower in Consideration and Tolerance of Freedom behaviours than those

persons lower in bureaucratic orientation.' Yukl
(1971) would stress, in addition, that the subordinate's preferences for Initiating Structure is partially dependent on his commitment to efficiency and
goal achievement. Korten (1968) associates degree of
goal structuring with different patterns of leadership.
The trend towards high goal structure is encouraged by
an increase in stress derived from internal motivational dispositions or external threats. Wispe and
Lloyd (1955) found a preference for a less structured
or permissive situation to emerge in the absence of
significant threats in the environment. However, the
greater the threat perceived the more highly structured the preferred situation. Stress and lack of
clarity as to the best plan of action to pursue in
given circumstances can give rise to the replacement
of one leader by another who is more able to tackle
the problems confronting the group. In the process
he may acquire greater power than previously bestowed
on the original leader (Hamblin, 1958). It would
also appear that in a low stress situation it is
difficult for an authoritarian leadership to sustain
itself. It is for this reason that an autocratic
leader, in order to maintain power, emphasises threats
from within and outside and strives towards high goal
achievement so as to keep the group united. This is
a ploy very evident at the macro level in the operation of totalitarian social systems. The power of
the situation is further evidenced by variations in
leadership patterns as a result of specific circumstances. For example, a crisis may call for immediate
decisive action without any reference to the group.
Outside a crisis situation different considerations
are likely to prevail. A competent leader who has a
record of success behind him may be able to resist
group pressures to conform to their demands, (high
idiosyncrasy credit), but if present non-conformity
does not generate more group success the leader's
idiosyncrasy credit will decline and he will then have
to operate within more constraining limits set by the
group (Hollander and Julian, 1970). Mulder and
Stemerding (1963) maintain that when subordinates are
committed to the attainment of group goals or survival

of the group, and the task or environment favours a
centralised style, then they are likely to expect the
leader to make most of the decisions. A person may
display qualities of leadership and prove effective
in a situation requiring diagnosis and prediction but
prove ineffective in situations where time for con-
templation and rigorous assessment of alternatives is
a very rare thing. A condition regulating effective
leadership performance is the degree of influence a
leader has at the higher echelons of the organisation
(Pelz, 1963). The standard of performance achieved by
the subordinate could have a material bearing on the
choice of style of leadership adopted by the superior.
Lowin and Craig (1968) believe that the more the subordinate contributes to the eventual desired outcomes
valued by the manager the more positive the manager's
attitudes will be towards the subordinate. This will
be reflected in the degree of freedom given to the
subordinate and is contrary to the oft quoted causal
relationship of leadership style determining productivity. They conclude from the findings of an experimental study that the causal relationship of performance influencing style is often ignored but is as
important as the opposite one of style influencing
performance. A similar view was forwarded by
Galbraith and Cummings (1967) who hypothesised that
a leader can improve the performance of a subordinate
by being highly considerate to him if task motivation
is impressive. Considerate behaviour is then used as
a reward and would be withheld from subordinates showing little motivation. Finally, Thompson (1961) doubts
whether democratic practices have yet taken root because of the existence of a fundamental superior/
subordinate conflict. This conflict is alleged to
express itself as a result of the demands made on the
subordinates - i.e., to be loyal, obedient and respect
the superior's veto - and the subordinate's need for
respect, and to be evaluated on the basis of merit.
Obviously tension would be reduced when the subordinate gives way to the superior's demands.

Perhaps the most influential situational theory is
that put forward by Fiedler (1967) in his Contingency

Model of Leadership. It attempts to predict how style of leadership, leader-member relations, the position power vested in the leader and the structure of the task harmonise to determine the leader's ability to achieve productive output. The measure of the style of leadership is the esteem of the leader for his least preferred co-worker (LPC). The LPC is the person the leader has found most difficult to co-operate with. To arrive at an LPC score leaders were asked to rate both their most preferred co-worker (MPC) and their least preferred co-worker (LPC). Leaders who describe their MPC's and LPC's similarly are classified as 'high LPC' leaders, whilst those who describe their LPC's much more negatively than their MPC's are classified as 'low LPC' leaders. The co-worker evaluated in this way need not be someone the leader is actually working with at the time. According to Fiedler the LPC score is best interpreted as a dynamic trait which results in different behaviour as the situation changes. A leader with a high LPC rating would be psychologically close to his group members; with a low LPC rating he would be psychologically distant. The leader who describes his least preferred co-worker in a relatively favourable manner (high LPC) tends to be permissive and considerate in his relationship with group members. He gains satisfaction and self-esteem from successful interpersonal relations. The leader who describes his least preferred co-worker in a relatively unfavourable manner (low LPC) tends to be autocratic, task centred and less concerned with the human relations aspects of the job. He gains satisfaction and self-esteem from successful task performance. Therefore, the high and low LPC leaders seek to satisfy different needs in the group situation. Applying this interpretation of leadership style to that of the Ohio State school we might conclude that a high LPC leader seems to rank relatively high on Consideration and the low LPC leader relatively high on Initiating Structure. Though this conclusion may have intuitive appeal, Weissenberg and Gruenfeld (1966) challenge it. Drawing on evidence from a field study of civil service supervisors they assert that a low LPC was associated with an inter-

mediate point between the extremes of Initiating
Structure and Consideration. They also challenge the
view that the LPC measure is a good predictor of
leadership behavioural characteristics, a point that
will be taken up later.

The three major variables in the work situation which
can impede or facilitate a leader's attempt to influence group members are, as stated above, leader-member
relations, the structure of tasks and the position
power of the leader. In the normal course of events
the organisation provides support for the leader by
structuring tasks with the help of procedures, rules
and regulations. The degree of task structure can be
measured by establishing the extent to which work
decisions can be verified, the degree of clarity surrounding the stating of the work goal, the number of
methods available for achieving the goal and the extent to which one can be specific about the solution
to the work problem. The leader finds it easier to
force compliance in a structured task situation than
in an unstructured task situation. In the latter
situation the leader may find it difficult to exercise
influence because neither he nor group members can be
dogmatic about what should be done; in fact, the
leader will have to pay attention to inspiring and
motivating his followers. Position power is the
authority vested in the leader's position as distinct
from any power arising from his skill and ability in
handling matters arising within the group. It would
include the rewards and punishment at the leader's
disposal; his authority to define the group's rules;
and his appointment being immune from termination by
the group. The most important of these three dimensions is leader-member relations. A liked and res-
pected leader, or one working in a smoothly functioning group can do what would be difficult for a leader
in different circumstances. Position power is the
least important of the three dimensions because a
well liked leader can get results without institutional
power, and likewise he will not need the power if the
task is clearly structured. Fiedler arrives at a
continuum depicting the favourableness of the situation

52

for the leader. Task-oriented leaders performed more effectively in situations which are either very favourable or very unfavourable for them. This was found to be so in basketball teams, surveying teams, military combat crews and in complex organisations when executive functions were examined. Relationship-oriented leaders perform better in situations which are intermediate in favourableness for them. Policy decision-making groups in complex organisations appeared to require a considerate, permissive, relationship oriented leadership where a good group climate existed.

Fiedler's theory tries to make situational leadership theory more convincing by isolating and identifying conditions under which different styles of leadership will be more or less effective. Group performance is therefore dependent upon the match between the leader's influence and power and his motivational disposition. Recognising Fiedler's work as an ambitious enterprise involving quite a few simplifications, Smith (1973) goes on to say –

> For example he assumes that the effectiveness of leaders is validly measured by the productivity of their subordinates, ignoring morale and other indicators. He assumes further that the leader's qualities need to be classified on only a single dimension. Finally he assumes that situations in which leaders operate can be classified in terms of their favourability to the leader.

Undoubtedly Fiedler's research methodology, along with most, suffers deficiencies. One recognises the selection of the situational dimensions as arbitrary, but his model has given a welcome emphasis to situational determinants of leadership effectiveness.

The findings of Fiedler and Likert – advocate of employee-centred leadership – could converge if one condition is met. That is if the immediate environmental factors in Likert's studies were intermediate in favourableness. However, we have no way of knowing that such a condition is met because Fiedler's situational measures were not used by Likert. Fiedler's model, often in partial form, has been subjected to empirical test with rather mixed results in different settings. In an experimental study in a laboratory setting Sample and Wilson (1965) examined certain aspects of the propositions put forward by Fiedler. They maintained that their investigation does not support Fiedler's notion that the unfavourable low LPC leader is generally socially distant and unfriendly. Both favourable and unfavourable styles of leadership - expressed in LPC terms - were used by superiors friendly to group members but at different times during the task. The unfavourable LPC leader quickly and firmly structures the group's procedures during the planning stage of an assignment and is then free later to play a less dominating and even jovial role. On the other hand, the favourable LPC leader holds a group discussion during the planning period when the work is not clearly organised. It is only with partial success that he attempts and achieves organisation of the work during the latter phases of task performance. This might be explained in terms of a lack of an adequate task orientation. However, it was found that the low LPC leaders displayed less positive socio-emotional behaviour during the early stages of an assignment when planning and organising was needed. The high LPC leader was more concerned with establishing warm interpersonal relationships with group members during the initial planning stage. But during the performance phase of the assignment high LPC leaders became more task oriented and low LPC leaders more human relations oriented. Graham (1968) in his study of life insurance agents endorses Fiedler's findings in one significant respect. Leaders with a high LPC score tend to be primarily human relations oriented whereas low LPC leaders tended to be more task oriented. Though variability did arise, when for example a low LPC leader becomes more considerate in his approach on some occasions, Graham concurs with Sample and Wilson (1965) in maintaining that high LPC leaders were not more favourably evaluated than the low LPC leader. Any differentiation

can be accounted for not on the basis of their primary
orientations but instead on how well they carry out
their particular leadership styles over a period of
time. In an investigation conducted in three organisations Hunt (1967) chose co-acting groups. Unlike
the groups chosen by Fiedler, co-operation between
group members was required to perform the task and
the leader's role consists of co-ordinating activities
of members. The leader is also required to provide
individual motivation and psychological support and
encouragement. Since position power of the leaders in
the organisations sampled was high, this variable was
not considered in Hunt's study. The findings suggest
that, to a large extent, variations in leadership
effectiveness are attributable to the leader-member
relations variable alone. This result is understandable given the nature of the leader's role in co-
acting groups. It appears to be imperative to foster
successful leader-member relations within co-acting
groups. An attack on a proposition of Fiedler that
creativity is discouraged under task-oriented leadership comes from Andrews and Farris (1967). They found
from their study of scientists that creativity flouri-
shed in such circumstances. In highlighting some desirable behaviour of a leader, particularly trust and
openness, Rubin and Goldman (1968) find it difficult
to concede that this kind of climate can be established by a low LPC leader who remains psychologically
distant from his group. They also criticise Fiedler
for a lack of explicit concern for the needs of individual employees and give us their version of the
effective leader as someone who is able to differentiate between subordinates in performance and culti-
vates open communication. As to task structure,
Greenwood and McNamara (1969) dismiss the idea that
this variable has any effect on leadership effectiveness, though their population sample has serious limitations.

More recent evidence is also critical of Fiedler's
model. Graen et al. (1970) criticise the research
strategy and the limited number of statistically
significant results and from a review of relevant

studies suggest that comparability is limited because different operational definitions of leader-member relations and position power have been used in different studies. Fiedler (1971a) throws doubt on the substance of this allegation. Graen et al. (1971) return with experimental evidence to discredit the LPC and conclude that there was no relationship between the leader's LPC score and the perception of group members of leader behaviour. The person they designated leader was chosen at random and completed the LPC form. At the conclusion of the experiment group members completed a questionnaire describing the behaviour of the leader. The force of this finding is however tempered by the fact that the researchers relied on undergraduate students as subjects and used a non-standard measure of leader behaviour. Fiedler (1971b) is quick to point out that the Graen experiments were unable to differentiate sufficiently between the situations constructed in the laboratory, and considers the work as a result an invalid test of his theory. However, the relationship between the LPC score and leader behaviour challenged by Graen et al. and defended by Fiedler was explored by Stinson and Tracy (1974). Using more realistic subjects - 21 general foremen from a metal processing factory - and a standard measure of leader behaviour - Leader Behaviour Description Questionnaire - they found, as did Graen, that leadership style (LPC) did not correspond to leadership behaviour as observed by subordinates.

A suggestion that there is a similarity between the scales used to measure LPC and leader-member relations, having the effect of considerably contaminating these measures by a measurement effect, comes from McMahon (1972). But perhaps the greatest weakness of the LPC is 'that it implies that a given leader has a fixed, invariant style of leadership which he uses in all situations' (Smith, 1973). The LPC scores for college students were found to have fluctuated over an eight week period, and though the LPC scores for industrial supervisors also fluctuated they were more stable than in the former case (Stinson and Tracy, 1974).

One discerns an inconsistency in Fiedler's position since he has modified his view of the relationship between the LPC score and leadership behaviour. He now contends that high and low LPC's might vary their behaviour in different types of circumstances (Fiedler, 1972a). The high LPC leader finding himself in an unfavourable situation, where leader-member relations are poor, position power is weak and the outcome uncertain, will behave in a manner to establish good relationships in order to prove to himself that he wishes to relate to others. In a favourable situation the high LPC leader will be motivated to seek secondary goals - i.e., luxuries such as recognition from superiors and admiration - and these goals are realised by 'playing the role of the responsible, efficient and even officious leader; that is by actually or seemingly attending to the task.' This is a rather interesting point because the behaviour of the high LPC leader in a favourable situation manifests itself as distinctly oriented towards his superior and expressing a concern for the task. On the other hand, the low LPC leader in an unfavourable situation will devote his energies to achieving the primary goal of task performance or accomplishment. But in a favourable situation he will seek pleasant work relations. His behaviour will then seem friendly and considerate toward co-workers. Therefore Fiedler concedes that leadership style or motivation as measured by the LPC and leadership behaviour are not directly related. Also a call for new methods for assessing situational favourableness originates from a group, one of whom is Fiedler (Mitchell et al., 1970). According to Rice and Chemers (1975) it is task structuring that is the single most influential factor determining behavioural modification, particularly for the high LPC leaders. The Contingency Model is obviously ready for a major overhaul but is showing remarkable resilience.

In comparatively recent times Kerr et al. (1974), representing the views of the Ohio State school of leadership, set about developing some situational propositions of leader effectiveness based on the

57

leader behaviour dimensions 'Consideration' and
'Initiating Structure' and acknowledge their indebt-
edness to House (1971) whose work on path-goal theory
has influenced the development of their ideas.   In
all, twelve propositions are put forward.   The situational propositions, with supporting evidence, are
specifically related to the Ohio State leader behaviour dimensions to disprove the notion that the Ohio
State school is not concerned with situational variables.   Wofford (1971) has also something to say about
the impact of situational factors.   Using a scheme of
leadership which incorporates the salient features of
both the Ohio State school and the Survey Research
Centre, Michigan, he found different characteristics
more effective in one situation rather than another.
Factors such as task flexibility, group size, managerial aspirations, degree of centralisation of operations called for a particular leadership approach and
the dimensions effective for production are not the
most effective for morale.   The impact of structural
factors will be examined later.   One thing seems certain from the discussion and that is that a study of
leadership is not meaningful without a recognition of
the importance of situational factors.

A LEADERSHIP CONTINUUM

The tendency in the literature, with minor exceptions,
has been to emphasise the polar ends of the leadership
style spectrum, leadership being viewed either as
task or autocratic on the one hand or permissive or
democratic on the other.   Heller (1971) argues that
power/influence concepts are of more relevance rather
than vague participation when looking at decision
processes.   However, these are rather elusive concepts.   Teulings (1971a) neatly defines power and
influence, and also authority -

> Power..... is the capacity to overcome resistance,
> to introduce changes in the face of opposition.
> The exercise of power is also visible to those
> subjected to it.

Influence on the other hand is by definition not
visible to the subjects; the subjects may find
their alternatives suddenly restricted but are
unable to trace the origin of this limitation.
Hence the exercise of influence is not faced by
opposition. If there is a choice men of position
in society prefer the use of influence over power.

Authority..... is legitimate power, that is power
with a socially fixed price for compliance.
Because the exercise of power faces opposition
the compliance of those subjected to it requires
a certain price. Power is converted into authority by fixing this price for a longer time period
in terms of scarce commodities (pay is the most
common example). Authority is therefore a more
stable form of power.

This definition of Power/Authority and Influence seems
to refer to processes moving down vertically or laterally in the organisational hierarchy and in leadership terms could be classified as directive. Another
way of looking at the power relationship is to observe the extent to which influence is exerted upwards
by those lower in the hierarchy. Mechanic (1962)
suggests that the most effective way for lower participants to achieve power is to obtain, maintain and
control access to persons, information, and instru-
mentalities. To the extent that this can be accomplished, lower participants make high ranking participants dependent upon them. Thus dependence together
with the manipulation of the dependency relationship
is the key to the power of lower participants. We
often tend to underestimate the amount of influence
subordinates exert in decisions made by superiors.
Drawing on the observations of Barnard and Simon,
Walter (1966) makes the point that, though policies
may be officially announced by superiors, they are
often initiated and elaborated by employees many
levels beneath them in the organisation chart. Heller
(1971) views the leadership process in organisations
as the sharing of influence to varying degrees between the superior and subordinates. A continuum of

59

leadership would then include own decision by superior; own decision with explanation by superior;
superior consulting subordinate; joint decision
making; and delegation. The distinctive aspect of
this model is the introduction of delegation as the
position of maximum subordinate influence, though the
area of choice is usually well specified and con-
strains behaviour. Heller maintains that delegation
is excluded from discussions of participation because participation is invariably associated with a
group-centred outlook - interaction, voting, consultation and consensus - but he believes there is no
reason why it cannot satisfy self-actualisation needs
(the justification for participation) as participation
is alleged to do. There is, of course, the danger
that it may be used punitively when only unpleasant
responsibilities are delegated.

Using a leadership continuum appears to mitigate a
problem identified by Kerr et al. (1974) as common to
both the Ohio State and Fiedler studies, that of what
befalls predictions when the leader's scores are
medium rather than high or low. The idea of describing decision-making behaviour along a continuum of
subordinate influence is certainly not new, but is a
departure from the well explored two-point scale discussed earlier. With the leadership continuum,
however, one could still arrive at centralised and
decentralised dimensions by aggregating the directive
and the permissive-oriented positions separately.

A number of authorities have presented individual
classifications of a leadership continuum. Strauss
(1963) draws a distinction between decisions made by
managers on their own, by managers and subordinates
jointly, and instances where the manager permits his
subordinate to make his own decision. March and Simon
(1958) also acknowledge a continuum of supervisory
styles, as does Likert (1967) when he puts forward his
four systems of leadership and shows a marked preference for system 4 - the participative style. In
addition Likert (1961) mentions a twelve-point scale
for describing the amount of subordinate participation

60

that occurs when organisational change is introduced. Blake and Mouton (1961) proposed a power spectrum which is a system for evaluating the amount of contribution a superior and subordinate make to decisions.

A leadership continuum is proposed by Tannenbaum and Schmidt (1958). Similarly Bass (1967) differentiated leadership patterns according to four types. Blankenship and Miles (1968) have also created a five category measure of subordinate influence in superiors' decisions. In recent times a contingency model based on the leadership continuum has been developed (Vroom, 1976). This approach to leadership style, proposed by Vroom and Yetton, is explicitly normative and situational in nature. Leadership style is seen as a process designed to maximise organisational outcomes, subject to the moderating influence of the organisational and task environment. Three criteria of effective decision making in organisations - the objective quality of the decision, the time required to make it, and the degree to which the decision will be acceptable to subordinates - are identified. To these are added various attributes of decision-making situations, for example, the extent to which information is at the disposal of subordinates to make high quality decisions, and the degree of disagreement among subordinates about preferred solutions. The above criteria and attributes would appear together on a flow chart which specifies the most rational decision making or leadership style to follow in any specified situation. It must be stressed that this model of leadership reflects what leaders should do in various organisational conditions. It does not attempt to suggest what leaders actually do.

The model of leadership style considered most suitable as an operational definition of managerial decision-making behaviour in the research study is the power/influence continuum adopted by Heller. This model could be equated with the Decision-Centralisation (DC) concept cited by Yukl (1971) which is also concerned with the behaviour of the leader, and with a number of diverse methods of decision making. Some may argue that Initiating Structure is similar to the directive end and Consideration is similar to the permissive end of the Decision-Centralisation Model, but Yukl maintains there are good theoretical arguments for treating DC as a separate aspect of leader behaviour. For example, though the Consideration factor incorporates several participative decision-making items it must be acknowledged that the desire for participation is not always present, it being dictated by personality and situational factors. Task-oriented behaviour is implicit in Initiating Structure, but this is not tantamount to denying the subordinate the chance to use his influence in the decisions of his superior. Almost certainly there is some form of relationship, more likely an indirect one, between Consideration and DC and the latter with Tolerance of Member Freedom, but Yukl (1971) considers it more practical to define Consideration as simply the degree to which a leader's behaviour expresses a positive rather than an indifferent or negative attitude toward subordinates. In the author's research instrument the above conceptual distinction is apparent. Decision-making behaviour, however, does not exist in a vacuum but has to bear some relationship to the type of decision considered and the structural features of organisation likely to impinge on it. If this is so, then a close examination of these factors is both desirable and appropriate. It is to this question that we now turn in Chapter 3.

3 Impact of decision processes and structural determinants

It is now patently clear that leadership is something which is subject to a number of influences. Two major influences, to be discussed in this chapter, are the decision-making process and selected structural characteristics of organisation. The decision-making process sets the scene for the behaviour involved in it, and decision-making behaviour takes place within an organisational framework.

DECISION PROCESSES

A brief moment's reflection on the claims made on behalf of parapsychology might dazzle one into a blind acceptance of precognitive powers as phenomena related to decision-making ability. Ever since Uri Geller's spectacular feats in precognition, telepathy and psychokinesis (Taylor, 1975), apparently it has stirred up interest in ways in which telepathy and precognition may be of help to the executive. No wonder then that in recent times a report on research carried out in the USA appeared in The Financial Times with the heading 'Why hunch may help the right decision' (Irvine, 1974). According to Irvine most top flight executives say they rely ultimately on their judgement or intuition. However, this is understandable since specialised decision-making techniques are not yet so advanced or sophisticated as to rule out the intervention of intuitive judgement or inspired guesswork. In fact, one can never deny the influence of intuitive judgement; what is more important is the reduction of the area conventionally reserved for intuitive judgement by the development and better use of decision analysis techniques.

Litchfield (1956) has put forward a proposition

63

viewing decision making as either rational, deliberative, discretionary, purposive, or irrational, obligatory and random. In the former instance we proceed
through somewhat of an idealised cycle. We begin by
clarifying and describing the issue in question. A
situational analysis then takes place with reference
to a variety of intelligence data. For the accountant
this obviously means a perusal of a variety of cost
and revenue data in addition to extrapolations. A
specification of alternative courses of action follows,
and where the likely consequences of each alternative
are known they are explicitly stated. Where they are
unknown, estimates are required and could take the
form of alternatives. Methods available in business
to tackle these quantities are, for example, economic
forecasting, market projections and linear programming.
The next step is to review the issues involved in the
decision in the light of what is known about the existing situation with reference to the alternative
courses of action which are now available. This is
the stage when values are assessed, probabilities
appraised and strategy is devised in conditions of
imperfect knowledge. The deliberative process now
approaches rationality as risk is calculated, normally
in mathematical terms, and values are explicitly
stated. A final choice is then made which will be
influenced by several considerations resting on the
rationality, mental faculties and discretionary
power of the decision maker. Obviously few decisions
in organisations are arrived at by means of this full
sequence of actions. This can be attributable to a
number of constraining influences. We are all prone
to irrationality at one time or another and invariably
we do not have enough time to methodically subject
each decision to such rigorous analysis. By implication Caplan (1971) recognises the accountant's sub-
scription to the idealised cycle view of decision
making when he states that accountants are deluding
themselves if they consider the activity of gathering,
processing, and interpreting data as an objective exercise, neither can they achieve the degree of certain-
ty and neutrality often attributed to them. Whatever
course of action is decided it must be executed and

subsequently verified as to its correctness. At the execution stage a decision has to be communicated, the superior taking the appropriate action or delegating to others the authority to act. He also has to provide for possible adjustment to and modification of the original decision in the light of changing circumstances (Martin, 1959). It is sometimes wrongly assumed that the conditions anticipated in the making of a decision will prevail, particularly when the time factor involved is long. We have only to consider the proposition of Merton (1936) as to the unanticipated consequences of purposive sociological action to realise that the interplay of forces and circumstances in a given situation is so complex as to render prediction of them quite beyond reach; this is apart from the handicap of incomplete knowledge, error and bias of interest which is likely to intervene.

When decisions are interpreted in the form of specific programmes they become guidelines to future action. We can then draw a distinction between programmed and non-programmed decisions. According to Simon (1970), a programmed decision is in essence repetitive and routine with a definite procedure - e.g., pricing ordinary customers' orders. On the other hand, a non-programmed decision could be considered novel, unstructured and consequential. This type of decision cannot be dealt with in a clear-cut manner, one finds difficulty in locating a precedent for it and the problem tends to be elusive or complex. Simon maintains that non-programmed decision making can be improved by orderly thinking; generalised operating procedures could, perhaps, be constructed, and the quality of both types of decision can be enhanced by the introduction of skilled participants to the organisation together with appropriate training and planned experience. There is also a danger that programmed activity will drive out that which is non-programmed, but the presence of staff activities in organisations ensures the survival of activities devoted to non-programmed thought.

Having observed a business decision Cyert et al.

(1970b) make a number of relevant points. First, alternatives are not usually given but must be sought. An important part of the process is therefore the search for alternatives and once a satisfactory solution is discovered, even though the field of possibilities is not exhausted, the search is discontinued. This is something that is neglected by the classical theory of rational choice. Second, consequences alleged to flow from each alternative are seldom given. It follows that a search for consequences is another important aspect of decision making. Third, a comparison of alternatives cannot be confined to analysis using a financial or quantitative criterion only because of consequences of an intangible nature which make comparison and evaluation difficult. Finally, in reality the problem itself may not be given and an important activity is searching for significant problems to tackle. Dufty and Taylor (1970), unlike Cyert et al's observation of the active phases of the decision process, studied the implementation stage of a non-programmed decision. The decision was connected with the transfer of personnel from one location of an organisation to another. Though the Chief Executive specified the outcome - the transfer of a specified number of staff - it was the Personnel Superintendent who had to connect the means to the end. He was given wide discretionary powers to use both his standard programmes and to develop new programmes or modify old ones through the processes of problem solving and learning. His first line of action was to initiate problem-solving activity by calling a conference of individuals qualified to contribute to the solution of the problem. From this conference resulted, where feasible, the preparation of programmes of activity. As the implementation processes neared the completion stage lack of optimisation of the operations was evident. Standards as to the calibre of staff, previously considered of vital importance, were relaxed because of a reluctance to move on the part of some staff. This had the effect of creating organisational slack, which was condoned by the men and union officials alike. The unanticipated consequences acted to the disadvantage of the company by creating a situation whereby organisational slack obtained at the old site and manpower at the new site fell below expectations in terms of quality.

Cyert et al. (1970a) feel that because information on the consequences of particular courses of action in business organisations is frequently hard to obtain and is likely to be unreliable, conscious and unconscious bias in expectations is introduced, and if perception is not aimed at realising hopes then new developments in reality are rationalised to fit in with expectations. As a result, they believe 'that research on selective perception and recall is of substantial importance to an empirical theory of business decision making.'

Programmed and non-programmed decisions also find expression in different terms by Drucker (1954). These are strategic decisions, involving risk, and tactical decisions, which are of a routine problem-solving nature. According to Drucker, strategic decisions involve the future, cover many aspects of business which are simultaneously affected, involve substantial sums of money or great unknown factors and are almost always taken by top management. Tactical decisions, on the other hand, are frequently taken every day within organisations. A tactical decision is taken by an accountant when he allocates a sum to a particular account.

Hickson (1966) maintains that the growth of programmed decisions leads to superiors paying too much attention to this type of decision to the neglect of non-programmed decisions, and he associates programmed decisions with a lack of power and non-programmed decisions with the acquisition of power. Using the dimension 'task structure', a variable not too dissimilar to the programmed decision, Fiedler (1972b) tends to share the view of Hickson. He believes -

tasks or assignments that are highly structured, explicit or programmed give the leader more

67

influence than tasks that are vague, nebulous and
unstructured. It is easier to be a leader when
the task is described step by step in a manual of
standard operating procedures.

With specific reference to the predicament of subordinates, Dill (1958) differs in his perspective from
that of Hickson and Fiedler and argues that the
autonomy of subordinates reaches a peak when making
routine choices in the decision process but declines
sharply on novel decisions. In the routine decision
situation the manner in which decisions are made is
governed in a detailed fashion by established precedent, explicit rules and regulations and standard
operating procedures, which almost certainly obviate
the necessity for overt supervision. This is a rather
interesting point because the routine decision situation of the type just described could give rise in
some circumstances to delegative behaviour on the
part of the superior. Dill goes on to emphasise that
important decisions of an infrequent nature that
culminate in committing scarce resources, generating
risk and uncertainty, are the type of decisions that
deny the subordinate the autonomy he enjoys in making
recurrent decisions. In fact Walter (1966) comes
closer to Hickson's premise - that more power is
associated with non-programmed decisions - when,
relying on data from empirical observation, he stip-
ulates that subordinate influence is very pronounced
in non-programmed decision situations. It is perhaps
to be expected for a superior to take advantage where
possible of a subordinate's technical competence,
previous specialised training and detailed information
about the immediate decision environment. If nothing
else, a superior is prone to rely on the knowledge of
a subordinate in order to save himself a lot of time
and effort. In such circumstances the superior is
doing little more than endorsing the subordinate's
field interpretations or decisions. As to what happens to subordinate influence in a programmed situation, a prior hypothesis by Walter that power would
be centralised, creating more superior influence and
less subordinate influence, fared very poorly.

Observations had shown that on some occasions the subordinate brought to the notice of the superior a situation requiring action and then proceeded to tackle the problem, having first received the superior's authorisation to do so. In another situation one might find the superior bringing to the notice of the subordinate a problem requiring attention with a directive to see to it. In other circumstances a subordinate's recommendations, requesting attention be given to a particular problem or issue, would be allowed to lapse because resources are scarce and consequently an emphasis is placed on priorities.

This led to a revision of the latter hypothesis which then took the form of, 'that the influence of superiors in programmed decision making lies chiefly in their ability to specify priorities among the alternative actions supported by their subordinates and clients.' This is a departure from Dill's total autonomy and Hickson's opposite presumption that subordinate power or influence is absent. However, Heller (1971) confirms Hickson's viewpoint in this respect. In seeking an explanation for the incidence of centralised decision styles in the areas of production and finance he postulates that tasks in these areas lend themselves to programmed decisions and as a consequence this leads to a centralisation of power. The refined hypothesis of Walter - superior/subordinate influence in programmed decision situations - is shared by the author. Equally subordinate influence in non-programmed situations, in line with the position of both Hickson and Walter, is something which appeals to one's impression of reality.

The distinction made between programmed and non-programmed decisions, in terms of subordinate influence, has received minor attention, though typical business decisions in relation to a continuum of decision-making behaviour have been considered by Blankenship and Miles (1968) and Heller (1971). In the former instance, programmed decisions only were examined and in the latter case no such distinction was made; instead the focus was on the nature of the decision and the level of organisation at which the decision was made. For example, one set of decisions were sub-divided into task-related and maintenance (personnel) decisions, the other set were categorised according to whether they affected the direct subordinate or the subordinate once removed from the superior. Heller and Yukl (1969) found that first and second line supervisors were likely to share more power with subordinates when task decisions, rather than maintenance decisions, were under consideration. Senior managers were more likely to allow greater subordinate influence in decisions affecting indirect rather than direct subordinates. Hill (1973) also recognises that interpersonal problems call for a different leadership style to that used for technical problems. It is now clear that decision-making behaviour is influenced by some features of the decision process. There are also structural features of organisation which are likely to produce a similar effect and it is to an examination of these factors that we now turn.

STRUCTURAL DETERMINANTS

A natural starting point for any discussion of the structural features of organisation is an acknowledgement of the contribution of Max Weber. Ever since his ideal type of bureaucracy came on the scene it has become a continuous source of fascination and theoretical controversy. Bureaucracy of the ideal type, according to Weber (1946), is managed by experts who are expected to subscribe to a highly impersonal rational perspective with the demands of positions requiring job holders to perform their duties as efficiently as possible. Rationality in decision making and obedience in the performance of duties are the keystones of the entire system. It appears emotion is something to be excluded from the bureaucratic process, though the administrator who exercises charismatic authority becomes emotionally important to his followers and must establish a right to lead. On the other hand, under the ideal type of bureaucracy the rational-legal administrator receives legitimate power from the system by virtue of his technical competence. Somewhat naively it is assumed that individual motivation is maintained by the processes of conformity, leading to acceptance of the demands of the organisation, and status-seeking, the urge to advance by acquiring and exercising technical competence.

Modification to this conceptual scheme has been suggested by a number of authorities. Some maintain that a number of dysfunctional consequences flow from it. Merton (1949) feels that the emphasis on reliability, efficiency and expertise has its limitations, and that bureaucracy engenders strong feelings because of the pressure to conform. This is further aggravated by mounting pressure, having its roots in individual expectation, that the organisation requires reliability, consistency, commitment and loyalty from the individual. Often in the process of enforcing compliance a high degree of emphasis is placed on discipline. The danger here lies in an over-emphasis on discipline, with the strong emotions attached to it, leading to a transference of sentiments away from the aims of the organisation to its detailed working, eventually resulting in the displacement of goals. As a result we expect to see the emergence of formalism and ritual as a consequence of a preoccupation with specified procedural matters. Excesses in this respect lead to diminishing awareness of organisational objectives and the development of 'red tape'. All this is apart from 'trained incapacity' whereby previous training and past skills elicit inappropriate responses to changed conditions.

The above interpretation opens the way for a systems perspective which Gouldner (1959) considers to operate side by side with the bureaucratic model. The distinctive features of the natural systems approach - also represented by Parsons (1956) and Selznick (1948) - is that the organisation as a system has survival and maintenance needs with an ability to respond in a spontaneous fashion to a changing environment, striving at all times to maintain a dynamic equilibrium. This is so irrespective of the fact that each part of the organisation has its own goals and needs and that organisational goals are but another set of goals. By way of contrast, an action perspective (Silverman, 1968) departs from a systems emphasis by maintaining that it is the individual's interpretation of the event that really matters.

In more recent times the preoccupation with rationality and formality appears to have suffered relegation in favour of a comparative analysis of formal structures. Blau and Scott (1963) constructed a typology based on the criterion of 'who benefits'. The prime beneficiaries, according to this scheme, are members or ordinary participants, owners or managers, clients and members of society at large; the respective organisations are mutual benefit associations, business concerns, service organisations and common-weal organisations. Etzioni (1961) in his comparative analysis of complex organisations treats compliance as the central theme. This is the power relationship which exists between those who exercise power and those subjected to it. Compliance is congruent when power is coercive and involvement is alienative (prison), when power is remunerative and involvement is calculative (work organisation) and, finally, when power is normative and involvement is moral (religious organisation). These approaches have raised the question of power and involvement as central differences between organisations at a general level of analysis. They can be contrasted with the more localised and detailed approach of Pugh et al. (1968) who rely on operational definitions of bureaucracy, with applicability across organisations irrespective of their activity or form of ownership, to create organisational profiles. The five primary variables or dimensions of organisation structure they used in their comparative study were specialisation (number of specialised activities and roles), standardisation of procedures and roles, formalisation (the extent to which things are written down), centralisation, and configuration or shape of the organisation.

An interesting finding emerged from this study in the form of a statement that bureaucracy is not a unitary concept, as conveyed by the Weberian model, but organisations may display different degrees of bureaucracy over a number of dimensions and that organisations may still be bureaucratic with a noticeable lack of centralisation. This was deduced from the non-significant correlation between centralisation and the variables overall standardisation, formalisation and shape of staff organisation.

The province of organisational analysis has also been the concern of various management theorists. An influential proponent of this school of thought is Urwick (1935). He and his contemporaries advocate principles of organisation not far removed from classical bureaucracy. Classical bureaucracy was then superseded by the classical theory of organisation, at the operational level, in which the following principles were enshrined. A vertical hierarchical structure embracing roles, optimally arranged, is required. Equal in importance is the precise definition of duties, responsibilities and the authority vested in a position. No ambiguity should surround the meaning attached to authority and channels must exist for effective delegation to take place, always remembering that authority and the related responsibility are co-equal. The chain of command, which facilitates communication and control, necessitates adherence to the principle of one man reporting to one superior. The principle of co-ordination ensures that individual or sectional effort is directed towards the achievement of common goals. On the question of the size of the span of control, it is asserted that it should be strictly limited, not to exceed five or six in situations where subordinates' tasks are inter-dependent. Finally, the functional authority (advisory) of the specialist is contrasted with the formal authority (executive) of the line manager. This is no doubt a very rational perspective and does not take seriously the needs of the individual and the constraints operating in different organisations.

It was perhaps for this reason that Woodward (1965) embarked on a programme of research examining the characteristics of a number of organisations in Essex. The main theme of her findings is the influence of technology or production systems in shaping organisational characteristics, though the importance of the history of the firm and the background of those who built it up is not discounted. She attributes a variation in structural features, such as span of control and number of levels within the hierarchy, to the production system (unit, batch, process) used by the organisation. The production system or technology is likewise held responsible for the extent of decentralisation or delegation, the form communication assumes, the quality of industrial relations and the strain experienced by individuals, the adoption of the staff-line concept and the friction or harmony generated, and the nature of the control systems used. In a later publication she tentatively suggests that management control systems have an influence on structure and behaviour (Woodward, 1970). The main conclusion of the Essex study is that the classical theory has high relevance to the operation of successful large batch and mass production firms, but firms outside this range depend on organic systems of organisation for their success.

Burns and Stalker (1961) maintain in addition that it is the instability of technology and the low level of market predictability that dictate an organic organisation structure. They, like Woodward, found that a mechanistic structure serves an organisation well if the conditions are appropriate; in this case the prevailing conditions need to be stable. An interesting variation on the theme of organic and mechanistic structures comes from Lansley et al. (1974) who extend it to form a four-fold typology of organisation, recognising different combinations of integration and control mechanisms. Different types of successful and unsuccessful organisations fit into the quadrant which expresses their unique organisational features.

A theme very much in evidence in the work of

74

Woodward and Burns and Stalker is the impact of the relevant environment on both structure and managerial behaviour. Without question the relevant environment has a significant impact on decision-making processes in business organisations. The disturbed reactive and turbulent field environments identified by Emery and Trist (1965) are two of the four ideal types of organisational environments, and are also the two impinging on the decision-making process. As yet we do not know to what extent these 'type abstractions' exist in reality; what activates a movement from one position to another is still uncertain. The full implication of each environment type for the organisation is also uncertain. The importance of the organisational environment is also emphasised by Lawrence and Lorsch (1967). They show us how the environment influences differentiation of sub-systems and cognitive sets of sub-system members. Since unity of effort is required to achieve organisational goals, diverse activities must be integrated. It hardly needs stating that future research will have to grapple with the distant organisational environment in a more sophisticated manner, than has hitherto been the case, when analysing interpersonal behaviour.

According to the results of a Canadian survey mentioned in an earlier chapter (Levesque, 1976), Chief Financial Officers are feeling a cold draught from certain regions of the relevant environment. Their main concern was the growing involvement of governments at all levels of the private enterprise system and the incidence of inflation and corporate tax changes. The author of the report concludes with the suggestion that in the future Chief Financial Officers will have to take economic trends into account when they design and recommend appropriate financing decisions; this is apart from advice they may receive from outside specialists. The importance of the relevant environment is also stressed by respondents in the present study. One respondent remarked that 'modern industry is very complex and interference from government through its agencies makes the role of the Financial Controller/Chief Accountant much more difficult.

Price control, for example, has shifted pricing decisions from the Marketing Department to Accountants. Developing financial acumen in business structures to deal with government policies is another.'

It appears that the debate as to which is the critical environmental variable dictating variations in organisation structure still continues. Pugh et al. (1969) discount the importance given to technology as an influential factor determining the structure of an organisation and consider size and dependence - the relationship the organisation has with any owning group, with suppliers, customers, etc., - as factors truly influencing structural features of organisation. It is size rather than technology - though technology will be related to structural variables close to the shop floor - which bears the strongest relationship to such dependent variables as specialisation, standardisation, formalisation and centralisation. In fact Woodward (1965) attached no great importance to size as a critical variable but, with due respect, her sample did not include many large-sized organisations. Lansley et al. (1974) also stress the importance of size, particularly in the printing industry, by suggesting that there is a clear tendency for larger organisations to have a steeper than average hierarchical structure, above average communication loads for individual managers and superiors, a high percentage of communications outside the chain of command and less mutual agreement about communication contacts both laterally and vertically. Small organisations were found to have flatter organisational hierarchies and more mutual agreement about communication contacts both laterally and vertically. Underlining the importance of size of organisation as a structural determinant Child (1973), using data from three different empirical studies, argues that it is size - rather than technology, magnitude of information flow, size of owning group, etc., - which appears to be the important predictor of role specialisation, functional specialisation and number of specialist staff. All these factors contribute to organisational complexity. It is this complexity that contributes to the creation of indirect and impersonal managerial controls and promotes delegation to qualified employees. They in turn are instrumental in setting up more standard operating procedures and records to facilitate control and consistency of performance, a preoccupation their professionalism encourages them to promote. Aiming his discourse at a different audience to that exposed to his 1973 interpretation, Child (1972) suggests that questions of performance could give rise to organisational decision makers taking decisions through which they influence organisational design. This view detracts from the general proposition that environmental variables exert the most influence on choice of organisational design. The question of strategic choice is then examined in which choice of organisation structure is to a large extent dependent upon decisions emanating from the dominant coalition within the organisation. But to complicate matters somewhat we are told that 'when incorporating strategic choice in a theory of organisation, one is recognising the operation of an essentially political process in which constraints and opportunities are functions of the power exercised by decision-makers in the light of ideological values.' Hall (1968) offers his explanation to account for structural variation. He postulates that there appear to be differences in bureaucratic structures adopted by professionals inside and outside a professional office and concludes 'that the nature of occupational groups in an organisation affects the organisational structure.' A shadow of doubt is therefore cast on the existence of any stable relationship between the contextual variables and structural variation examined earlier.

STRUCTURE AND ATTITUDES AND BEHAVIOUR

Already the 'dysfunctional school' has identified the weaknesses of classical bureaucracy in terms of its human repercussions. Therefore it seems appropriate to examine, in the first instance, features of bureaucracy that affect attitudes and behaviour generally

77

and then proceed to suggest that bureaucracy is also likely to influence patterns of decision-making behaviour that lie within its boundaries.

Argyris (1959) believes that structure is one of the key variables - the others are restrictive leadership and management controls - which promotes dependence and is anathema to the 'mature' individual; though he ascertains from empirical evidence that certain personality types, those who had not proceeded beyond the infant end of the personality continuum, were congruent with formal structure. This is also a theme running through a more recent publication (Argyris, 1973) with the emphatic acknowledgement that bureaucracy generates alienation. Support for this latter proposition comes from Aiken and Hage (1966) who report that organisations conforming more to the formal bureaucratic arrangements are more likely to have a greater incidence of alienation, with the conspicuous presence of greater dissatisfaction in those organisations in which jobs were fragmented and rigidly structured. The power of bureaucratic structures, in terms of the demands imposed on role occupants, has been generally recognised. Merton et al. (1957) state that individuals not initially suited to the demands of a bureaucratic position progressively undergo modifications to personality. But equally one could validly assert the view that it is both the demands of role and personality which bring about individual adaptation in the organisation (Levinson, 1959). One type of structure may be more amenable to one type of personality than another. Tannenbaum and Allport (1956) related personality types to 'autonomous' and 'hierarchical' structures of organisation and found that where structure was compatible with personality subjects were more satisfied, liked the structure better and were keen to remain in it. There is, however, one minor qualification to this finding. Although the hierarchical structure suited those who were that way inclined, on average the 'autonomous' structure produced more satisfaction than the 'hierarchical' one. Thompson (1961) believes that bureaucratic structures tend to pose constraints on group effectiveness by interfering with the development of cohesiveness and encouraging competition rather than co-operation.

Having explored briefly a global impact of bureaucracy, we shall now select certain characteristics of organisation structure and relate them individually to attitudes and behaviour. One such characteristic is level within the hierarchy. In a way it is not surprising to find differentiations in attitudes and behaviour associated with status differentials since differentiations are so prevalent in society at large. Porter (1961) examined the relative importance attached to thirteen different personality traits at two levels of management. The higher-level managers considered aggression, dominance, independence and originality more important for managerial success, with a lesser degree of importance conferred on conformity, co-operation, flexibility and sociability. The first group of traits show a strong emphasis on personal and individual capabilities, while the second group contain traits which show a capability for adapting to the feelings and behaviour of others. As the findings of this study were considered to be suggestive only, Porter and Henry (1964a) felt it necessary to pose two problems for further investigation. These were concerned with whether the perception of personality qualities needed for job success changes from lower to higher levels of management, and whether the protestant ethic based inner-directed traits (forceful, imaginative, independent, self-confident, decisive) rather than the other-directed traits (co-operative, adaptable, cautious, agreeable, tactful) are regarded more important for success at progressively higher levels of management. The results of the study show that the inner-directed cluster of traits were regarded more important the higher the level of management; the reverse was true for the cluster of other-directed traits. Though we may conclude from this result that an 'organisation man' is more likely to be found at the bottom rather than at the top of the organisation, an important qualification is required. That is, the trait caution – other-directed – was regarded as slightly more important at

79

the higher than at the lower level, but the trait
self-confidence - inner-directed - varied little between levels. Relying on the self-perceptions of top
and middle managers, Porter and Ghiselli (1957) report
different qualities endorsed by the two groups. Members of top management are more likely to see themselves as active, self-reliant, and generally willing
to take action on the basis of their own faith in
themselves and in their abilities rather than simply
being influenced by objective evidence. They appear
confident in the job and in social interaction,
display certain cultural refinements and feel it necessary to ingratiate themselves. Members of middle
management, by way of contrast, are more likely to
see themselves as careful planners, prone to thought-
ful actions and well controlled behaviour, inclined
seldom to take rash decisions, tend to consider proposed actions from many angles with a reluctance to
take hasty or unfounded decisions, tend to conform to
the rules of the system and are unwilling to take risks
in times of uncertainty. They are also unlikely to
display the same brand of confidence as displayed by
top managers; they do not wish to be controversial,
neither do they exhibit self-centred behaviour and
they describe themselves as stable and dependable individuals who try to avoid making mistakes. Given
the authenticity of these profiles, it would be interesting to try and establish whether the individuals
concerned possessed these orientations to begin with
or whether the nature of the job and the level of
organisation were the true catalyst forces in the
cultivation of these orientations.

Level within organisation is also a variable which
appears to influence the degree of job satisfaction
experienced. Rosen (1961) analysed the conditions of
work in a single plant and attributed a higher level
of satisfaction to top and middle managers, almost in
equal proportions, than to first-line supervisors.
Porter (1962) considered hierarchical level in relation to the extent to which subjects had gratified
psychological needs. Using a measure of satisfaction
which looked at differences between obtained and

expected fulfilment, he found that for the esteem, autonomy and self-actualisation needs satisfaction increased relatively more at the higher-level management positions; the security and social needs were roughly equally satisfied across all organisational levels. Pellegrin and Coates (1957) lend support to this finding when they state that top level executives emphasised intrinsic features of the job, but off-the-job rewards were given more emphasis by first-line supervisors. In a cross-cultural survey of management attitudes in fourteen countries, Haire et al. (1963) associated greater degrees of satisfaction with higher, rather than lower, levels of management. One critical variable absent from all these studies is the difference in formal education which Porter and Lawler (1965) believe should be identified. However, the studies reviewed serve to impress upon us the importance of hierarchical level as a determinant of attitudes and behaviour.

Another important factor is size, which has already been considered in the context of structural variation in response to an environmental variable. It can be viewed from two angles: size of department and size of company. Frequently one hears claims extolling the benefits of small size in terms of absenteeism, staff turnover, accident rates and productivity. According to Worthy (1950), in the smaller organisation there are fewer people, fewer levels in the hierarchy and less minute sub-division of labour. Employees find it easier to adapt and work is more meaningful because of being able to overview the scene. 'The organisation operates primarily through the face to face relationships of its members and only secondarily through impersonal institutionalised relationships.' This view of Worthy is based on impressions gained from observations of organisational functioning. Before analysing data from an empirical study in which size of organisation featured prominently as a variable, Talacchi (1960) postulates a theoretical proposition governing size of organisation and its impact on morale. As one might expect, large size leads to increases in division of labour and the development

of status differentiation which leads to a falling-off
in employee satisfaction. Division of labour narrows
jobs and areas of functional responsibility. A dep-
rivation of psychological rewards - pride in workman-
ship, recognition, responsibility and so on - ensues,
with the almost inevitable result of a deterioration
in efficiency and morale. Large size also affects
interpersonal relations. More interaction between
people and departments in the execution of a single
task develops, bringing in its wake an increase in
complexity which generates conflicting technical
interests among departments and a reduction in their
informal interaction and communication. This increases the potential for personal and group conflict,
leading to a lower level of satisfaction. Size is
also held responsible for promoting a hierarchy of
formal status relationships which has little connection with the various networks of informal group relationships. It creates an attitude of mind in which
the organisation and its goals are regarded as impersonal entities. There is a greater likelihood of
communication becoming distorted and a climate of
social distance between the upper and lower strata is
established. The way people feel and react, as a
result, is not very likely to reduce internal organisational friction. Therefore the growth in status
differentiation promotes interpersonal conflict with
undesirable behavioural consequences. Talacchi
maintains that in the small organisation this type
of thing does not happen because of the likelihood of
overlapping formal and informal status, due in part
to the fact that authority relationships are seen and
accepted in terms of natural requirements to achieve
organisational goals.

Perhaps the bureaucratising effect of size is something one could leave unchallenged, but the dysfunctional aspects of large-sized bureaucracy appear to
be over-exaggerated and the beneficial aspects of the
smaller organisation are uncritically accepted by
Talacchi. However, he found that as an organisation
increases in size, particularly a manufacturing organisation, the general level of satisfaction decreases,

and as administrative units grow in size the level of satisfaction with interaction episodes, both laterally and vertically, decrease as does the level of satisfaction derived from non-material rewards. From a behavioural, rather than an attitudinal, perspective the influence of size is in no way clearcut and definitive. Grusky (1961) produces an empirical association between rapid turnover in top management positions and increasing organisational size. But Gordon and Becker (1964), having reanalysed the data used by Grusky, were unable to establish any reasonable relationship between size and the rate of managerial succession.

Apparently size of organisation is an important consideration when managers endorse certain personality characteristics (Porter, 1963a). He found that managers from larger companies were slightly more likely to describe their jobs in terms of challenging, interesting and competitive, thereby placing the greatest emphasis on inner-directed as opposed to other-directed traits. In another context Porter (1963b) found hierarchical level as a factor which modified the relationship between size and motivation. For example, the manager from the small organisation, occupying a lower or lower-middle position, is more likely to be more satisfied. A high level of satisfaction is likewise experienced by an upper-middle manager or vice-president in the larger company. Porter and Lawler (1965) feel that the available evidence is more convincing in pointing to a better relationship between sub-unit, rather than total, size and relevant variables. So it appears that size of department is the more influential variable, with hierarchical level generally mediating the importance of size.

An organisational relationship which has attracted a fair amount of comment and analysis is that of line/staff. The role of the line manager has been conventionally viewed as that of a generalist concerned with the primary activities of the organisation. The efforts of the staff specialist are directed at supplementing the contribution of the line manager by

providing specialised assistance. Dalton (1950)
believes that the assumptions governing line/staff
relationships ought to be highlighted so as to establish whether they are realistic. These assumptions
suggest that the staff specialist is quite content to
function without formal authority, though it could be
argued he wields informal authority since he stands
to influence line policy, and that the staff specialist's suggestions as to the improvement of processes
and techniques to control more efficiently production
and people would be eagerly embraced by line managers
and applied by them. But we know that conflict situations do arise and interfere with the harmonious
functioning of this ideal relationship. It is
therefore interesting to note the impressions gained
from an observational study conducted by Dalton in
three related plants. Recognising that it is extremely difficult to withdraw or isolate staff/line conflict from general conflict, he ventures to suggest
that three conditions were basic to staff/line
struggles: conspicuous and individualistic behaviour
among staff specialists; complications due to staff
people having to justify their existence and getting
acceptance for their contributions, and as a consequence, the realisation that to secure a higher-level
staff position they were dependent upon the approval
of line personnel. It was found that line managers
disliked receiving what amounted to instructions from
younger men, and staff specialists were conscious of
this. Staff specialists who were relatively inexper-
ienced were somewhat disconcerted when their ideas
were treated lightly or frivolously. Though often
possessing impressive academic backgrounds it appeared
they suffered a deficiency in social skills and compensated for this disadvantage by endeavouring to
create informal relationships with powerful line managers. There was also a noticeable tendency on the
part of staff specialists to enhance their hierarchical structure in order to create greater opportunity
for upward mobility. Differentiation on the basis of
class and formal education manifested itself in the
way staff specialists displayed an air of superiority
in image, dress and speech, which invited anything but

complimentary remarks from line managers. Line managers who were suspicious of the intentions of staff specialists, because of their eagerness to introduce new techniques, considered their actions as something designed to usurp their own authority. As a result a power conflict inevitably ensued. Without antagonising his colleagues the staff specialist had somehow to reach a tacit agreement with line managers so as to foster a workable relationship. Otherwise there is the danger of line personnel seeking to jeopardise proposals with which they disagree. It is perhaps understandable why line managers should resist innovative proposals because, in Dalton's view, line managers may look stupid because they themselves were unable to make suggestions for improvements; the changes in methods may break up cliques and existing informal relationships and dent their authority, and changes in techniques may expose forbidden practices and departmental inefficiency. Dalton is not alone in highlighting the difficult relationship between line and staff; there are other authoritative studies which report staff/line conflict and ill-feeling (e.g., Woodward, 1965).

In seeking an explanation for the alleged disharmony and friction we shall turn to an examination of personality differences between line and staff personnel. Thompson (1961) expects to find some form of natural selection as responsible for bringing into line hierarchies people with great dominance and status needs, whereas people whose dominance needs are satisfied by mastery over materials, rather than people, will probably become specialists of some kind. This observation appears to be at variance with that of Dalton (1950) who observed staff specialists as ambitious, restless, individualistic and keen to make the right impression with the expectation of receiving individual recognition. In fact the drive for personal distinction tended to corrode group cohesiveness and cause intra-staff tensions. When managerial respondents were asked to express preferences for both inner and other-directed personality traits in terms of their importance for job success, it was found that staff specialists placed relatively more emphasis on the other-directed traits and less emphasis on the inner-directed traits than did line managers. Managers holding down combined line/staff jobs occupied an intermediate position between the other two groups (Porter and Henry, 1964b). These managers place less importance on inner-directed traits than do line managers, but consider them more important than do staff. For other-directed traits they place more reliance on them than line managers, but less reliance than staff. As is customary when interpreting data with the aid of typologies, certain traits showed reverse trends. The differentiation between line and staff personnel in the form of need gratification is reported by Porter (1963c) where higher level needs were given the greatest emphasis by line managers. From a study conducted in one company Davis (1953) considered staff specialists to be better informed than line managers because of their greater freedom and mobility within the organisation. In the light of the evidence introduced above it is no wonder that friction and conflict arise between the two groups.

As organisations become more complex in our society it is increasingly hard to identify the functions of a particular organisational unit as productive or non-productive or as line or staff (Logan, 1966). Teulings (1971a) is of the opinion that the implementation of the staff/line concept is no more than 'front-stage' behaviour in the service of actual 'back-stage' behaviour, covering up basic authority and power conflicts. The staff/line principle deludes the line manager that he only has the right to exercise power. Teulings offers an explanation of the staff/line relationship in terms of coalition theory, adopting five different models. From an empirical study in a British context he found that effective staff managers tend to form alliances of the counsellor type with line managers, where the staff department head develops a personal contact with the higher line manager and the staff subordinate with the middle and lower line managers. The staff role in such a coalition is not always as consultative and therapeutic as a 'human

relations school' interpretation might suggest. To
be effective the staff man has to be somewhat independent, able to manipulate situations informally and
generally machiavellian in approach (Teulings, 1971b),
a view not much at variance with that of Dalton (1950).
Fisch (1961) also questions what he calls the wisdom
of slavish adherence to the staff/line concept and
sets about proposing an alternative organisational
scheme, believing that staff/line has been at the root
of many of our post-war organisational problems. He
considers it a useful concept when a company's product
lines are simple and subject to infrequent changes
over time. But with diversification of product lines
and growth in complexity of operations staff specialisms proliferate. Some of these specialisms (e.g.,
research and development and finance) are so vital to
organisational success that it is perhaps unwise to
treat them as staff functions. Fisch has some flat-
tering remarks in store for accountants. 'I am sure
you can find in your company many instances where, if
the controller had more authority to initiate action
to remedy inefficiency in both manufacturing and
sales, substantial savings could be achieved faster
than under the pure line/staff system where the controller may only function as an adviser.' The alternative system he proposes is the functional-teamwork
concept which advocates the breakdown of artificial
barriers between activities and functions, regrouping
allied functions with the emphasis on organic structures. This scheme has a lot to commend itself and
could go a long way towards removing some of the
friction and conflict that beset staff/line relations.

It appears accountants adopt a directive stance when
acting a staff role in the area of budgeting. Argyris
(1953) feels that the way in which accountants operate
budgetary control systems is punitive rather than supportive and that budget staff view their role as essentially one of criticism. They also view their role
as one of policing, reporting deviations from target
to top management and view the budget as a device to
pressurise and challenge line employees. As one
might expect, line supervisors did not respond in a

favourable fashion to these attitudes and behaviour.
They tended to view the budgeting system as a mechanism reporting results without commenting on the reasons for the results, that targets were set at an
unrealistically high level with a tendency to go on
increasing them, and that the accountant's approach
was generally inflexible. Line supervisors felt that
these problems could be overcome if the accountant
recognised that budgetary standards have no firm factual basis; they are merely calculated statements of
opinion, and that matters could be improved if the
accountant was prepared to see the other man's point
of view. Argyris mentions the remarkable degree of
aggression levelled at the budget department, a not
altogether surprising phenomenon given their perceived
policing role, and also given the situation that success for the budget supervisor means failure for the
factory supervisor. Wallace (1966) commenting on some
aspects of Argyris's study suggests that budgeting
practice not only generates a department-centred
mentality with parochial views prevailing which act
to the detriment of organisational based goals, but
also that the planning and control aspect of budgeting
is sometimes over-emphasised and tends to remove the
opportunity for the exercise of personal initiative.
A number of dysfunctional consequences - defensive
behaviour, anxiety, tension and manipulative tactics
designed to produce a favourable variance - were
associated with the imposition of rigid budgets, but
apparently a profit conscious approach to budgeting
where supervisors are technically efficient and
psychologically close to their subordinates produces
a different effect (Hopwood, 1973). Another recent
study highlights the reaction of middle managers to a
budgetary control system. Unlike senior managers who
tended to view it as an instrument to provide better
control for middle management, middle managers felt it
was a policing mechanism based on inaccurate information (Beresford Dew and Gee, 1973).

The criticism of the accountant's staff role is not
confined to budgeting practice. It is alleged that
accounting as a service falls short in adequately

assessing the information needs of management. This
deficiency is exemplified in an observation by Tricker
(1967): 'The provision of information for management
through the management accounting system tends to be
haphazard. In many concerns such systems study that
there has been, has concentrated on the paperwork
systems without becoming involved with the people and
the use made of the data.' Robson (1965) takes on a
similar perspective when he maintains that many accountants do not see themselves as part of an alliance
with managers in the processing and dissemination of
information. Rather they are preoccupied with techniques without paying sufficient attention to management's information needs. Still on the same theme,
Lee (1968) suggests that the accountant operating in
the area of management information should broaden his
horizon. Elgin (1965) also admonishes the accountant
to consider the genuine needs of management for information and quotes the example of one British company
- Boots Limited - who took some positive moves by officially stressing the inter-dependent roles of management accountants and managers.

This theme of general criticism still seems to have
at least some relevance in the light of more recent
observations. Firnberg (1973) relates the deterior-
ating position of a Financial Director whose position
was gradually undermined as a result of the appointment of a Planning Director who introduced a comprehensive information system which seemed to become
the main source of information for all significant
decisions. The role of the Finance Director appeared
to be relegated to that of 'keeper of the purse'.
Although traditionally the accountant belongs to a
discipline frequently laying claim to presenting the
whole picture of what happens in the organisation,
Firnberg expresses grave doubts as to the authenticity
of this claim in reality in terms of both reflecting
the events happening and the speed with which the
happenings are being reported. Support for this position comes from Young (1973) who maintains there has
been a failure on the part of the accountants to fur-
nish the right sort of information. This failure is

attributable to two main causes: first, the accountant's lack of understanding of the decision-making
process and lack of sensitivity to the needs of the
participants in these processes; and second, that the
traditional role of the accountant in providing information more to describe or highlight a particular
manager's responsibility does not adequately equip
him to directly assist managers in decision making.
His solution to counteract this unsatisfactory state
of affairs, now used in his company, takes the form
of a 'decision analysis' technique whereby a series of
interviews with the managers concerned are arranged -
with the blessing of the Chief Executive - resulting
in a pattern of decision making devised to highlight
information requirements of assistance in decision
making. Recent empirical evidence throws further
light on the inadequacy of certain information provided by accountants to help managers. Beresford Dew
and Gee (1973), investigating the use of accounting
control data by middle managers, showed that a significant amount of information prepared for control purposes was not properly used due to the following reasons: it was not totally relevant, it was too detailed
or not detailed enough and it arrived too late. It is
therefore not surprising to find classical staff/line
friction, of the type discussed earlier, developing
between the accountant and the manager he serves.
Woodward (1965) accounted for the ill-feeling between
accountants and line managers in the sphere of production administration by asserting that management accountants were reluctant to accept the role of management accounting as a servicing or supporting function.

Span of control has been considered traditionally
an important structural variable. Its size featured
prominently in the thinking of the classical theorists
(e.g., Urwick, 1935) who viewed it as having an optimum size. Later, empiricists (Woodward, 1965; Pugh et
al., 1969; Child, 1973) considered it a function of
contextual variables - size and technology - and attributed its different magnitudes to changes in these
variables. Dale (1952) has shown how progression from

medium to large-sized organisation results in an increase in the number of subordinates reporting to one superior. Entwisle and Walton (1961), drawing on a study of spans of control in both college and small company organisations, maintain that there were small positive correlations between size of organisation and span of control, and in any case the span of control does not dramatically increase with increasing size.

It is worthwhile exploring the main reasons why the classical school show such a strong attachment to the almost constant narrow span of control. First, there is the question of span of attention. This view subscribes to the contention that a person is psychologically incapable of attending to more than seven items at the one time. Therefore the span of attention dictates the size of the span of control. But one can argue that the conditions prevailing in the psychological laboratory in which optimum spans of attention are measured do differ, often quite substantially, from ongoing organisational conditions. It is highly unlikely for an executive to have to attend to his subordinates simultaneously. But one must concede that 'the span of attention is probably a contributing factor toward limiting the span of control, but it seems unlikely that it is the only factor' (Entwisle and Walton, 1961). Second, with a larger span of control there are more possibilities for the formation of sub-groups and each sub-group produces its own unique social interaction with the superior. There are also greater opportunities for the formation of cliques with self-advancement as their primary aim. Entwisle and Walton, having invoked evidence from studies of small groups, believe that continuing external pressures are required to bind groups larger than five into cohesive spans of control. Also it is maintained that larger groups require a longer time to reach consensus with less opportunity for members to participate, and as a result members experience less satisfaction from interactions. Third, the possibility of a multiplicity of relationships inevitably acts as a constraint on the size of the span of control.

However, a positive disadvantage of the narrow span of control can be expressed as close supervision and a stifling of initiative.

Worthy (1950) equates wide spans of control with company success, posing a direct challenge to the position of the classical school. With a wide span of control, he believes close supervision becomes impossible and devolution of authority and responsibility becomes possible, though he stresses that this requires a fair measure of self-confidence and personal capacity on the part of subordinates. His recipe for success is a flat, less complex structure, with a maximum of administrative decentralisation; it is only then that one can expect an improvement in attitudes, more effective supervision, and a climate in which people are keen to assume responsibility and use their initiative. Fisch (1963) substitutes span of management for span of control and considers it in relation to different hierarchical levels of organisation. At the general manager level, with the exception of this level in medium to small companies and the management of sub-units in very large corporations, very wide spans of management are the rule rather than the exception. Middle managers on the other hand, tend to supervise subordinates with well structured jobs, and in any assessment of the optimum size of the span of management at this level one has to be cognizant of the functional and geographical diversity of company operations; the quality of company planning and control; the freedom to delegate; the amount of information at the disposal of the decision maker; the adequacy of the remuneration system and the qualities and characteristics of superiors and subordinates. Obviously this poses difficulties when trying to arrive at a figure for the span of management because of the complexity of the constraints, but the figure of fifty is suggested by Fisch and is based on his own personal observations. A much wider span of control is recommended for the supervisory level. A recognition of size and product diversification as influential agents determining the width of the span of control is very much in evidence, with the important proviso that one should always remember that companies organise themselves in diverse ways depending on the type of business, its history, location, facilities, personalities and so on. It appears that a departure from the optimum number is now well overdue, and size, hierarchical level and technology deserve our attention as mediating influences.

STRUCTURE AND LEADERSHIP

What remains to be examined is how the structural variables mentioned above, together with any relevant organisational phenomena not acknowledged so far, are likely to influence leadership or managerial decision-making behaviour. The relationship between leadership and structure is widely acknowledged. This will be explored, to begin with, at a global level of analysis, to be followed by specific reference to the impact of selected structural variables.

In his analysis of the contribution of the neo-human relations school, Strauss (1968) maintains that there is a tendency to consider their assertions as having universal applicability irrespective of prevailing situational and structural variables. He cites a case in point, that of Likert's system four style of leadership, 'which calls for high individual identification with the organisation as a whole and a great deal of interaction between groups.' This he believes is appropriate only in certain areas of work, especially where technology is complex, change is rapid and novel problems are frequently encountered for which there are no simple answers. Janowitz (1959) maintains that with the development of new weapons military authority has shifted from an emphasis on explicit instructions to manipulation with an air of paternalism appended to it. He sees a similar trend in non-military organisations. The existence of 'structural looseness', according to Thompson (1965), implies the dispersion of power in organisations with ramifications for problem solving. Argyris (1964) makes the suggestion that it might not be a bad thing if we were to accommodate

93

structure to the type of decision faced. In a similar vein, Whyte (1948) considers the prospect of organisational flexibility ruling during the discussion stage of decisions, but greater structuring to be introduced at the implementation stage. The influence of structure on leadership style is forcefully put by Worthy (1950) who contends –

> that the over-complex, over-functionalised
> organisation structure is likely to require the
> driver type of leader; the over-use of pressure
> as a tool of supervision is thus related primarily to the character of the structure and only
> secondarily to the character of the individual at
> the head of it.

Already in our discussion of Fiedler's contingency model of leadership we have noticed the prominence given to the favourableness of position power and job structuring as important variables determining the effectiveness of leadership style. Likewise, Wofford (1971) found different situational factors eliciting different leadership responses.

In a specific reference to functional specialisation Heller and Yukl (1969) reported that production and finance managers tended to use centralised leadership styles whereas non-specialised general managers and personnel managers tended to behave in a more permissive way. Purchase and sales managers were found to occupy a position between two extremes. In accounting for the differences in leadership style the authors are inclined to the view that the nature of the task is instrumental in bringing about the above result, but the answer may also lie in an analysis of the degrees of freedom in the different functions. One would expect to find a lesser degree of freedom in the finance and production departments because of the incidence of more programmed decisions. In the personnel and general management fields, on the other hand, there are likely to be relatively more unprogrammed jobs. Leadership style was also found to be influenced by job tenure, but here again hierarchical

94

level was a mediating force. Heller and Yukl feel that the longer the time spent by first and second-line supervisors in their job, the greater is the tendency to experience a shift from a permissive to a directive leadership style. In contrast, senior managers tended to use more 'delegation' as their stay in the job increases. The differences in leadership style are considered to be a function of the different perceptions of the qualities and skills in the subordinate; it appears that more power-sharing is associated with less perceived differences in skill between superior and subordinate levels in the organisation. This amounts to a question of confidence in the subordinate. It is not altogether clear why the more experienced supervisor is less willing to share his decisions with his subordinate.

An interesting theoretical question is posed by Hage and Aiken (1967) when they ask whether centralisation of power is associated with high formalisation and low complexity. The measure devised to gauge centralisation or distribution of power was aimed at establishing the amount of influence exerted by subordinates in decisions concerned with resource allocation and policy determination on the one hand, and the extent to which hierarchical authority was relied on for normal work decisions on the other. Formalisation embraced the use of rules, their description and whether they were adhered to. It would appear that formalisation is firmly established in the finance function. Complexity refers to the amount of occupational specialisation, amount of professional training and involvement in the activities of professional bodies. In circumstances where centralisation of power exists there is every likelihood of adhering to the practice of codifying past decisions to form organisational rules so as to avoid overloading the centralised decision-making unit. Decentralisation of power would then be associated with a lower degree of job codification. Earlier in this chapter reference was made to attempts at devising operational definitions of bureaucracy using dimensions not too dissimilar to those mentioned above (Pugh et al.,

1968). In a study of social welfare and health
agencies Hage and Aiken found that the relationship
between formalisation and centralisation did not
stand up to empirical test, though the extent to which
rules were enforced and expected to be observed bore
a weak or minor relationship to participation in
decision making. Therefore to counteract the lack of
commitment arising from a low level of participation
in decisions affecting organisational objectives,
rule observation is something to be considered.

When we move to a consideration of occupational
specialities a clearer picture emerges. There is
evidence to suggest that as the number of occupational specialities increases inevitably there is a movement towards decentralisation (Thompson, 1961). In
the study conducted by Hage and Aiken (1967) they
report the greater the level of professional activity
the greater are the demands for participation. This
can be explained with reference to the unique predicament of the professional in the organisation. He
normally demands more power and autonomy, and as he
becomes more competent and expert decision makers
consult him and share decision making with him. Participation in decision making, rather than reliance
on hierarchy of authority, is the 'centralisation'
dimension offering the greatest association with the
structural properties under discussion. It was found
also that wide participation in decision making appears to go hand in hand with lesser resort to job
descriptions, less close supervision, more specialisation and better trained and committed professionals.
The main message emanating from this somewhat pro-
longed deliberation is that decentralisation is associated with a reliance on skills and expertise and
the exercise of self-control; centralisation is associated with a reliance on rules and close supervision
- mechanisms of control which are unsuitable when
organisational participants are professionally
trained. Chandler (1966) lends some support to the
above findings. He reports that large corporations
in the USA were more likely to become decentralised
after becoming involved in the manufacture of vastly

diversified products as if to suggest that product diversity leads to an increase in occupational specialists, eventually resulting in decentralisation of decision making. This was more likely to happen when managers were more professional, suggesting that professionalism may hasten the process of decentralisation. In a study conducted in the UK, already referred to, delegation and decentralisation were most prominent in industries which had a high concentration of skilled personnel (Woodward, 1965).

A finding at variance with those mentioned above – again in a British context – whilst acknowledging that the more structured of two small-sized organisations had an organisational climate where people are more concerned with rules and regulations, administrative efficiency and conventionality in dress, manner, etc., states that participation on the part of group members is slightly lower in the less bureaucratic organisations in spite of the greater autonomy (Payne et al., 1971). In defence of the position of Hage and Aiken it should be stressed that the work environment they studied was likely to be conducive to the particular needs of a professional group. The conclusion of Payne et al. is not substantiated by the findings of a more recent study (Bass et al., 1975). They associate a tight structure with a directive style, and a participative style with a non-bureaucratic organisational environment.

The remainder of this chapter will be devoted to a further examination of the impact of the structural variables that were the subject of comment earlier, but this time they will be specifically related to decision-making behaviour. Level within the organisation is one of the variables which affects leadership status (Stogdill and Shartle, 1948). Drawing on evidence which they classify as expert opinion, training practices and empirical data, Nealey and Fielder (1968) advance the view that different levels of organisation place somewhat different demands on leaders. The higher the position in the organisation the more one felt it necessary to offer work groups more Initiating Structure and less Consideration (Fleishman, 1953). The independence of both Consideration and Initiating Structure is mediated by level within the organisation (Weissenberg and Kavanagh, 1972). In a different context, Martin (1959) related hierarchical level to decision situations in terms of time, continuity, duration and tempo. At the lower level the foreman, for example, operates in the immediate present with only a slight extension into the past and future. The time from the inception to the conclusion of the decision is relatively short, but at the higher level it is likely to be considerably greater. The verification of the correctness of a decision is almost immediate at the lower level, whilst at the higher level wide intervals of time can separate the various components of the decision situation, resulting in discontinuity. The duration is longer as one moves upwards from the lower to the higher levels; at the higher level the decision enquiry stage alone could last for over a year as opposed to a day or a week at the lower level. Also the frequency of decision situations is greater at the lower level but there is a greater opportunity to exercise flexibility in choice of time to take action at the higher level. Obviously immediacy of action is paramount at the lower level; a broken pipe or defect in product quality requires immediate attention. Variations in decision-making behaviour were found to occur at different hierarchical levels by Blankenship and Miles (1968) who report that freedom of action believed to be enjoyed by a manager is associated with his position in the hierarchy. Those occupying positions at the upper echelons of the organisation enjoy considerable autonomy in the sense that their superiors did not initiate action for them, nor did they consult their superiors. But 'they relied heavily on subordinates to bring problems to their attention and to offer ideas and recommendations.' Managers lower in the hierarchy relied less on suggestions and ideas emanating from subordinates and were more inclined to accept guidance from above. This result is supported by Heller and Yukl (1969) who indicate that the higher the leader is in the hierarchy of authority, the less centralised is his decision making.

As the size of social groupings increases so does the size of the leader's authority, his personal power and the amount of delegation permitted in the decision-making process (Michels, 1949). More specifically, as the size of organisational groups increases direction of group activities which is leader-centred is associated with members expressing attitudes of greater tolerance for this type of leadership (Hemphill, 1950). Wofford (1971) found the manager whose style is oriented towards personal security and group maintenance to be the most effective in the large complex organisation. A different type of leadership - group achievement and order - was most effective for the smaller groups. Blankenship and Miles (1968) also comment on the influence of size but make the point that any relationship between size and decision-making behaviour is modified by hierarchical level. Those occupying positions at the bottom of the hierarchy enjoy greater freedom in small sized organisations. Managers exercising considerable influence on their superiors and endowed with the ultimate right of choice in the making of a decision were more likely to be found in the upper levels of the hierarchy. Differences were not so marked between large and medium-sized firms.

The relationship between line/staff organisation and decision-making behaviour is not at all clear. Heller and Yukl (1969) found it difficult to classify senior managers as either line or staff but eventually were able to choose twenty six managers (line) who implemented and controlled policy and sixteen managers (staff) who advised and made recommendations on policy. They report that there is a small likelihood of line managers being authoritarian or less permissive than staff managers.

Reliance on subordinates - a facet of managerial decision-making behaviour - was the dimension related to the span of control (Blankenship and Miles, 1968).

99

A greater number of managers, with thirteen or more
subordinates reporting to them, said they frequently
depended on their subordinates for ideas and the
initiation of decisions. With a narrower span of
control - four or less - managers were less dependent
on subordinates, but yet again the influence of hierarchical level was felt. Regardless of the size of
the span of control, upper rather than middle or
lower-level managers are likely to depend more on
their subordinates. Areas where subordinate influence could be felt - consultation and joint decision
making - were almost dispensed with the larger the
span of control (Heller and Yukl, 1969). From their
investigation - which reverses the trend depicted
above - they found a tendency on the part of senior
managers and second-line supervisors to centralise
their decisions when the span of control was large.
However, the senior managers resorted to delegation
as their alternative style in such circumstances.

4 Research design and hypotheses

Before undertaking the field work required by the research project alternative approaches to the collection of data were given consideration. The anthropological approach, resulting in qualitative description, and action research, whereby the researcher can act as a catalyst to initiate change and observe its consequences, are valuable techniques at the disposal of the researcher. The natural experiment in a field setting also offers a lot of potentiality and is most useful if the researcher gains access to an organisation to investigate social phenomena before and after a major change in an organisational process is executed.

Because of the author's full time commitment to teaching it was felt that the final choice of instrument would rest on either the mail questionnaire or the interview and discussion. Each approach has its own advantages and limitations, as we shall see later, and any one approach could be supplemented by the other. In choosing the mail questionnaire as the main research instrument one was partially influenced by the trend in empirical psychology towards quantitative analysis. It is of course possible to use a questionnaire as an interview schedule, but such an approach would of necessity be costly in terms of reaching the number of respondents who might participate in the research study. To reinforce the questionnaire as a research tool it was always my intention to use a flexible structured interview with a sample of respondents.

RESEARCH METHODS

Though suffering a deficiency as an efficient instrument to study social processes, the questionnaire is particularly suitable for studies of attitudes, values, beliefs and perceptions of informants. As a method it offers great efficiency in gathering data and by lending itself to quantification opens the way to statistical analysis and data processing. The use of the questionnaire for a simple inquiry among people of a certain educational standard − a professional group − and concerned with a subject of particular interest to them is considered valid (Moser and Kalton, 1971). Without specifying the complexity of the inquiry, Cartwright and Ward (1968) would endorse this suggestion when they maintain that 'postal question- naires offer an efficient method of collecting infor- mation. They are cheap and relatively quick and can be widely scattered geographically. In approaching professional groups there are no problems of illiter- acy or inarticulateness to set against these advan- tages.' There are other advantages attributable to the postal questionnaire, among them being that the greater proportion of returns will be returned in a few weeks; problems associated with interview errors which affect the reliability and validity of survey results are avoided; the likelihood of respondents making critical remarks and uttering less socially acceptable responses is that much greater than in the interview situation; and finally the accuracy of responses is greater if questions require the respon- dent to consult documents or reflect on matters for a while (Moser and Kalton, 1971).

There are, however, drawbacks surrounding the questionnaire as a research tool. It would appear that all too frequently questions are not sufficiently simple and straightforward to be understood with the help of printed instructions and definitions. The danger of ambiguity, vagueness and inappropriate use of technical expressions creeping in is always present. Speak (1967) has much to say about the deficiency of question wording on questionnaires. Her main concern is that not enough thought and care is given to the wording of questions and that we are too ready to accept that interpretations of words and phrases depend upon their context. But research evidence suggests that certain words and phrases may have a unique interpretation in their own right - something that could be quite independent of context. It is also her contention that in order to check distortion we must try to avoid the use of emotionally charged questions and those affecting the prestige of respondents, just as we should avoid phrases or words which elicit varying frames of reference among respondents. Machlup (1946) feels that we must be on our guard against the danger of artificial responses, misinterpretation or failure to comprehend meaning of questions. The questionnaire may not be completed with due care; there is no check-up on the validity of the responses, bias is likely to enter and the end result may be but an abstraction of real life situations.

Other criticisms levelled at the questionnaire are that it is an unsuitable technique where spontaneous answers, without any reference to a colleague, are required and where the respondent can see all the questions before answering any of them, particularly where a subsequent question gives a clue as to what is required previously. In addition one cannot always be sure that the right person receives the questionnaire (Moser and Kalton, 1971). Commenting on the disadvantages of closed questions so frequently found on a questionnaire, Oppenheim (1972) makes the point that we tend to lose the respondent's own thoughts on the matter in question, albeit it is only fair to add that the open-ended question can somewhat counteract this flaw. Also we introduce bias by forcing the respondent to choose among alternatives not of his own making, and consequently the prospect of irritation arises because the choice of answers do not coincide with his own.

The activity of self-description or self-reporting which occurs through the medium of the questionnaire has been the subject of much comment. Though recognising some of its limitations in the form of distortion and ambiguity, Blankenship and Miles (1968)

believe it facilitates the undertaking of a study
and enables the researcher to contact a large number
of organisations. Mahoney et al. (1965) commenting
on measures of performance used in their studies
suggest that 'the reliability and validity of self-
reported performance patterns equal that of other
commonly accepted measures' and justify their use.
However, Burns (1954) having compared behavioural
profiles of managers on self-recorded forms with a
subsequent verbal description of behaviour on similar
dimensions found a number of disparities. Apparently
the managers concerned were astounded by the incon-
gruities. Relying exclusively on a respondent's
appraisal of his own behaviour is to accept perceptual
errors, particularly in a situation where perceived
status clashes with what appears in reality. Hopwood
(1973) and Heller (1971) report perceptual gaps when
a superior and subordinate were asked to express a
view on social phenomena common to both. Even outside a situation of this nature significant discrep-
ancies between reported and actual behaviour are
likely to arise (Whyte, 1971). Evidence also exists
pointing out a discrepancy between reported feelings
on the questionnaire and what people really felt
(Cummings et al., 1958). Poor response rates are
often cited as the preserve of the postal questionnaire. This is a point which will be discussed later
in the context of the survey response. One must, as
a result, offer qualified acceptance of the questionnaire. But equally alternative methods, such as the
interview, possess flaws.

Follow-up interviews are a means of overcoming
some of the disadvantages of the questionnaire but
the interview is not immune from criticism. It is
much less structured than the questionnaire, but since
research requires the securing of comparable data from
a number of respondents it would be almost pointless
if the interview was to be non-directive, as found in
psycho-therapy. The research interview requires the
interviewer to maintain some control but the pivot of
success is flexibility. One advantage of the interview is the intervention of the interviewer when

questions appear ambiguous. Nevertheless, an inter-
viewee may give a false reply because he misunderstands
the question or consciously or unconsciously he dis-
torts the answer for reasons connected with prestige,
or he gives the answer expected of him (Moser and
Kalton, 1971). Likewise the interviewer may uninten-
tionally offer an insight into his opinions or expectations by his tone of voice, the way in which he
reads the questions, or simply by his appearance,
dress or accent (Oppenheim, 1972). Problems common
to both the interview and questionnaire are: the
absence of motivation on the part of the respondent
to co-operate; questions are considered irrelevant or
inappropriate by the respondent and access to the
requisite information is difficult. Whether the
questionnaire stands on its own as a tool, or is
combined with the interview, Heller (1971) considers
the use of both techniques together or the questionnaire on its own to be less than satisfactory. To
him the real alternative is Group Feedback Analysis
(GFA) because it incorporates some aspects of the two
major approaches to the study of human behaviour, the
idiographic and nomothetic.

This is a technique which, to begin with, requires
a group to be seated around a table. Then members of
the group are presented with standardised instructions
and a definition of the research objectives by tape
recorder. Reinforcement of the research objectives
appear on the short questionnaire they receive. Some
verbal reinforcement can also come from the researcher.
A simple statistical analysis is performed and some
time later the results are fed back to the group for
interpretation. This stimulates group discussion
with a movement, as the process continues, from the
unstructured to the structured and quantifiable.
Heller, in general, seems to be satisfied with the
questionnaire he used in management research when he
states, 'the evaluations of the group discussions do
not contradict the conclusions from the statistical
results, rather they provide a second dimension and
enable us to see some of the findings in a rough perspective.' But in the case of a particular result he

expresses reservations about the efficacy of the
questionnaire when he states, 'this statistical
result is not congruent with the strongly expressed
views of the feedback discussion, and it seems likely
that the discrepancy points to a difficulty in using
questionnaires for complex, subtle and emotionally
charged concepts.'

Systematic observation in organisations is put
forward by one writer as a procedure of greater value
than reliance on retrospective questionnaires and
interviews (Walter, 1966). But equally one could
argue that observers can also misinterpret reality
since our perceptions can be influenced and distorted
by values, motivation, prior expectations, social
norms and so on (Hyman, 1964). Also the observer who
is interested in events in the past will have to rely
on records or the memory of the respondent, both of
which may not be entirely dependable. Lowin (1968)
attacks both self-reporting and observation as procedures 'vulnerable to observer halo or rationalisation and need to be replaced by objective measures or
experimental methods.' He quite rightly advocates
the adoption of longitudinal studies and the use of
control groups which are not unduly influenced. This
is admirable as an ideal proposition, but the problem
of access to organisations to conduct such studies is
by no means an easy one.

THE RESEARCH QUESTIONNAIRE

With full cognizance of the observations in the pre-
ceding discussion the author set about the preparation of a questionnaire suitable for collecting the
required data. Particular attention was given to the
layout of the questionnaire, to the clarity of instructions and to the adequacy of questions in terms
of being simple, acceptably technical and free from
ambiguity. From the initial reaction to a pilot
questionnaire this objective was not wholly realised.

106

First pre-test

Ten subjects were chosen in an arbitrary fashion to participate in the pilot scheme. They all occupied senior positions in the field of industrial accountancy, invariably occupying positions of the rank of Chief Accountant or Financial Controller. Eight expressed a willingness to participate in the study by completing the questionnaire they received with an accompanying letter soliciting their co-operation. Subsequently, after receiving the completed questionnaire, a personal interview was arranged with four respondents. Around the same time consultations took place with a few academic and senior accountants in industry when the contents of the questionnaire were discussed. These meetings I believe had the effect of subjecting the contents of the questionnaire to quite an intensive and penetrating analysis, producing a crystallisation of scattered ideas to a far greater extent than did discussions with two senior industrial accountants prior to the pilot scheme. The instrument was tested in order to establish the clarity of the instructions and questions, its validity in the light of the research objective, its reliability as far as one could tell, and finally the ease with which the requisite information could be recalled. What immediately came across was that the questionnaire was too long and likely to discourage even the most eager and enthusiastic respondent. In addition, it was felt necessary to modify its layout and contents as a result of a perusal of the completed questionnaires and the interview results.

The number of decision types in question 2 of the questionnaire - see Appendix 'A' - was reduced from 23 to 14 and it was felt that the decision types finally chosen more accurately reflected those normally taken by, or within the province of, the Financial Controller or Chief Accountant. Also in question 2 the columns dealing with the frequency with which a decision is taken in the course of a year and the approximate time interval between the commencement and conclusion of the decision-making process were deleted.

107

This was because the completion of these columns posed a problem for respondents by taxing their abilities to accurately recall the number of times a particular decision was taken and the length of time between the initiation and completion of the decision-making cycle. The distribution of scores from the pilot run, as one would expect, seemed rather skewed. A less severe rationalisation of question 3 dealing with the extent of specialisation within the finance function was also undertaken. Job areas of a unique but not widespread nature were deleted to allow a portrayal of a more representative view. This had the effect of reducing the job areas from 19 to 13. In question 4 the section concerned with the 'importance' of certain qualities or skills was removed because in the circumstances it was considered both confusing and redundant, leaving the respondent to grapple with the extent to which the qualities or skills are desirable in, or actually possessed by, subordinates in the final survey. Perceived characteristics of the respondent's superior in question 6, originally designed to reflect certain leadership patterns of behaviour at the highest level of the organisation, was considered to be too crude a measure and as a consequence was removed. Absent from the pilot questionnaire were questions referring to the size of the company and size of the finance function. It was felt that size was too important a variable to be omitted and was, as a result, incorporated in the final version of the questionnaire. There were other instances of very minor adjustments to the layout and content of the questionnaire.

Second pre-test

Whilst attending a one-week programme on behavioural accounting at Brunel University in June 1975, the author distributed the modified questionnaire to nine participants whose profile closely resembled that of the respondents in the pilot survey. Seven of the participants completed it. As a result of the analysis of the completed forms a very minor modification to the content was executed in the form of an improvement to the wording in a few instances. The layout of the questionnaire was much improved in the final version.

Before the preparation of the final questionnaire a number of factors were considered with a view to creating a favourable response rate. To begin with, the length of the questionnaire is likely to be a critical factor. Stanton (1939) reports that a double postcard containing a single question which could be answered with a tick received a 21.9 per cent increase over a three page questionnaire. A similar result is reported by Brown (1965). The difference in effort required of the respondent in both cases is quite staggering. However, when the nature of the project dictates a somewhat complex questionnaire which is also lengthy - e.g., 14 pages - of the kind used in the present research study, then we must expect a relatively low response rate. This view is to some extent implicit in a comment made by Cartwright and Ward (1968) -

Meanwhile many researchers will have to face the dilemma and choose between a low response rate with more information and a high one with less data about the individuals who respond.

Sponsorship of the survey is another factor to consider. The author unsuccessfully approached both the Institute of Chartered Accountants and the Institute of Management Accountants with a view to funding the project, in effect sponsoring it. It has been suggested that sponsorship of surveys by government is instrumental in achieving a high response rate. This is discounted by Scott (1961) when he maintains that the use of three different letterheads (Central Office of Information; London School of Economics; British Market Research Bureau) produced no significant variation in response. Kanuk and Berenson (1975) are of the opinion that there is little experimental evidence on the effects of sponsorship, but maintain that when government sponsorship is compared with the pooled results of the two non-governmental sponsors, referred to above, a significant advantage for government sponsorship is revealed. Birmingham Polytechnic provided support for the survey conducted by the author, and one is convinced that the appearance of the Polytechnic's name and address on the covering letter was beneficial in authenticating the study, which in turn could be reflected in a favourable response. The same is likely to be true of an association with any charitable or non-profit making institution. The introductory instructions and the first question on the questionnaire were printed on the back of the covering letter. Scott (1961) found a significant difference in favour of printing the questionnaire on the back of the covering letter instead of enclosing it on a separate sheet of paper. Using both sides of a separate sheet of paper was followed throughout the questionnaire, a measure also endorsed by Scott. The covering letter started by acknowledging that not enough was known about an influential body of people, senior accountants in industry, and continued with a general statement of the purpose of the survey; finally, emphasising the confidentiality of information provided, anonymity of company, that a copy of the synopsis of the findings would be sent on request and that the respondent by his co-operation would be helping the researcher in this worthwhile venture or endeavour. The author felt it essential to emphasise the points mentioned, but in some respects Linsky (1965) holds an opposing view. He concludes that inserting a piece to convince the respondent that the research is worthwhile, and making an appeal to help the researcher had no effect on the final response rate.

Anonymity of the respondent, by name and work telephone number, was not envisaged simply because one required a means to contact him, if necessary, subsequent to the completion of the questionnaire. On the face of it anonymity of the company was more fictional than real if the respondent provided his name and company telephone number, and if the identification number on the questionnaire remained intact. Anonymity of respondent may ensure a high level of voluntary response, and may minimise invalid responses when response is mandatory. The benefits of anonymity have, however, been challenged. Brayfield and Crockett (1955) feel that anonymity as such does have little or no bearing on the willingness to respond, albeit respondents may of course be reluctant to provide certain information about their department or company. Rosen (1960) likewise maintains that anonymity per se has little or no effect, and concludes that the identification of respondents in attitude questionnaire surveys in circumstances less than threatening is unlikely to result in serious statistical or practical distortion. However, one must concede that the incidence of social desirability responses is likely to be minimised by respecting the anonymity of the respondent (Cannel and Fowler, 1963). Therefore, in the research study this is unlikely to be an important factor.

Since the identity of the Financial Controller or Chief Accountant was unknown one had to ensure that either of them would receive the questionnaire by specifically stating on the covering letter that it was for either of their attention. This in effect determined the form of salutation - 'Dear Sir'. Apparently a personal salutation has no significant advantage over an impersonal one (Kimball, 1961). Nevertheless in order to give the communication a somewhat personalised flavour the date and signature were hand-written. Though this may not produce the desired effect. Kawash and Aleamoni (1971) tested the effect of a hand-written signature on the covering letter against a facsimile signature and found an insignificant difference. Using designatory letters to denote qualifications and official job title of the author was considered relevant. Roeher (1963) obtained a significantly larger response by using a title after the signature on the covering letter.

The questionnaire was produced on an offset litho process; white paper was used and the questionnaire was precoded where this was feasible. It seems there is no difference between printed and stencilled

111

questionnaires in terms of response rates (Scott, 1961). Though Plog (1963) is of the belief that an individually typed letter accompanying the questionnaire, explaining the nature of the research study and couched in such terms as to secure the co-operation of someone hostile to mail surveys can have a tremendous impact in promoting a high response rate. Apparently it does not really matter if the questionnaire is printed on green rather than white paper (Gullahorn and Gullahorn, 1963). Perhaps the same applies to any other colour. It appears that no disadvantage is suffered by using precoded questionnaires (Linsky, 1975). Finally the only tangible reward offered the respondent for his efforts was the promise of a synopsis of the findings of the survey.

Contents of questionnaire

The final questionnaire, containing thirteen questions, shall now be analysed.

Question 1, biographical detail, including the experience variables - age and time spent in job.

Question 2, decision-making behaviour in relation to different types of decisions. This question focuses on the dependent variable - the major variable - and requires of the respondent the identification of his decision-making approach when confronted with different types of decisions. The fourteen decisions, applicable to the role of the Chief Accountant, can be classified as either programmed or non-programmed; programmed or non-programmed decisions could also be classified as task and personnel decisions, the latter consisting of non-programmed decisions. Decisions are arranged by category in the section on Methods of Analysis. Arriving at the final selection of decisions for incorporation into this question was a lengthy process. Numerous conversations took place with senior industrial accountants and academic accountants before, during and subsequent to the pilot survey on the representativeness of the decisions. One also solicited observations on the degree to which some informants considered each decision as either structured or non-structured. The manner in which the later analysis reflects the decision categorisation process is the author's responsibility. The measure of leadership or decision style is that used by Heller (1971) who successfully tested it for reliability and validity. Test - retest reliability of this measure with an interval of seven weeks was 0.82 (n = 32, $p < 0.01$). The measure is illustrated in Figure 4.2.3 as the decision style continuum.

Style A	Style B	Style C	Style D	Style E
Own decision without explanation	Own decision with explanation	Prior consultation	Joint decision-making	Delegation

Figure 4.2.3 Decision style continuum
(Heller's Influence/Power Continuum)

It shows the extent to which a superior shares influence with subordinates and is very much in the tradition of a power spectrum or leadership continuum. Each point on the continuum is said to be as effective as any other, and each respondent who has the authority to make a particular decision or make a recommendation that will lead to one is asked to indicate the approach to decision making he normally adopts. Though encouraged to opt for one approach entirely in connection with a decision, if more than one approach was applicable then 100 per cent was to be distributed across the relevant approaches according to the weight given to each approach. There were a number of instances where the 100 per cent was split. If a decision was not relevant to the work role of a respondent, he was expected to place 'not applicable' opposite the appropriate item. For example, this would apply in the case of decisions connected with debtors if the

respondent worked in a retail food establishment.
Another example would be where the respondent does not
assume responsibility for all finance function activities due to split financial responsibilities. Likewise a respondent would be unable to respond to a
decision item related to costing where such an activity, though anticipated, nevertheless does not exist in
his company.

Question 3, specialisation and specialism. This
question sets out to measure the extent to which job
areas within the finance function are established
and the level of expertise possessed by those responsible for operating or managing each individual area.
Key activities or specialised functions within the
finance function are well documented (Weston, 1954;
Henning and Moseley, 1970). Thirteen job areas were
finally selected to reflect the main operational
centres. A high rating on this dimension would denote a high level of specialisation. The specialism
factor was a rather crude one, relying on the degree
of qualification of a section head or sub-system head.
Fully qualified and senior unqualified could be considered by some to run closely parallel to each other.
There could also be a slight danger of semantic error
being introduced. Fully qualified to one respondent
could mean professionally qualified, and to another
it could have a different connotation; for example,
highly qualified in the area in question irrespective
of professional qualification. This is precisely what
was intended and by all accounts was interpreted as
such. Where an activity is performed by subordinates
of equal rank, the respondent was asked to choose the
individual with whom he had most contact, otherwise
unnecessary confusion would arise. If one or more
job areas are not relevant, the respondent was directed to place 'not applicable' opposite the appropriate item. This answer would be forthcoming in conditions exactly the same as those stated in question 2.

Question 4(i), perceived qualities or skills in
subordinate. Respondents are presented with fifteen
personality related characteristics and skills and

asked to specify the extent to which these are desirable in and actually possessed by a subordinate. Where the respondent has more than one direct subordinate he is asked to focus his attention on the subordinate he meets most frequently. A small difference between the aggregate score for desired and actual qualities or skills denotes a higher regard for the subordinate, and conversely with a large difference. A number of qualities or skill items used in previous management research programmes were adopted. For example, seven items can be found in Heller and Porter (1966), four in Porter and Henry (1964a) and one in Miles (1964). The remaining three were derived empirically from observations at the pilot survey stage.

Question 4(ii). The respondent is given the opportunity to add any further qualities or skills he considers important.

Question 5, power, status and influence. This question was designed with the express purpose of gauging in rather general terms whether or not the respondent's position is endowed with an impressive degree of authority, status and influence at both superior and subordinate levels. A 'Yes' or 'No' answer to each of the five or six items is required. Power vested in the leadership position is one of Fiedler's key situational variables. A biased response to this question cannot be ruled out entirely due to its connection with status and influence.

Question 6, leadership behavioural characteristics. Already we have conceptually distinguished leadership behaviour expressed in terms of the Ohio State leadership school from leadership style manifest in Heller's power/influence continuum. The four operational definitions of leadership behaviour chosen and presented in this question, though condensed, coincide with major themes running through the literature (Bowers and Seashore, 1966), particularly Initiating Structure or task orientation on one hand and Consideration or employee orientation on the other.

In question 6, items (i) and (ii) fit the latter and (iii) (iv) fit the former. The respondent is asked to indicate the extent to which he considers these characteristics a manifestation of his own leadership style.

Question 7. Space was provided for comments on any other characteristics, not listed in question 6, which the respondent feels ought to be emphasised.

Question 8, psychological closeness of the leader. The measure available to the respondent in this question is almost identical to the LPC measure used by Fiedler. The only variation is that the least preferred co-worker of the leader in Fiedler's research need not be a person working with the leader at the present time. In question 8 the respondent is asked to give his immediate first reaction to sixteen pairs of words opposite in meaning and describe the subordinate whom he prefers the least by placing a mark in one of the eight spaces on each bi-polar line. This type of scaling procedure is known as the semantic differential technique and was developed by Osgood et al. (1957). Fiedler uses this measure to gauge the motivational disposition or style of the leader. Its use in the present study is confined to acting as an indicator of the psychological closeness of the leader to his subordinates.

Question 9, hierarchical level in the organisation. This question aims at establishing the level within the hierarchical structure occupied by the respondent. Because of the enormous variability of positions, seemingly similar across organisations, one recognises the difficulties inherent in a comparison of levels. In order to help the respondent locate his particular level the following guideline was offered. Top managers of a company or division are designated 'level 1'. Managers one step removed from them on the organisation chart are considered to be at 'level 2'; those two steps away constitute 'level 3', and so on. Though four levels are given it is unlikely that many of the respondents would be categorised by level 3 or 4.

Question 10, span of control. The respondent is asked to indicate the number of subordinates he is responsible for supervising directly, by choosing a number opposite the appropriate range.

Question 11, size of finance function. This question asks the respondent to indicate the size of the finance function, expressed in terms of number of employees, by choosing a number opposite the appropriate range.

Question 12, size of company. This question asks the respondent to indicate the size of the company, expressed in terms of number of employees, by choosing a number opposite the appropriate range.

Question 13, nature of role within the company. This question is akin to a question specifically concerned with the outline ingredients of the classical notion of staff/line relationships. It endeavours to establish the nature of the authority relationship between the Chief Accountant and the managers he serves or for whom he provides essential financial information. The respondent is asked to indicate (a) whether his role as representative, or acting for the representative, of the finance function is purely advisory, or (b) whether his role capsulates direct authority to implement recommendations of an accounting and finance nature in functional areas such as production and marketing, and finally (c) whether he is unable to identify his role in accordance with the above definitions.

The absence of a measure of the efficiency of the finance function on the questionnaire is conspicuous. It would appear somewhat unrealistic to invite a respondent to express a view pertaining to the efficiency of the department he manages. It is commonplace in studies of leadership in the USA to introduce a productivity criterion and relate it to leadership style. But it is very difficult to evaluate producti-

117

vity for a service function. Evaluation criteria in the form of standards are difficult to define, performance is difficult to measure and a comparison of performance with standards is difficult to make. When giving consideration to this question some tentative measurement criteria, open to elaboration and refinement in the future, came to mind.

(i)   Cost of the finance function as a proportion of total turnover.

(ii)   Time-lag between the publication of the statutory accounts and the end of the financial year.

(iii) Speed with which monthly comparative figures are available and the adequacy of the detail.

(iv) Cash flow: the adequacy of cash - with or without debtors - in relation to creditors. A liquidity ratio (cash + debtors $<$ creditors) could be used. A very fine ratio, 1.1 or 1.2, may be symptomatic of good management; alternatively in some circumstances it may be construed as a danger signal.

(v)   If it is the company's policy to take advantage of discounts receivable and if the liquidity position facilitates it, the speed with which creditors are paid. Equal in importance is the effectiveness of the function in securing receipts from debtors.

All the above factors would then be considered in the context of the number of staff employed and the extent of mechanisation. One should point out that the absence of an efficiency criteria does not detract from the importance and validity of the present research study. When we understand to a greater extent the impact of situational and structural factors on leadership style or managerial decision-making behaviour, then our attention can be diverted to a consideration of concrete efficiency criteria.

THE SAMPLE

Considerable difficulty was experienced at the first attempt to choose a sample of companies representative of a cross section of industry and commerce, excluding banking, insurance and related financial services companies. A good example of an index of companies, often referred to by researchers, is The Times 1000 Index. This lists the top 1000 companies trading in the UK. Unfortunately, from the author's point of view, some of these listed companies are either holding or parent companies, proving unsuitable for the purpose of the research. It was important to choose operating companies because it is in these companies that one normally finds a fully developed finance function, unlike the customary situation in the parent company, particularly the large company, where the major preoccupation appears to be consolidation accounts work and the monitoring of financial operations. Another type of company which was considered unsuitable for the purposes of the research was that which employed 100 employees or less, because of the real likelihood of it having an underdeveloped or practically non-existent formal finance function. Woodward (1965) deleted from her sample 93 companies employing 100 employees or less because she felt these companies had few hierarchical levels and few organisational problems. Added to this were bank, insurance and finance companies because their accounting procedures differ from those of an industrial and other commercial type. Eventually one managed to secure a relatively recent copy of The Guide to Key Industrial Enterprises (Dun and Bradstreet) which contains a cross section of industrial and commercial enterprises. Putting to one side the very small company, the very large group or parent company and the financial services companies, one was left with approximately 7,000 companies of varying sizes, located in the UK, to choose from. The intention was to select roughly 1,000 companies evenly distributed as to size, and

119

because of this condition a systematic random selection was not possible in the circumstances. Instead an arbitrary selection within the constraints specified was the only feasible course of action. The manual extraction of 989 companies from the Dun and Bradstreet Guide, on average one company per page, was both a burdensome and time-consuming task. The name, address and telephone number, if available, of each company was noted, and companies were classified by type of industry and size. The size classification was decided on after consultation with two senior executives in industry, finally taking the following classification: < 500; 500-2000; > 2000 employees. One feels confident in suggesting that the sampling frame is very representative of British industrial and commercial companies, bar financial institutions.

The next step was to consider the despatch of the 989 questionnaires. Each questionnaire bore a serial number to facilitate the identification of respondents, and obviate the likelihood of sending a reminder letter to a respondent. One was aware that in the eyes of some respondents this could amount to an infringement of the notion of company anonymity. A company on the sample list was given an identification number which was cross referenced to the number on the questionnaire and the outgoing addressed envelope. It was then a matter of matching the appropriate questionnaire and envelope. Enclosed with the questionnaire was a self-addressed envelope which was unstamped. It would be preferable to enclose a stamped addressed envelope but the cost of doing so was a discouraging factor. A compromise was reached in the line of action taken. Ferris (1951), however, provides convincing evidence for using a stamped return envelope to increase the response rate. The outgoing envelope bore the addressee's title 'Financial Controller' or 'Chief Accountant'; this title order was reversed if the company concerned had less than 500 employees since it is unlikely to use the title 'Financial Controller'. So that the envelope would appear less stereotyped than correspondence of this kind normally reaching a company, it was decided to

opt for handwriting when addressing the envelope.
In addition the word 'personal' was prominently displayed on the top left hand corner of the envelope.
It was felt that first-class postage would be preferable to second-class in creating a sense of urgency
and a better impression. Also the threat of a rail
strike, likely to disrupt the postal service, lingered
on the horizon. However, the evidence on the superiority of first-class mail is inconclusive. Watson
(1965) found a small advantage accruing to first-class
over second-class mail but Kernan (1971) found no
advantage either way. Finally no deadline date for
questionnaires to be returned was specified as it was
felt unrealistic to do so at a time of the year when
holidays are taken. It has been suggested that the
setting of a deadline date for completion and return
of a questionnaire encourages an early reply (Kanuk
and Berenson, 1975).

The first batch of questionnaires, numbering roughly
500, were despatched on the 19 June 1975 and the remainder on the 30 June 1975. One felt it might have
some beneficial effect, in terms of response, if
subjects received the questionnaire early rather than
later in the week; though according to Scott (1961),
it makes no difference what day of the week the
questionnaire reaches the prospective respondent.
The response rate to the first mailing was as follows:

Table 4.3.1

Response to despatch of 989
questionnaires

Accept-ances	Refusals	Returned 'gone away'	Returned company liquidated	No response
144	28	25	4	788

Roughly a month later, on the 18 and 30 July 1975, a reminder letter (Appendix 'E') bearing a pre-printed date and signature, together with a copy of the questionnaire undated also bearing a pre-printed signature, were forwarded to non-respondents. This time no self-addressed envelope was used, the address-ees name and address was typewritten and second-class postage was used. It was felt that the original copy of the questionnaire would have been mislaid in many cases by this time, so it was decided to attach another copy of the questionnaire to the reminder letter in order to encourage the respondent to reply. A reasonable response followed the despatch of the reminder letter. This is illustrated in Table 4.3.2.

Table 4.3.2

Response to despatch of 788 questionnaires and a reminder letter

Accept-ances	Refusals	Returned 'gone away'	Returned company liquidated	No response
64	37	4	1	682

It would be difficult to differentiate late replies to the original request to complete the questionnaire from replies activated by the reminder letter. What is interesting, however, is that the bulk of accept-ances in Table 4.3.2 appears on the original copy of the questionnaire. Obviously in most cases, contrary to one's expectations, the original copy of the questionnaire was not mislaid by interested subjects. Non-respondents who replied giving their reasons for not participating in the study offered some initial appreciation of the problem of non-response. The following remarks reflect the main reasons given and

122

appear in the original and in paraphrased form -

We would like to help academics bridge the gap
between theory and practice but the half-
psychological questionnaire does not ask sensible questions.

In view of the nature of some of the questions
I am afraid that I felt unable to complete it.

We are inundated with a multitude of forms from
government departments and trade associations,
and since your questionnaire requires an appreciable amount of time to complete, I am afraid
we cannot waste company time in this way.

We are very busy at the moment with year-end
accounts and feel at this time we are unable to
participate.

Current volume of work aggravated by holidays.

We are unable to assist you due to a substantial
cut-back in staff because of the current economic
climate.

I don't wish to participate.

I am not prepared to provide the information
requested.

The centralisation of the accounting function in
the group to which my company belongs rules out
I completing the questionnaire.

My job would not fit the pattern of your questionnaire.

At the time we received your questionnaire we
also received two others, and although we are
sympathetic to your aims we find we are unable
to complete it.

> I take exception to having to disclose my
> identity.

It was not my intention to remind non-respondents,
for the second time, to complete the questionnaire as
one felt such an effort would produce a marginal
benefit in terms of extra response. But one recognises it is conceivable that the issue of more than
one reminder letter is a powerful means to promote an
increase in response (Kemsley, 1962), but as we have
already noted there are a number of other determining
factors as well. To gain some insight into the reasons why people did not bother to respond it was
decided to contact a random selection of non-
respondents, numbering thirty five, by telephone.
This presented some difficulties when endeavouring
to locate the person who ought to have received the
questionnaire. One resorted to asking the telephonist
could I speak to the Chief Accountant or Financial
Controller. In some instances I was unable to establish contact with the appropriate person. The non-
respondents I contacted offered a number of reasons
for not responding, ranging from having insufficient
time available to complete the questionnaire because
of normal work pressures and mandatory form filling,
to lack of interest and pleading not having received
the questionnaire. In some instances a Financial
Director received the questionnaire and, perhaps
recognising that it was not totally relevant to his
job area, retained it instead of passing it on to the
appropriate subordinate to complete. By seeking an
explanation for non-response on the telephone one
could easily have forced the non-respondent into a
situation whereby he offers a plausible rationalisation for his failure to co-operate. This rationalisation may be at variance with his true intentions.
Non-respondents were contacted in early September
1975 and during the course of the conversation I
availed of the opportunity to remind them that it was
still not too late to complete the questionnaire.
About ten respondents requested a further copy of the
questionnaire. Shortly afterwards thirteen completed
questionnaires were received. The final response,

expressed by company size, is shown in Table 4.3.3.

Table 4.3.3

Number of respondents classified
by company size

n = 955

Size of company			
Small	Medium	Large	Total
% 64(29)	% 86(38.9)	% 71(32.1)	% 221(23)

On comparing the stratification in Table 4.3.3, with
that which constitutes the original sample, illustrated in Table 4.3.4, no great divergence is evident.

Table 4.3.4

Sample of companies classified
by company size

n = 989

Size of company			
Small	Medium	Large	Total
% 336(34)	% 322(32.6)	% 331(33.4)	989

After deducting the number of questionnaires (34)
representing those returned as 'gone away' and
'company liquidated' from the total sample number,
a response rate of 23 per cent was achieved. Having
discarded nine incomplete questionnaires, the final

125

distribution of responses appears as depicted in
Table 4.3.5.

Table 4.3.5

Final distribution of responses
by company size

n = 955

	Size of company		
Small	Medium	Large	Total
			%
59	86	67	212(22)

The questionnaire, as stated earlier, was designed
with a view to it being completed by a respondent who
possessed operational responsibility for a reasonably
developed finance function. Those who were unable to
complete the questionnaire to an acceptable standard,
but tried to do so, did not normally satisfy this
requirement. For example a respondent - a Financial
Controller of a large group of companies - recognised
the limitation of his position in this respect when
he maintained that each operating company within the
group had its own qualified Financial Controller or
Financial Director which precluded his involvement
in the sort of decisions, of an operating nature,
envisaged by the questionnaire. At the other end of
the scale three Financial Accountants obviously had
very restricted authority attached to their positions,
so much so that the questionnaires were grossly incomplete. Another respondent, a Managing Director
and Financial Controller, submitted only two pages
of the questionnaire with a note to the effect that
the company was a small private one, and 'I do not
think my answers to your questions would be very
representative.' A number of unanswered questions
was a prominent feature of a questionnaire coming
also from a respondent in a small company. The

fragmentation of the finance function, a concomitant of which was the allocation of responsibility between two accounting managers, led the respondent to submit an incomplete questionnaire. These then were the type of questionnaire not processed.

Poor response rates are often cited as the preserve of the postal questionnaire. 'Response rates reported for mail surveys have been very much lower than those for interview surveys...... Mail surveys with a response of as low as 10 per cent are not unknown while rates of over 90 per cent have been reported on a number of occasions' (Moser and Kalton, 1971). Gray (1957) contends that with specialised populations it seems possible to obtain an 80 per cent response rate without the issue of a reminder letter. He attributed the good result, however, to the simplicity of the questionnaire. As far as one can see, a good result in the context of a relatively complex, lengthy questionnaire is possible given the presence of favourable influencing factors. Hopwood (1973) reports that each questionnaire in his study conducted in one company was accompanied by a letter from the general manager confirming that the study had been approved by the senior managers of the company. In addition two reminder letters with accompanying copies of the questionnaire were sent to non-respondents. A response rate of over 87 per cent was obtained. A similar response rate was achieved by Bass et al. (1975). They attributed the high return rate to the fact 'that respondents were informed that the data would be summarised for each individual manager so that he would be fed back a 'profile' of the situation in which he and his subordinates worked.' A group of forty two managers, attending a short course at the Ashridge Management College in 1971, were addressed by the author with a view to seeking their co-operation by participating in a research study. Having spent ten minutes explaining the purpose of the study and its value, stressing the anonymity of the respondent and the confidential nature of the inquiry, a fairly long, cognitively taxing questionnaire was distributed to each person present with the specific request that it should be completed while I waited. On average it took thirty minutes to complete the questionnaire. The response rate was very impressive at 98 per cent. There is no doubt that one confronted a receptive audience, coupled with the fact that the Course Director had approved the survey as a legitimate educational pursuit. A similar questionnaire was distributed in the same year to a group of accountants attending a short course at Cambridge University. This time I instructed the Course Director to distribute the questionnaires, which he received from me, to the course participants, which he did towards the end of the course. He spent little time introducing the questionnaire to the audience, and suggested that those interested could collect a copy of the questionnaire as they left the lecture room. After the despatch of one reminder letter to non-respondents, the response rate was 46 per cent.

These generally favourable response rates can be contrasted with the rate of 23 per cent obtained in the present survey. But one must be fully aware of the favourable conditions prevailing in the above circumstances which, in my opinion, facilitated an impressive response rate. However, when one compares the response rate of 23 per cent with that of 22 per cent achieved by Santocki (1975) who conducted an ICMA sponsored research study, using the postal questionnaire, into various aspects of the management audit, one begins to appreciate some of the difficulties in securing a high response to a technical questionnaire from a remote sample population, widely dispersed geographically, but representative of the population as a whole.

The problem faced with a low response rate is that non-respondents may differ in some material respect from respondents, so that any judgements based on the views of respondents are biased. From a brief conversation with thirty five non-respondents, undoubtedly a small proportion of the non-response population, the author failed, from a superficial assessment of them, to subscribe to the view that they were a unique or special breed of Chief Accountant or Financial Controller. Already reasons have been put forward for refusing to respond and outright non-response. When 13 of the 35 non-respondents returned the completed questionnaire subsequent to the telephone conversation, their profile and distribution of responses on the questionnaire showed a similarity to the pattern of the initial respondents. In connection with bias due to non-response, Ferber (1948) maintains that it does not follow that all questions on the questionnaire will be similarly affected. In fact some questions may be totally unaffected.

McDonagh and Rosenblum (1965) maintain that the mail questionnaire may reveal representative responses in spite of a partial return from a sample of the selected population, and that researchers should have greater confidence in the questionnaire method as an initial tool of research. They conclude from the results of a study that there were no significant differences between the responses on a mailed questionnaire and those given by interviewed respondents who had not answered the questionnaire. Identical questions were asked of both groups. There is a contention that respondents and non-respondents can be differentiated on the basis of socio-economic and personality characteristics, but the evidence available to support it is not very convincing. Wallace (1954) reported that respondents and non-respondents were virtually the same on a number of socio-economic characteristics. Ognibene (1970) found respondents to be high on gregariousness and leadership traits, but Vincent's (1964) typical respondent did not fit this profile; instead he showed a tendency towards conformity and co-operation. Finally, the representative nature of the sample can be gleaned from the sample characteristics set out in Appendix 'B'.

THE RESEARCH INTERVIEW

The questionnaire was primarily designed as an instru-

ment to collect data lending itself to quantifiable
analysis. There were of course open-ended questions
to offer the respondent the opportunity to expand,
add to or qualify a given observation. However, it
was felt necessary to conduct follow-up interviews
with a sample of respondents in order to allow qualitative judgements or comments to be made on issues
covered by the questionnaire. The sample list was
compiled from respondents whose companies were located in the south east of England, particularly the
Greater London Area, and the West Midlands. Respondents chosen for interview were selected from the
list in a random fashion. Only three respondents
refused to participate and this was justified on the
grounds of pressure of work. In all thirty two
respondents participated and their distribution over
company size is shown in Table 4.4.

Table 4.4

Number of respondents interviewed,
by company size

n = 221*

Size of company			n=32
Small	Medium	Large	Total
%	%	%	%
10(31.2)	10(31.3)	12(37.5)	32(15)*

Sub-sample - interview sample - characteristics appear
in Appendix 'B' where they are contrasted with total
sample characteristics. The number of respondents
interviewed as a percentage of the total number of
respondents is 15 per cent. The interview programme
started in September 1975 and was concluded by the
end of February 1976.

In order to facilitate the smooth operation of the

130

interview and collect a wide range of pertinent data an interview schedule was prepared and used. This had the effect of structuring the interview but it offered also a lot of flexibility. The questions on the Interview Schedule (see Appendix 'F') covered most of the points raised by the questionnaire and acted as a catalyst by promoting a very useful empirical enlargement of responses on the questionnaire. At the outset of the interview the author stressed the strict confidentiality of the inquiry, which was educational in nature, and the anonymity of respondents and that if one's curiosity led to asking delicate or sensitive questions the motives of the researcher were purely educational. One tried to explain to interviewees how their company came to be chosen as part of a sample of companies in the first place and the reasons for the follow-up interview.

At the time of arranging the interview a large number of the selected respondents expressed the view that the most time they could devote to the interview was thirty minutes, preferably less. In actuality the time allocated to the interview was considerably greater. Everybody interviewed was co-operative and helpful and the interviews varied in length from $1\frac{1}{4}$ to 2 hours, averaging $1\frac{1}{2}$ hours. One felt that as the interview progressed it assumed a therapeutic value for many interviewees. A number of interviewees also welcomed the opportunity to give serious consideration or reflection to aspects of their jobs normally taken for granted but present at the level of dim awareness. Wax (1952) would view this situation as a form of exchange in which the researcher and informant consciously or unconsciously give each other what they both desire or need. She quite rightly states that most informants will resent manipulative and patronising behaviour on the part of the researcher. It is important to listen attentively with respect to suggestions or advice; and the rewards received by the informant are many, ranging from relief from a boring work episode to allowing a bitter informant to obtain relief from divulging his frustrations.

METHODS OF ANALYSIS

Hypothesised and other relationships in the data were
subjected to statistical analysis. A computer programme was specifically compiled in order to examine
simple correlative associations. Later a statistical
computer package - SPSS - was extensively used. The
statistical tests used were :-

Tests of Hypothesis - comparison of proportions
using the Normal Statistic
Test

Pearson's Product Moment Correlation Coefficient

Kendall's Tau Rank Order Correlation Coefficient

Coefficient of Multiple Correlation

Partial Correlation

Chi-Square (χ^2), Kruskal-Wallis One-Way Analysis
of Variance

The relationships examined with the aid of these tests
are discussed below. In addition, in order to obtain
an overview of patterns of questions, on a tabular
and cross-tabular basis, percentage or index tables
were produced. All statistical work was carried out
on the computer.

Each question on the questionnaire (see Appendix
'A') will be examined with a view to identifying the
statistical treatment it received. The variables
which were subjected to statistical test will be
examined first. The decision-making behaviour variable in question 2 (hereafter referred to as decision
style) is the major dependent variable and has a
relationship with all other variables on the questionnaire. The latter comprise the independent variables.

Decision style in relation to different types of
decisions (Question 2). Programmed decisions are
identified by the numbers 3, 6, 10, 12, 14; non-
programmed decisions are comprised of the remaining

132

numbers - 1, 2, 4, 5, 7, 8, 9, 11, 13. Task decisions
are identified by the numbers 1, 3, 4, 5, 6, 7, 9, 10,
11, 12, 14; personnel decisions are comprised of the
remaining numbers - 2, 8, 13. This probably reflects
reality, with a preponderance of emphasis given to
task decisions. For each decision style the mean of
the stated percentages was extracted over all applicable decisions. An identical calculation was made
when all applicable decisions were sub-divided into
the categories enumerated above. A comparison of the
percentage time usage of the decision style for the
different categories of decision was made. For each
decision style the number of respondents actually
using a given style more for non-programmed than programmed decisions was calculated. This was achieved
by comparing the mean percentage time allocated to a
decision for non-programmed decisions with the mean
percentage time allocated to a decision for programmed decisions. The proportion of all respondents
using a decision style more for non-programmed than
for programmed decisions was then compared with 0.5
using the normal test statistic. An identical calculation was made when comparing the usage of the
various decision styles for task as opposed to personnel decisions.

Decision style in relation to the
independent variables

The experience variables - time spent in job and age -
(Question 1) were related individually and combined to
decision style using the Pearsonian Product Moment
Correlation, Kendall's Tau Rank Order Correlation and
the Coefficient of Multiple Correlation. The individual relationships were then mediated by level in the
organisational hierarchy (Question 9) and size of both
finance function and company (Questions 11, 12) using
the Partial Correlation Coefficient.

The variable Specialisation - extent to which a job
area is established - (Question 3) was derived from a
Likert five-point scale by summating the ratings for
the thirteen areas. It was then related to decision

style by category of decision using the Pearsonian Product Moment Correlation and Kendall's Tau Rank Correlation. Specialisation and specialism - degree of qualification of person operating or managing a job area - (Question 3) were together related to decision style using the Coefficient of Multiple Correlation. Specialism was also related, on an individual basis, to decision style using the Pearsonian r and Kendall's Tau. The scale used to arrive at a score for the variable specialism was almost identical to that used for specialisation.

Perceptions of desirable and actual qualities or skills (Question 4) were recorded on ordinal type scales. Integers ranging from 1 to 7, denoting minimum and maximum scores respectively at the extreme points, were assigned to the scales to indicate relative positions. The difference between the actual and desirable score for each of the fifteen types of quality or skill was calculated and the differences were aggregated. The aggregate difference was then related to decision style over all decisions and by category of decision using the Pearsonian r and Kendall's Tau. The individual types of quality or skill discrepancy were also related to decision style using the Pearsonian r. The mediating effect of level within the organisational hierarchy (Question 9) was measured by using the Partial Correlation. The Kruskal-Wallis One-Way Analysis of Variance was used to test the hypothesis that the mean index scores of quality or skill discrepancy for the three company sizes were equal.

The status, power and influence variable (Question 5) was obtained by aggregating the affirmative responses in columns 57 to 62. This variable was related to decision style, using the Pearsonian r and Kendall's Tau, over all decisions.

The managerial behaviour characteristics variable (Question 6) was sub-divided into two categories - employee orientation (i) (ii) and task orientation (iii) (iv). It was obtained from a five-point Likert

134

scale by summating the ratings for the four characteristics, and was related to decision style using the Pearsonian r and Kendall's Tau. Using identical tests the ratings for the dimensions employee orientation and task orientation were summated and each dimension was related to decision style. Combined with LPS - opinion of least preferred subordinate - (Question 8) both dimensions were related to decision style using the Coefficient of Multiple Correlation.

The Semantic Differential scale (Question 8) was adopted in order to measure the attitude of the superior towards his least preferred subordinate (LPS). It was used by Fiedler in a similar capacity and can be viewed, like a Likert scale, as a summated rating scale. The total attitude scale is derived from sixteen bi-polar rating scales, each being an eight point scale, with 8 representing the most favourable response. A respondent's total score is the measure of his attitude. To counteract a biasing effect the position of the poles was varied between scales. The LPS variable was related to decision style over all decisions using the Pearsonian r and Kendall's Tau. When relating LPS and employee orientation and LPS and task orientation to decision style the Coefficient of Multiple Correlation was used. Ignoring decision style, LPS was related to both employee orientation and task orientation individually using the Pearsonian r and Kendall's Tau.

The 'level' variable (Question 9) was related to decision style using the Pearsonian r and Kendall's Tau. The mediating effects of size of company and size of finance function (Questions 12, 11) individually and collectively on the relationship between decision style and hierarchical level were measured using the Partial Correlation. The same statistic was used to establish the mediating effects of level in the following relationships: the individual relationship between age and decision style and time spent in job (job experience) and decision style; age and job experience together in relation to decision style; the relationship between the aggregate quality or skill discrepancy and decision style; the relationship between span of control and decision style. In addition hierarchical level was combined with size of company to mediate the relationship between span of control and decision style.

The number of subordinates reporting directly (span of control) variable - Question 10 - was related to decision style over all decisions and by category of decision using the Pearsonian r and Kendall's Tau. The relationship between decision style and span of control was then mediated by hierarchical level (Question 9) and by both size of finance function (Question 11) and size of company (Question 12) individually, and by hierarchical level and size of company together using the Partial Correlation.

The size of finance function variable (Question 11) was related to decision style using the Pearsonian r and Kendall's Tau. It is used as a mediating variable in the relationship between hierarchical level (Question 9) and decision style. It was also merged with size of company (Question 12) to mediate the latter relationship. To measure its mediating effect the Partial Correlation was used. Similarly this variable mediated the relationship between job experience and age (Question 1) and decision style, and the relationship between span of control (Question 10) and decision style.

The size of company variable (Question 12) was related to decision style using the Pearsonian r and Kendall's Tau. It acted as a mediating variable in the relationship between hierarchical level (Question 9) and decision style, fusing with size of finance function (Question 11) to mediate the latter relationship. The Partial Correlation was used to measure its mediating effects. It also mediated the relationship between span of control (Question 10) and decision style and together with hierarchical level (Question 9) mediated this relationship. The relationship between age and job experience (Question 1) and decision style individually was also mediated by size of company.

Nearly all relationships between the dependent and other independent variables were classified by size of company in an endeavour to assess the influence of company size.

The role of the Chief Accountant variable (Question 13) was related to decision style using the Chi-Square test (x^2).

Index and Percentage tables were compiled in order to highlight the pattern of data distribution on a tabular and cross-tabular basis. In three instances graphs were prepared from the Percentage tables.

Percentage cross-tabular tables

Size of company related to job experience; Size of company related to hierarchical level; Size of company related to span of control.

Graphs. Decision style profile; Decision style profile by company size; Size of company related to size of finance function.

Percentage tabular tables

Functional role of Chief Accountant; Status, power and influence.

Index tabular tables

Specialisation and specialism; Employee and task orientation.

Table of differences

Discrepancy between desirable and actual qualities or skills related to size of company.

Comment on the statistical tests

Confronted relatively frequently with a skewed distribution of data and the use of ordinal scales, the

logical course of action would appear to be the choice
of non-parametric tests. Siegel (1956) has championed
these tests in psychological research when conditions
surrounding the use of parametric tests are not fully
satisfied. Constrained by the confines of the statistical package used - the SPSS - all multivariate
analysis had to be conducted through the medium of
parametric tests which are underpinned by the assumptions of normality of distribution and interval scaling. This being so, in order to achieve uniformity
of testing methods a parametric bivariate correlation
coefficient - Pearson's Product Moment - was considered an appropriate test to use. However, as a pre-
cautionary measure Kandall's Tau Rank Correlation
Coefficient was used in nearly all the cases where
the Pearsonian r was considered relevant as an exercise in verification. No substantial differentiations
are discernible when we compare the results of both
tests (see Appendix 'D'). Though Spearman's Rank
Order Correlation Coefficient is generally considered
preferable to Kendall's Tau, the incidence of a number
of ties in the data makes the latter the more suitable.

Parametric tests are frequently used in psychological research in circumstances when the conditions
attached to them are not fully met. In highlighting
the limitations of his research method, Heller (1971)
goes on to say: 'It is known that rating scales such
as those used in nearly all research on participation, including the present one, do not meet all the
assumptions of the Pearsonian r.' A widely held view
explaining the attachment to the parametric test
(even when its conditions are not satisfied!) is that
it is better at detecting significant differences between two sets of scores, making use of all information in the data, whereas the equivalent non-
parametric test simply takes into account the rank
order of the scores. Miller (1975) states that
'statisticians have recently examined what happens
to the accuracy of certain parametric tests (i.e.,
the t-tests) when the basic assumptions of normality
and homogeneity of variance are systematically violated.

Happily these studies show that the results of the
t-tests are not seriously distorted even when quite
marked departures from the basic assumptions are
introduced.' There appears to be no reason to suspect the robustness of other parametric tests unless
there are glaring departures from normality and homogeneity. This is unlikely to be the case with the
present research data.

Though the dependent variable, depicting the time
spent on each decision style, may satisfy the interval
level measurement criteria, since it possesses the
characteristics of a ratio scale, the same cannot be
said of the independent variables measured on a Likert
scale. Since the Likert scale does not offer a zero
point for subjects who feel neutral about an item, it
facilitates statistical analysis at the cost of reducing validity by forcing some subjects to express
a view they do not hold. It is argued that the Likert
scale is not tantamount to an interval scale because
of its ordinal status and therefore no conclusions
can be drawn about the meaning of distances between
scale positions (Moser and Kalton, 1971). Nevertheless, many psychological variables are measured on
scales which cannot be classified as interval scales
of measurement. However, under certain circumstances
a seemingly ordinal attitude scale may satisfy the
requirements of interval scaling. Stone and James
(1965) offer as a major finding the view that 'education students perceive the prestige of teacher specialities reliably enough so that their judgements
can be measured on an interval scale.'

It is evident that when interpreting the significance of a correlative association between variables
there are no imputations of cause and effect. A
5 per cent level of significance will be used (i.e.,
one-tailed test) when a hypothesis postulates a direction in the differences between two variables. The
size of the sample for any statistical table will
depend on the completeness of the information on the
questionnaires.

139

HYPOTHESES

The hypotheses were formulated subsequent to an exhaustive review of the relevant literature, and reinforced by empirical observations obtained during the pilot stage of the research study. The dependent variable - decision style - is featured in every hypothesis along with the relevant independent variable(s). One should emphasise that the hypotheses centred on the mediating effects of size and level are somewhat speculative.

Hypothesis I. The Chief Accountant displays a tendency to manage in a directive fashion.

Hypothesis II. Programmed decision situations lend themselves to both directive and delegative styles of decision-making behaviour.

Hypothesis III. Non-programmed decision situations lend themselves to consultative or participative styles of decision-making behaviour.

Hypothesis IV. Task decision situations are more likely to be associated with a directive and a delegative style of decision-making behaviour.

Hypothesis V. Personnel decision situations are more likely to be associated with a consultative or a participative style of decision-making behaviour.

Hypothesis VI. The more experienced - age and time spent in job - the Chief Accountant the greater the likelihood of he using a moderately directive style of decision-making behaviour.

Hypothesis VII. A high level of specialisation is likely to be associated with a directive style of decision-making behaviour.

Hypothesis VIII. A high level of specialism is likely to lead to the use of a less centralised style of decision-making behaviour.

Hypothesis IX. When the Chief Accountant perceives a larger discrepancy between actual and desirable skills or qualities in the subordinate he is more likely to use a directive decision style. The opposite is true when he perceives a smaller discrepancy.

Hypothesis X. Chief Accountants enjoy a high level of organisational status, power, and influence and this is likely to be so irrespective of the style of decision-making behaviour.

Hypothesis XI. Employee-oriented behaviour, rather than task-oriented behaviour, is associated with decision style.

Hypothesis XII. A directive style is likely to be associated with a low LPS and a permissive style with a high LPS.

Hypothesis XIII. When the span of control of the Chief Accountant is wider a directive decision style is more likely to be used, whereas a permissive decision style is more applicable when the span of control is narrower.

Hypothesis XIV. The Chief Accountant whose functional role embraces the use of direct authority to implement his recommendations is likely to have a penchant for a directive decision style.

Hypothesis XV. The larger the size of the company and finance function the greater is the likelihood of a permissive-oriented decision style prevailing.

Hypothesis XVI. Size of company and finance function mediates the relationship between decision style and the experience variables.

Hypothesis XVII. Size of company and finance function mediates the relationship between decision style and span of control.

Hypothesis XVIII. Size of company and finance func-

tion individually and combined mediate the relationship between decision style and hierarchical level.

Hypothesis XIX. Overall the Chief Accountant's
decision style is likely to be influenced by the
size of the company.

Hypothesis XX. The higher the organisational level
the greater is the likelihood of the Chief Accountant
exercising a permissive-oriented style.

Hypothesis XXI. Hierarchical level mediates the
relationship between decision style and the experience variables.

Hypothesis XXII. Hierarchical level mediates the
relationship between skill discrepancy and decision
style.

Hypothesis XXIII. Hierarchical level mediates the
relationship between decision style and company size.

Hypothesis XXIV. Hierarchical level mediates the
relationship between decision style and span of control. It produces a similar effect when combined
with company size.

5 Results

Having specified the hypotheses in Chapter 4, the stage has now been reached where data and observations derived from the questionnaire and interviews are subjected to analysis, and inferences are drawn from the trends and patterns that develop. In the next chapter, under the heading of Discussion, the empirical evidence will be discussed further with specific reference to the hypotheses and the relevant literature.

Before examining the impact of category of decision on decision style, the distribution of the Chief Accountant's decision style over all types of decisions ought to be acknowledged. The decision style profile is shown in Figure 5.

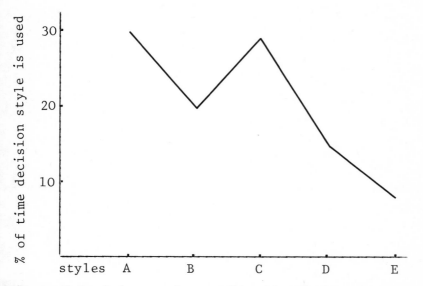

Figure 5 Decision style profile of Chief Accountants

We find that almost equal emphasis is given to restrictive and permissive decision styles with a marginal advantage in favour of a directive style whose
closest rival is a consultative style. Styles D and
E - joint decision making and delegation - appear to
be used sparingly.

DECISION-MAKING BEHAVIOUR (DECISION STYLE)
IN RELATION TO DIFFERENT TYPES OF DECISIONS

The main consideration to bear in mind is whether the
type of decision faced by the Chief Accountant has
any bearing on his decision style. The manner in
which decision styles are used more for non-programmed
and task decisions than for programmed and personnel
decisions is depicted in Table 5.1.

Table 5.1

A comparison of the percentage time
usage of decision styles for the
different categories of decision *

Decision type comparison	Decision style				
	A	B	C	D	E
Non-programmed - Programmed	-3.39^d	-0.07	6.40^d	7.43^d	-5.01^d
Task - Personnel	6.78^d	8.04^d	-4.12^d	-4.43^d	5.76^d

d = $p < 0.001$
* Normal Statistic test

The finding in the upper part of the table suggests
quite emphatically that decision styles C and D -
prior consultation and joint decision making - are used

more frequently for non-programmed than programmed decisions. Alternatively, it can be expressed in a slightly different form. Decision styles A, B and E - own decision without detailed explanation, own decision with detailed explanation and delegation - are used more frequently for programmed decisions than for non-programmed decisions. Though the statistic for B was not significant, nevertheless the pattern of positive and negative values was maintained.

The finding in the lower part of the table suggests equally emphatically that decision styles C and D are used more frequently for personnel than for task decisions and that decision styles A, B and E are more frequently used for task as opposed to personnel decisions.

In the relationship between programmed decision situations and decision styles A, B, E the strongest statistical association is reserved for the delegative style 'E', and the weakest association (non-significant) for the semi-directive style 'B'. This then might suggest that the two most appropriate styles for programmed decisions are delegation and own decision without explanation. We shall now turn to the field observational data to see to what extent it endorses the statistical prediction.

For programmed decisions delegation is prevalent. There is extensive delegation with a cut-off point beyond which variances have to be reported by the subordinate.

In the larger company control data (e.g., sales and profit analysis) and the audit function tend to be relied on as monitoring devices in addition to placing trust in the subordinate. One respondent in a large company said:

Because of the size of the company extensive delegation is applied. I rely on my fortnightly meetings with subordinates to keep me informed. In addition there is the internal audit to keep me in touch with any irregularities and defects in the content of records and systems. And of course there are the impersonal control techniques – budgets and profit statements to keep me in the picture.

In the smaller company there appeared to be more direction emanating from the Chief Accountant. Generally, the calibre of his subordinates was relatively lower and the size of operations lent itself to a higher degree of informality. Every effort was made however to delegate when the circumstances justified it. The following remarks are attributable to Chief Accountants in the smaller company.

Subordinates operate under guidelines, subject to periodic checks – browsing through the control data and a reliance on informal contacts.

In a programmed decision situation you would delegate where possible, but exceptional matters – e.g., when to take a discount on a payment to a supplier in certain circumstances – would require my attention. In other situations you would take action on your own if, for example, the accounts did not look right. But you must always rely on your subordinates, your success depends on them.

Delegate with clear terms of reference. Where a formal control device does not exist, then control is likely to be exercised surreptitiously. It is essential to be informed, particularly when you have to face the external auditors, so periodic checks are essential, though the number bears a relationship to the calibre of staff. The need for periodic checks is also important in another sense because sometimes subordinates fail to understand instructions.

Irrespective of size certain similarities were discernible in the comments made by respondents. Confidence in subordinate's ability is an important determinant of decision style, particularly of delegation in this context. Conversely, matters of an exceptional nature arising from a programmed decision situation - e.g., where payment to a foreign supplier in his currency exceeds £50,000, though individual sums in excess of this figure on aggregation are exempt - were likely to call forth a directive style. In practically all situations where authority to take programmed decisions was delegated the use of monitoring devices, be they personal or impersonal, were considered justifiable. Cross-functional contacts and hearsay also had their uses as sources of information. In addition subordinates were encouraged to bring to the notice of the Chief Accountant matters of a unique kind both within and outside their level of competence. They were also allowed to conduct a dialogue on a cross-functional basis, e.g., discussions with marketing personnel on matters connected with credit control, provided in the event of a disagreement or anything of significance arising from such contacts the Chief Accountant was fully aware of developments. The Chief Accountant would also be likely to interfere more in so called sensitive areas - e.g., debtors - with a moderating influence in case an over-enthusiastic credit controller pressurises unduly a valued customer.

Though some form of checking book entries was an organisational reality universally, checking reached almost obsessional proportions in two construction companies. Both companies evolved from humble beginnings and their overall management still resided in the entrepreneurs responsible for their development. In a sense the Chief Accountants concerned were perpetuating a practice initiated by the owner manager in the early formative days and still actively pursued. One respondent said he was perfectly satisfied with the competency of his immediate subordinate and tended to delegate but felt it necessary to retain control by a random selection of entries in the books of account, so as to verify their accuracy. Another checked the cash book once a month and performed a periodic check of the plant register. In other

situations pressure of time tended to elicit a directive response from the Chief Accountant.

Non-programmed decisions elicit different decision
styles. The decision styles C and D - consultation
and joint decision making - are significantly associated with non-programmed decisions in Table 5.1.
The observational data certainly confirms this finding. Various forms of consultative and joint decision-
making behaviour were, for example, attributable to
situations in which a major overhaul or modification
to an accounting system was contemplated. Often in
addition to the vertical contact with the subordinate
the Chief Accountant would involve interested parties,
from other functional areas, likely to be affected by
any changes. This was exemplified in a number of
comments made by respondents.

> In a decision connected with the redesign of the
> accounting system consultation took place between
> the computer man, my deputy and myself. My
> deputy, who favoured the retention of the manual
> system, exerted great influence in the final deci-
> sion.

> The involvement of subordinates was conspicuous
> throughout the discussions related to the central-
> isation of accounting.

> With reference to the centralisation of the ac-
> counting function subordinates were asked to
> examine their areas; time targets were set and
> a programme of action, decided jointly, was initi-
> ated. Subordinates exercised a fair degree of
> influence, e.g., in the matter of staff redundan-
> cies.

> I was presented with the idea of developing a
> computerisation programme. Having considered the
> problem and broken it down into manageable parts,
> a steering committee was formed and my deputy along
> with a systems analyst were seconded full-time to
> conduct a feasibility study. A number of managers

from other departments were involved in the deliberations at the committee meetings, but unfortunately this gave strong members the chance to influence events. Only my deputy was involved in the discussions before the report to the board was finally produced.

Because of a need for a new accounting system due to a significant increase in capital expenditure I conveyed to my subordinate what I thought it might look like. He listened, went away, thought about it, sorting out any snags as necessary. Hopefully he will come back to me having clarified the situation and then we shall discuss the scheme together.

Numerous instances could be quoted of subordinate involvement in non-programmed decisions other than those relating to a modification of accounting systems. At the same time one can identify situations in which the Chief Accountant is reluctant to involve a subordinate, or if he does he appears not to treat the subordinate's contribution as such all that seriously when arriving at a decision. The confidential nature of a decision and whether the subordinate can make a worthwhile contribution appear to be important constraining influences. Here are some comments which reflect certain reservations.

As far as modification to procedures is concerned subordinates can exercise tremendous influence; for example, they make suggestions, we engage in joint facts-analysis exercises, and it is not difficult to reach agreement with them or endorse their views. However, there are times when I make the modification proposals and present them to subordinates as decisions, giving reasons for the line of action suggested.

Because of the secretive nature of disposals and acquisitions, the subordinate's role is merely that of collector of relevant information.

Faced with a complex situation - profit projection - I seek information from a number of quarters, e.g., production and sales. I would also seek the suggestions of subordinates in certain circumstances but at the same time I would refer to the documentation they prepare in the normal course of events.

I discuss matters connected with the finalisation of cost statements when the person in charge is competent.

In many complex or uncertain situations I tend to make decisions on my own because of the limitations of subordinates. Subordinates usually have realistic expectations of the quantity and quality of their contributions and are aware of their limitations.

A subordinate's influence in a decision to change the accounting system is only felt if, having consulted him, his contribution appeals to sound principles of logic.

If the problem concerned is within the orbit of the subordinate's experience, by all means involve him in the decision. Otherwise, the inclination is to tackle it oneself. Where decisions are based on information of a secretive or confidential nature, this rules out the involvement of the subordinate.

In a problem or special situation the subordinate may be involved in the decision process as the provider and interpreter, exercising a strong influence on the final decision. But this is subject to the competence of the subordinate.

Circumstances in which I decide on my own are those in which I feel my knowledge or skill is superior to that of my colleagues or subordinates.

There appeared to be a greater tendency for respondents

150

in the smaller organisation to express a reluctance
to involve subordinates in non-programmed decisions,
apparently due to their lack of an acceptable level
of competence. Generally speaking the subordinate
of the Chief Accountant in the larger organisation is
more able, perhaps because of better job prospects
and remuneration. Some Chief Accountants felt participation by subordinates in a problem decision area
was beneficial in circumstances where their influence
was negligible.

I involve the subordinate in a problem situation
so as to give him the opportunity to assimilate
it and I would suggest certain courses of action
for his consideration, but from the beginning I
knew what the answer would be. It's an educational experience for the subordinate.

Where I am very knowledgeable about something
(e.g., setting guidelines for the investigation
of variances) I initiate action with predeterm-
ined notions about the likely outcome, and though
I have made up my mind I involve my subordinate
out of courtesy.

A number of other factors received a minor emphasis
as phenomena likely to influence the adoption of a
permissive decision style.

Consensus decision making is a striking feature of
this organisation.

I would like to be able to engage in the style I
like (lots of consultation) but the company environment seems to discourage it.

Group guidelines forced a decision on subordinates which they felt to be unsuitable for the
company.

It's likely one is more friendly and considerate
towards subordinates when their contribution to
a decision is valued.

Avoid the danger of being manipulated by having decisions imposed on you. To guard against this, it is necessary to build up confidences.

A similar statistical pattern presents itself when types of decisions are dissected into personnel and task decisions. All the personnel decisions have already been classified under the label of non-programmed decisions. On the other hand, five of the eleven task decisions are programmed decisions. The evidence in Table 5.1 suggests that decision styles A, B and E are significantly associated with task decisions, and C and D are significantly associated with personnel decisions. This is not a surprising result if we lend credence to the observational data as to the appropriate style to use for personnel decisions when the subjects concerned are indirect subordinates.

In connection with personnel decisions related to indirect subordinates I enter into discussion with my immediate subordinate before taking the final decision.

Joint decision making is a normal occurrence when it comes to the upgrading of indirect subordinates.

There appears to be an expectation on the part of the Chief Accountant that his subordinate would initiate the consultation.

I like to receive early notice of significant personnel decisions, which is required in a medium-sized company. I like to play the devil's advocate, e.g., in contemplated dismissals, when I try to extract from my immediate subordinate the consequences of dismissing an indirect subordinate.

With personnel decisions I would like to know what is being done and why.

As to staff decisions, I feel I must be consulted by my subordinates.

Of course there will be times when consultation and joint decision making will be forfeited in favour of a more directive style, and if consultation is used it is not altogether genuine.

The promotion of an indirect subordinate is a decision I am likely to take on my own. There is an able accountant working in the management accountant's section and he could benefit from broadening his experience and assuming new responsibilities. I know the management accountant is likely to resist such a move because he does not want to lose his services. My mind is made up and any 'consultation' I use in such circumstances amounts to no more than a diplomatic ploy.

Finally, the impact of programmed decisions in the relationship between task decisions and decision style is likely to be critical.

DECISION STYLE IN RELATION TO EXPERIENCE VARIABLES (TIME SPENT IN JOB AND AGE)

The relationship between decision-making behaviour (decision style) and both age and job experience individually and combined is shown in Table 5.2.

Table 5.2 illustrates a significant statistical association between decision styles A and C and job experience. This suggests that the more time spent in the job the more directive the Chief Accountant becomes, whereas when he is relatively new to the job he is essentially consultative in his approach; though in the small company there is a likelihood of a shift from consultation to joint decision making materialising (see Table 1, Appendix 'C'). Age does not seem to be an important factor in this respect. No significant statistical relationship emerges when the

Table 5.2

Correlation between decision style
and experience variables

Decision style	Experience variables		
	n=212	n=209	n=209
			Age and
	Job experience	Age	job experience
A	0.15^b	0.07	0.15
B	-0.07	-0.10	0.10
C	-0.12^a	-0.04	0.12
D	-0.01	0.04	0.09
E	-0.01	0.02	0.03

a = $p < 0.05$
b = $p < 0.025$

experience variables are combined and related to
decision style. In an attempt to rationalise the
two significant relationships between job experience
and decision style we shall refer to the observational
data.

Respondents showed a certain unease when trying to
recall and articulate style differentiation due to
job tenure. A number of those interviewed had spent
a relatively short period of time in their present
job, though obviously they were able to draw on experience of similar jobs which preceded the present
one to help them distinguish between behavioural
dispositions on assuming a new job and subsequently
on having behind them the benefit of a reasonable
amount of job experience. Resorting to delegation as
a style with growing job tenure was something which

received some emphasis in the interviews with respondents but is not borne out by the statistical evidence. However, we must acknowledge that delegation in many circumstances within the finance function does not carry with it the autonomy often alleged to encompass it. The issue of guidance and monitoring of events can be quite prevalent in conditions of delegated authority. The consultative nature of decision-making behaviour when job experience is shallow was forcefully endorsed by the observational data.

Newness to the job promotes a consultative style. As one acquires knowledge of the critical operations in the department and absorbs the expertise of subordinates, one could easily become less consultative and take more decisions on one's own.

It took some time to get to grips with the job and during the first six months I tended to consult peers and subordinates quite a bit. I was many times disposed to condemning a particular practice or procedure but always felt it necessary to consult the appropriate person to discover the reasons behind it. You are likely to take more decisions on your own as familiarity with both subordinates and the technical nature of the work grows.

While maturing in the job you listen a lot but I must admit you feel vulnerable in situations where knowledge or information is lacking. At the early stages you go through the phase of getting to know your subordinates better, and they you, and it is critical to gain their respect. In developing goodwill with subordinates you take longer to explain things.

You are inclined to consult subordinates more in the early days in a job as a means to remove uncertainty and introduce a clearer perspective of the situation. With the passing of time however you are more likely to take decisions on your own.

At the beginning I was rather anxious in the job, faced with the difficulty of learning the company's practices and procedures as well as having to size-up my subordinates. Having now spent ten years in my present job I feel that maturity, greater know-ledge of the requirements of the job and the right people as subordinates give me greater scope to delegate. Increasing time spent in the job also gives you the opportunity to recruit 'your type' of subordinate and train those you inherited.

On taking over a new job you would almost as a matter of course consult, up and down, if only as a means to spread the blame if need be.

Respondents who experienced procedural deficiencies in the past felt that improvements in systems would relieve them of a detailed preoccupation with day to day administrative matters, and foster delegative behaviour.

At one time panic situations were frequent due to grave defects in various procedures. Now proce-dures have been tightened and perfected to the extent that so much of the processing of the work load is a matter of routine and can be safely delegated.

With such a highly proceduralised environment and a young team of subordinates, this respondent has tried to sustain interest and motivation of staff by initia-ting group discussions and target setting, where the meeting of targets is viewed competitively across companies within the group. Also in an endeavour to create an 'exciting' environment, his office walls carry different diagramatical representations of per-formance.

Assimilating the style of the boss was considered by some respondents to be the end result of the passing of time in the job.

The chief influence is the boss's style. If he

likes to work in a directing way then you should
do likewise.

The main influence on one's own style over time
is the management style of one's superior.

RELATIONSHIP BETWEEN DECISION STYLE AND EXTENT TO
WHICH JOB AREAS ARE ESTABLISHED (SPECIALISATION)
AND DEGREE OF QUALIFICATION (SPECIALISM)

The impact of both specialisation and specialism individually and combined on decision style is depicted in
Table 5.3.

Table 5.3

Correlation between decision style
and Specialisation and Specialism

n=211

Decision style	Special-isation	Specialism	Specialisation and specialism
A	0.15^b	0.04	0.17^a
B	−0.02	−0.10	0.11
C	$−0.11^a$	0.06	0.20^b
D	−0.03	0.01	0.04
E	−0.07	−0.04	0.07

a = $p < 0.05$
b = $p < 0.025$

Before commenting on the results in Table 5.3 one
should emphasise the fact that specialisation was
found to be fairly high and specialism comparatively
low in the finance function (see Index of Specialisa-

tion and Specialism Table 5, Appendix 'C'). Table
5.3 illustrates significant statistical relationships
between decision styles 'A' and 'C' and specialisation, suggesting that in conditions of high specialisation a directive style may prevail; whilst a
consultative style may be more relevant in circumstances where specialisation is relatively lower.
No statistically significant relationship emerges
when decision style is related to specialism. However, when this relationship is expressed by size of
company - see Table 1, Appendix 'C' - a highly significant statistical association exists between the
directive style 'A' and specialism for the small
company, implying that the Chief Accountant resorts
to this style when those in charge of the many job
areas are well qualified. A very plausible explanation to account for this result is that in many instances the Chief Accountant himself takes over responsibility for and direction of a number of these
areas in the small company. In the medium-sized
company high specialism invites consultation (see
Table 1, Appendix 'C'). When the variables specialisation and specialism are combined and related to
decision style the pattern of the relationship subsisting between style and specialisation is repeated,
conveying to us the impression that the Chief Accountant may consider it necessary to be directive in his
approach when jobs are highly structured and specialised and managed or operated by well qualified personnel. By way of contrast, the Chief Accountant may
feel a greater need to involve himself, through consultation, when he is confronted with a lesser degree
of specialisation and where the person in charge is
not so highly qualified. The authenticity of this
proposition can now be examined with reference to the
observational data.

There appeared to be a general belief that once
areas of work activity are well specified and prescribed, constant interference is necessary and justified, be it as a result of what was said at progress
meetings, hearsay and perusal of formal control data;
or in the absence of the latter, matters coming to

light as a result of frequent informal contact. Interference was not confined to areas of activity where the Chief Accountant suffered a lack of adequate knowledge of operations or technicalities, but it extended to situations where he was very conversant with the technical nature of the activity.

Even in highly specialised areas, keep your eyes open and do dip checks.

You've got to know whats going on. Credit Control is a great responsibility for one man; pick his brains and spend at least two hours a week with him. Constant liaison is a wise course of action.

I must be convinced of the justification for the action suggested by subordinates on major issues.

Because of the size of the company I possess comprehensive knowledge of all accounting activities. In selected areas, e.g., credit control, I am fully aware of what's going on but still I sit down with the person in charge of it to discuss problems and offer guidance monthly.

The budget officer is given strict guidelines to adhere to in the preparation of the budget. I will critically review the end result. I make it my business to be familiar with the main stream of each activity I am responsible for, even where the detail of an activity is not fully comprehended.

You tend to formalise things, e.g., meetings and reports, when you are not too sure of the core of an area you are responsible for.

Computer programming is an activity in which I plead a certain ignorance, and difficulties in understanding arise even at progress meetings. As a form of self-protection I enlarge the responsibilities of the computer manager into areas with which he is not totally familiar. You must not give him the chance to act in a cocky manner.

There are times when the subordinate with specialised skills 'takes exception to the fact that he has
to submit a summary of his price commission submission' to the Chief Accountant. The respondent to
which this remark is ascribed disapproves of his own
boss's 'style of remote supervision or complete delegation without checks.' He maintains 'people don't
mind providing information on their performance because it shows their boss the progress they are making
so he can, where necessary, compliment them on their
performance.'

The interdependence of job areas was in itself a
good reason to maintain control.

> Activities within organisations are interdepend-
> ent, so deadlines must be met and pressure applied,
> if necessary, because falling behind would disrupt
> the sequence of events.

The benevolent nature of the organisational environment may sustain the expectation that procedural
change can be legitimately initiated and implemented
by the person in the position of authority.

> The old budgeting system had well defined rules,
> and all variances were brought to my notice. The
> budgeting system is now creative and flexible.
> When it was first introduced it encouraged a lot
> of contacts, exchange of views and positive par-
> ticipation. Because of the attitudes of most
> people to the atmosphere created by benevolent
> management in the company, they are a pretty
> docile lot. They neither resist change, nor are
> they inclined to use initiative. They expect any
> changes to come from my position.

Probably because of a lesser degree of specialisation
and a lower level of specialism a less clear picture
of the organisational situation is visible. This
forces the Chief Accountant to consult his section
head to establish his depth of understanding of a particular issue, more so because procedures are not

efficient at registering and analysing developments. Some of the comments made by respondents who experienced such conditions are as follows:

> From recent experience I can recall a section head who performed adequately but lacked foresight in the identification of problems. In these circumstances it is necessary to spend more time finding out what is going on and then offer leadership.

> One is inclined, so to speak, to hold their hands a lot more, at all times trying to encourage them with a considerate form of supervision which amounts to guidance. One tries to strike a balance between involvement and non-involvement.

> In conjunction with the subordinate in charge we review and try to improve the procedures.

It appears from the evidence presented in Table 5.3.1 below that the weight of a high degree of specialisation could be instrumental in forcing the Chief Accountant to use a directive style in non-programmed decision situations. This can be gleaned from the statistically significant relationship under style 'A'.

Table 5.3.1

Correlation between decision style,
with regard to decision type,
and specialisation

n=211

| Type of decision | Specialisation | | | | |
| | Decision style | | | | |
	A	B	C	D	E
Non-programmed	0.15[b]	−0.11[a]	−0.07	0.01	−0.01
Programmed	0.05	0.02	−0.08	−0.02	−0.01

a = p $<$ 0.05
b = p $<$ 0.025

161

One might conclude from this result that a high level
of specialisation may elicit attempts to structure
decision processes, with the Chief Accountant resorting to a directive style. Without the mediating effect of specialisation we could expect a consultative
and joint decision-making style to be more applicable
to non-programmed decision situations. This is shown
clearly in Table 5.1.

RELATIONSHIP BETWEEN DECISION STYLE AND
PERCEIVED QUALITIES OR SKILLS POSSESSED
BY SUBORDINATE

A pertinent question to ask is whether the size or
magnitude of the discrepancy between desirable and
actual qualities or skills appertaining to the subordinate, as perceived by the Chief Accountant, bears
any relationship to decision style? It should be
noted that the greater the discrepancy over the selected items on the questionnaire the less favourable
the impression of the subordinate's qualities or
skills. The converse is true of a smaller discrepancy. Table 5.4 shows the relationship between decision style, over all types of decisions and by category of decision, and the aggregate skill discrepancy
score. Where the Chief Accountant perceives a large
difference between what he considers desirable and
what his subordinates actually possess in terms of
qualities or skills related to job performance he is
inclined to use a semi-directive style 'B'. On the
other hand, where he perceives a small difference he
is likely to involve his subordinates by sharing influence with them through the medium of joint
decision making. This finding, shown in the bottom
row of Table 5.4, appeals to commonsense by suggesting that one is more likely to involve a subordinate
in the decision-making process if he has the requisite
qualities or skills likely to permit him to make a
valid and effective contribution. Turning to the
category of decision one row removed from the bottom
of the table, we find that the statistical associations for task decisions are almost identical to that

Table 5.4

Correlation between decision style, analysed
by decision type and aggregate decisions,
and perceived qualities or skills in subordinate

n=212

| Decision type | Perceived skill discrepancy | | | | |
| | Decision style | | | | |
	A	B	C	D	E
Programmed	-0.03	0.11[a]	0.02	-0.02	-0.11[a]
Non-programmed	0.11[a]	0.07	-0.01	-0.19[c]	-0.01
Personnel	0.13[b]	0.03	-0.00	-0.14[b]	0.01
Task	0.01	0.12[a]	0.00	-0.13[b]	-0.08
Aggregate	0.05	0.12[a]	0.00	-0.18[c]	-0.07

a = p < 0.05
b = p < 0.025
c = p < 0.01

for aggregate decisions. However when the relationship is viewed from the position of other categories
of decision, differentiations do emerge but the underlying pattern of influence sharing remains unperturbed.
For example, in the context of programmed decisions a
large skill discrepancy will again call forth a semi-
directive style 'B'. But where the discrepancy is
small, delegation is the style considered most appropriate. This is understandable given the nature of
this type of decision. Where a skill deficiency is
experienced it seems logical for the superior to take
the decision and provide the subordinate with some
form of learning experience by explaining to him the

reasons for the course of action taken. In the event
of the subordinate possessing the requisite skill,
there is no reason why the subordinate should not exe-
cute the requirements of a programmed decision on his
own. As we have seen earlier in the discussion, he is
in any case likely to operate within an elaborate
framework of performance monitoring. The emphasis
changes when the scene of action shifts to a non-
programmed venue. Where the superior has a low esti-
mation of the subordinate in an ill-structured decision
situation he opts for a directive style probably in
the belief that it is the more practicable because the
subordinate may be out of his depth in the event of
the superior trying to explain to him the intricacies
of the decision. Should the superior hold the subordinate in high esteem then circumstances change. He
is now prepared to share non-programmed decision
making with the subordinate by engaging in joint decision making - style 'D' - no doubt convinced that the
subordinate has a positive contribution to make to the
final outcome. The statistical pattern applicable to
non-programmed decisions and perceived skill discrepancy practically repeats itself when we glance at the
result for personnel type decisions in Table 5.4. It
is well to bear in mind that all the personnel decisions listed in the research instrument are classified
also as non-programmed, though the majority of non-
programmed decisions are task rather than personnel
decisions. The presumption that the Chief Accountant
faced with a delicate personnel issue, in circumstances where he has a low opinion of his subordinate's
skills, will take decisions affecting indirect subordinates on his own has a lot of intuitive appeal.
Conversely, the Chief Accountant who holds his subordinate in high esteem is likely to endeavour to create
a relationship in which the subordinate has a significant part to play in reaching a final decision.

So far we have viewed the perceived qualities or
skills in the subordinate variable as an aggregate
score, sub-divided by type of decision and decision
style. We shall now relate each individual skill item
to decision styles in order to establish the items

which have the greatest effect on the decision style
of the Chief Accountant. A matrix of correlation of
perceived skill discrepancy over the individual items
by decision style appears in Table 5.4.1. In accordance with the earlier aggregate finding the pattern
of signs in Table 5.4.1 suggests that positive values
are more likely to be associated with restrictive
styles and negative values with permissive styles.
Out of 75 correlations only 11 are statistically significant. The strongest statistical association
(-0.24) is reserved for the relationship between
technical ability and decision style 'D'. This tells
us that when the Chief Accountant perceives a small
discrepancy between what is desirable and what the
subordinate possesses of this attribute (knowledge,
skill and current information related to industrial
accountancy) he is likely to enter into joint decision
making with him. Conversely, if the discrepancy is
large, a directive style 'A' is employed. Other
skills which can be singled out for comment are self-
confidence; calmness under pressure; tactful; willingness to pass on information; acceptance of new ideas.
Where the subordinate is seen as lacking in self-
confidence the superior adopts a semi-directive style
'B', but where the subordinate suffers no deficiency
in this respect and possesses enough self-confidence
he is likely to be considered a partner in the
decision-making process. Being endowed with an acceptable level of calmness under pressure of work is
certainly to the subordinate's advantage if he wishes
to be involved in joint decision making with his superior, because of the relationship between style 'D'
and this attribute. Should the subordinate be lacking
in adroitness in his dealings with others, particularly
when the issue is a sensitive one, it would appear the
superior is unlikely to hesitate in using a directive
style. But where the subordinate is capable of being
tactful in a delicate situation to the satisfaction of
his boss he is allowed to share influence with him in
the decision-making process. The less the willingness
to pass on information to others on the part of the
subordinate, the greater the likelihood of he being
subjected to a semi-directive style 'B'. Finally, the

Table 5.4.1

Correlation between individual skill discrepancy and decision style

n=212

Type of quality or skill	Decision style				
	A	B	C	D	E
Rapid decision ability	0.09	0.05	-0.10	-0.07	-0.02
Verbal ability	-0.06	0.08	0.13^b	-0.08	-0.10
Technical ability	0.19^c	0.05	-0.10	-0.24^d	-0.04
Forcefulness	0.00	0.09	-0.03	-0.07	0.00
Perseverence	0.06	0.01	-0.02	-0.08	-0.02
Sensitive	-0.03	0.08	0.05	-0.08	-0.04
Intelligent	0.01	0.06	-0.02	-0.06	0.01
Imaginative	-0.02	0.04	0.06	-0.06	-0.03
Responsible	0.06	0.05	-0.04	-0.08	-0.05
Self-confident	-0.04	0.15^b	0.06	-0.13^b	-0.09
Calm under pressure	0.07	0.09	-0.04	-0.13^b	-0.05
Tactful	0.13^b	0.01	0.02	-0.19^c	-0.06
Considerate of the views of others	0.02	-0.01	0.03	-0.05	-0.01
Willingness to pass on information	-0.04	0.19^c	-0.07	-0.05	-0.01
Ready to accept new ideas	0.05	0.10	0.04	-0.18^c	-0.11

a = $p < 0.05$ c = $p < 0.01$
b = $p < 0.025$ d = $p < 0.001$

Chief Accountant shows a willingness to engage both in joint decision making and delegation where he is assured of the subordinate's readiness to accept new ideas.

We shall now focus attention on the material derived from 4(ii) on the questionnaire, which afforded the respondent the opportunity to present qualities or skills additional to those listed, and to the observational data derived from the interviews. Technical ability - manifest predominantly as professional skill, coupled with knowledge of the relevant problem or issue under review - was overwhelmingly endorsed as the skill in the subordinate most valued when considering his true involvement in the decision-making process. This item along with five other items already listed in Table 5.4.1 is excluded from Figure 5.4, which only depicts additional qualities or skills influencing subordinate involvement in the decision-making process. They are listed in order of importance, 1 being the most important. In many organisational settings the existing distribution of responsibility among subordinates is obviously a key factor in determining the choice of subordinate to perform a particular task. It would appear, however, that the degree of involvement of the subordinate in the decisions of his boss must be strongly influenced by his suitability as perceived by the boss.

DECISION STYLE IN RELATION TO STATUS,
POWER, AND INFLUENCE

One might expect to find the role of the Chief Accountant to be endowed with high position power, authority and status because of the importance attached to financial control, particularly in times of economic difficulties. If he is reasonably competent there is no reason why his influence is not felt in the higher echelons of the organisation. Equally, because of his training and career progression he should possess a high degree of technical influence with his subordinates. These presumptions are substantiated by the

1. Able to communicate clearly in writing

2. Able to liaise effectively with non-financial personnel

3. Able to think analytically and logically

4. Able to motivate staff

5. Commitment
   Loyalty
   Pleasant personality

6. Balanced judgement
   Able to delegate
   Honest and trustworthy

7. Able to meet deadlines

8. Commercial insight
   Ambitious

9. Respects confidentiality
   Able to control staff
   Sense of humour
   Objectivity

10. Initiative
    Persuasiveness
    Determination
    Punctuality

11. Numerically exact
    Reliable

Figure 5.4 Additional qualities or skills

data in Table 2, Appendix 'C', where a high score for this variable is established. When status, power and influence is correlated with decision style no significant statistical association emerges between the two. This is demonstrated in Table 5.5. Though an important variable it is difficult to fathom how it affects decision style directly. Generally respondents scored high on this dimension. They tend to view vertical respect as emanating from it when it is of sufficient

Table 5.5

Correlation between decision style and status, power and influence

n=212

Decision style	Status, power, influence
A	0.02
B	0.04
C	−0.04
D	0.02
E	−0.08

magnitude. A falling-off in respect is attributable to lower doses of it. In either case a number of behavioural ramifications are said to flow from it, some directly filtering through to leadership behaviour, but all affecting the general personality disposition of the Chief Accountant. The following comments extracted from the observational data emphasise this point.

High incidence of respect

It has the effect of making life easy and relaxed, encourages openness and allows one to intercede on behalf of subordinates rather than trying to protect oneself.

It enables you to be more definite in comments or views about situations as well as about figures, generally feeling more self-assured.

It would promote self-confidence that would show itself in a keenness to assign jobs to subordinates. A person would feel freer to act and feel less threatened.

169

It allows you to be creative and outspoken and permits you to experiment and take risks.

It provides the atmosphere in which you explain to subordinates the reasons for doing things, keeping them informed of developments and the consequences of not pursuing a particular line of inquiry. This encourages subordinates to bring problems to you, and shows them that you care about their difficulties.

Low incidence of respect

Without it you are inclined to be ratty, blowing your top and keeping things close to your chest.

We have a manager in the organisation whose influence has deserted him and his respect is at a low ebb. He is really twisted inside desperately trying to woo popularity. As a result his style is nondescript and in exercising it he loses the respect of all concerned.

Particularly in relation to the boss, one could become more protective, less open, a tendency to double check, feeling inhibited and trying to cover-up. In relation to subordinates there could be a tendency towards a dictatorial approach, directing people to do jobs rather than asking them to contribute.

There was a general view that influence and the concomitant respect were a function of the technical and social skills of the job occupant. Where they were lacking every effort should be made to redeem the situation, if of course the person is aware of the deficiency. Where position power is weak this predicament may be eased or reversed. As one respondent remarked, 'I involved myself in a significant area – corporate planning – where once I had no influence at all. Now they consult me on matters connected with it.'

DECISION STYLE IN RELATION TO
MANAGERIAL BEHAVIOUR CHARACTERISTICS

One recognises that a measure of leadership behavioural characteristics should ideally be more comprehensive, in terms of the quantity of items, than that used in the questionnaire. Nevertheless, one is confident that question 6 does emphasise, albeit in a condensed fashion, the salient features of the leadership behavioural dimensions - employee and task orientations. These characteristics are possessed by respondents overall to a fair degree (see Table 3, Appendix 'C'). In Table 5.6 these dimensions are related individually and together to decision style.

Table 5.6

Correlation between decision style
and managerial behaviour characteristics

n=212

Decision style	Managerial behaviour characteristics		
	i and ii Employee orientation	iii and iv Task orientation	i, ii iii, iv
A	−0.10	−0.01	−0.07
B	0.08	0.04	0.07
C	−0.06	−0.03	−0.06
D	0.06	−0.01	0.03
E	0.12[a]	0.05	0.09

a = $p < 0.05$

The relationship between the combined characteristics and task orientation and decision style fares poorly. However, the statistically significant relationship between decision style 'E' and employee orientation tends to suggest a linkage between a permissive style and employee-centred behaviour. It appears to be necessary to distinguish between delegation as a style contributing to high subordinate autonomy with the minimum level of performance monitoring, and a delegative style offering some autonomy but with the subordinate primarily operating within well prescribed procedural boundaries and subject to a fair amount of control. When asked how they would behave in relation to a subordinate, deserving their confidence, at the inception of a delegated assignment which was not procedurally circumscribed, respondents invariably remarked on the necessity to be considerate in behaviour in such circumstances. Where confidence is lacking, one respondent was convinced that his behaviour 'was likely to become somewhat formal, punctuated with social unease or distance, always operating in the knowledge that one day in the future one may have to reprimand him for something.' This may offer an explanation for the statistically significant result. The next best statistical association (-0.10) between decision style 'A' and employee orientation is also an interesting result, though it fractionally falls short of significance. It assumes a position of statistical significance on the Kendall Tau non-parametric test (see Table 6, Appendix 'D'). This might offer some form of endorsement of the oft quoted association between a directive style and less considerate managerial behaviour. By way of contrast task-oriented behaviour, manifest in a preoccupation with achieving impressive performance standards and ensuring that expertise and resources are mobilised to attain work targets, is not the preserve of any one style. Question 7 asked the respondents to specify any other managerial characteristics not listed in question 6 which they felt ought to be emphasised. This elicited a number of responses, the majority emphasising the characteristics contained in the previous question in a different or more explicit form. The greater number of remarks hovered on the employee-centred aspect of the leadership role concerned with individual development and fostering group harmony and integration. Typical comments were as follows:

172

I believe everybody desires to be good in his or her eyes at the job they are doing. Our management by objectives scheme requires staff to do their own appraisal at the end of the year and submit it to their superior for comment.

I am responsible for encouraging my subordinates to develop ideas and carry them through on their own initiative. I allow them to work without close constant supervision and to expose them to outside influences, i.e., other companies and technical courses.

I believe I am responsible for the broadening and development of my subordinates and in influencing them to similar action vis-a-vis their staff.

I believe I am responsible to a fair degree in encouraging my subordinates to work as a team rather than as individuals.

I believe I should be responsible for ensuring that all staff are tolerant and work together on a proper working relationship basis.

One respondent mentioned a less acceptable behavioural view of management as the 'art of being a good 'nag' - of demanding, expecting, and getting a certain standard or objective.' Another felt that different accounting functions demanded different managerial qualities. 'Routine accounting functions require administrative, technical, innovative and men management abilities. Commercial activities need different abilities, viz., commercial flair, imagination, persuasiveness and the power to influence (hopefully for the good!).' The projection of charismatic leadership qualities, enhancing the status of the finance function, removing obstacles likely to induce frustration, and relieving subordinates of some of their work load in times of pressure were qualities which received minor emphasis.

DECISION STYLE IN RELATION TO OPINION OF
LEAST PREFERRED SUBORDINATE (LPS), AND THE
LATTER IN RELATION TO MANAGERIAL BEHAVIOUR
CHARACTERISTICS

The LPS measure touched a raw nerve in some respondents - 'I cannot see that it can be of significant
interest to you'; 'I do not psycho-analyse my subordinates. We work as a team and objectives appear to
be satisfactorily achieved.' If this reaction was
widespread it may cast doubts on the authenticity of
the profile. It was therefore very reassuring when,
in one instance during the interview stage, I played
back the profile of the least preferred subordinate
to the respondent and he was remarkably impressed by
its accurate reflection of what he considered to be
key aspects of the personality of the subordinate in
question. The relationship between decision style and
LPS, and decision style and (a) LPS and employee orientation (b) LPS and task orientation appears in Table
5.7.

Table 5.7

Correlation between decision style and LPS, the
latter combined with both employee orientation and
task orientation and correlated with decision style

n=212

Decision style	LPS	LPS and employee orientation	LPS and task orientation
A	-0.12^a	0.15	0.12
B	-0.01	0.08	0.04
C	0.06	0.09	0.08
D	0.03	0.07	0.04
E	0.13^b	0.17^a	0.14

a = $p \leqslant 0.05$
b = $p < 0.025$

174

It is particularly apparent from a scanning of Table
5.7 that the high LPS Chief Accountant, who we claim
establishes a friendly and warm relationship with his
subordinates, resorts to a delegative style. Conversely, the Chief Accountant with a lower LPS score
becomes directive in his approach. When LPS is combined with employee orientation and related to decision style a significant statistical association emerges between style 'E' and this combined variable,
reinforcing the earlier result of a high LPS leader
embracing or clasping a delegative style. The association with style 'A' is marginally short of significance. So we might expect the employee-centred leader
who happens to be warm and friendly to choose the permissive style 'E'. As is demonstrated in the right
hand column of Table 5.7 the strength of the relationship between LPS and decision style cannot compensate
for the lack of a significant association between
decision style and task orientation in Table 5.6 when
the independent variables are combined and related to
decision style. As a result, no significant relationship is found. Though this may be so when LPS and
task orientation are integrated and related to decision style, something quite different arises when
LPS is related to managerial behaviour characteristics
without the intervention of decision style. This relationship is depicted in Table 5.7.1.

Table 5.7.1

Correlation between LPS and managerial
behaviour characteristics

n=212

Opinion of least preferred subordinate	Managerial behaviour characteristics	
	Task orientation	Employee orientation
LPS	0.19^{c}	0.08

$c = p < 0.01$

The significant statistical relationship between LPS
and task orientation may appear on the face of it to
be a rather surprising result, particularly in the
light of a non-significant relationship between LPS
and employee orientation. A feasible explanation to
account for it at this juncture may be that the leader
who enjoys a warm and friendly relationship with his
subordinates feels it now necessary to place priority
on the task-related ingredients of his role.

DECISION STYLE IN RELATION TO
THE SPAN OF CONTROL

The pattern of relationships between the span of control and decision style over all decisions and by
category of decision is shown in Table 5.8.

Table 5.8

Correlation between decision style, with regard
to decision type, and span of control

n=212

Decision style	Span of control				
	Decisions				
	Aggregate	Programmed	Non-programmed	Personnel	Task
A	0.16^c	0.04	0.21^d	0.35^d	0.07
B	-0.04	-0.06	-0.01	-0.03	-0.03
C	-0.08	-0.01	-0.09	-0.11^a	-0.05
D	-0.11^a	0.05	-0.14^b	-0.17^c	-0.02
E	-0.02	-0.01	-0.01	-0.05	0.01

a = $p < 0.05$
b = $p < 0.025$
c = $p < 0.01$
d = $p < 0.001$

176

In the second column from the left under the heading 'Aggregate' are listed the statistical associations between decision style and span of control over all decisions. We may conclude that, as a result of the statistically significant associations between decision styles 'A' and 'D' and span of control, the Chief Accountant is less likely to use a permissive style, instead preferring a directive style, when a large number of subordinates report to him directly. On the other hand, he is more likely to resort to a permissive style where a small number are directly responsible to him. When we explore the other significant trends highlighted in Table 5.8 we begin to realise that the best predictors of the relationships just specified can be located in the non-programmed and personnel categories of decision. We find also that when confronted with personnel decisions the Chief Accountant adopts a consultative style in addition to joint decision making as an approach when his span of control is narrow. No significant statistical relationships emerge between decision style and span of control when programmed and task decisions are considered. The above finding would appear to suggest that in decision situations of an ill-structured or personnel nature, where one might expect to find a high level of interaction between the superior and subordinates, a permissive style - deeply consultative or participative - would be too cumbersome, and a directive style would be more appropriate when the number of direct subordinates is large. In these decision situations, however, a permissive style would be suitable when the span of control is narrow. As to the non-significant relationship between decision style over programmed decisions and span of control, one could subscribe to the view that the superior's span of attention is not heavily taxed, irrespective of the size of the span of control - within reasonable limits - in decision situations which are procedurally well prescribed. One is forced to rely on conjecture to explain the non-significant relationship between decision style over task decisions and span of control. Perhaps the instrumentality of programmed decisions, which along with non-programmed decisions are responsible for the creation of this category of decision, was most strongly felt.

The observational data lends support to the central theme manifest in the statistical results. The general consensus appeared to be that a small span of control - in the region of 2 to 4 - offered the superior the opportunity to become more involved in his subordinates' work problems, more aware of developments conducive to a problem-centred approach, more able to concentrate on matters of policy freed from numerous co-ordinating functions and generally able to act in a more informal fashion. There was a feeling however that the danger of interfering too much in the subordinate's work province was omnipresent. The above emphasis was reversed when respondents commented on the consequences of a large span of control (e.g., 6). There was a general belief that the wide span of control was instrumental in encouraging remoteness, detachment, less time spent with subordinates, formalised access to the superior and structuring of contacts, and generally provided a sympathetic climate for the exercise of a directive style. Swimming against the tide, two respondents expressed a marked preference for a flat organisational structure. One of them equated good working relationships with a large span of control, maintaining 'that nobody is then the teacher's pet.' Others rightly pointed out that both the calibre of subordinate and task similarity were influential determinants of the optimum size in given circumstances. One might also add that supervisory capability is equally a determining influence.

DECISION STYLE IN RELATION TO THE FUNCTIONAL
ROLE OF THE CHIEF ACCOUNTANT

Respondents had to choose from three role categories (executive, advisory and neither) on a nominal scale in the questionnaire. Establishing exactly the true nature of their authority in cross-functional contacts which results in action or inaction is evidently fraught with difficulty for respondents. This may be reflected in the distribution of their perceptions in Table 5.9.

Table 5.9

Perceptions of functional role occupancy

n=212

Functional role	Percentage distribution
	%
(a) Advisory	30.7
(b) Executive	42.9
(c) Neither (a) or (b)	26.4

Though 42 per cent of respondents see themselves as possessing direct authority to implement recommendations of an accounting and finance nature in other functions (e.g., Production, Marketing), the majority consider themselves to act in a purely advisory role, or are unable to perceive their role definitively as either advisory or executive. This tends to conform to the weight of observational data indicating that pragmatism in the presence of formidable constraints is the only sensible course of action. We shall delve into these observations shortly, but first an examination of the relationship between decision style and functional role is called for. It is illustrated in Table 5.9.1. The data lends itself to a Chi-Square test after creating categories based on the time spent on a decision style - $< 19.9\%$; $20 - 49.9\%$; $> 50\%$ - and relating them to each functional role. There is no reason to suspect a differentiation in the decision-making behavioural patterns exhibited by the Chief Accountant due to the nature of the functional role he performs. The functional role, embracing cross functional contacts, is politically a delicate one in the eyes of a number of respondents.

Table 5.9.1

Relationship between decision
style and functional role

n=212

Decision style	Chi-Square observed values
A	2.83
B	2.88
C	1.63
D	1.36
E	4.41

0.05 tail of $x^2 = 9.49$. As the observed values are less than 9.49 we cannot claim a significant relationship.

It would appear that the Chief Accountant most frequently resorts to formal recommendations on financial matters in his dealings with non-financial managers but he is always prepared to institute persuasive powers when considered necessary.

I have probably a 90 per cent success rate in getting my recommendations accepted, but I still have to make a conscious effort to sell my ideas.

The status of the finance function is high in this company but nevertheless I have to rely on political processes to get things accepted. It's not infrequent for me to take managers in other departments to lunch and explain to them the desirability of accepting a certain line of action.

Advice is challenged as a normal occurrence. You have to use persuasion because figures alone cannot do the talking, e.g., price increase. Managers are anything but weak and humble as far as financial matters are concerned - they challenge you and question you and it's up to you to prove your position.

I recommended that stock be reduced by £100,000 in three months time. I explained to the production manager the beneficial effect this would have on the cash flow position. No progress on this issue was reached within a reasonable length of time, so I was forced to repeat the recommendation. It was at this stage that a meaningful exchange of views happened where we explored the reasons behind the production manager's objections, e.g., the consequences in redundancies due to a cut-back in production; the impairment of service to marketing. This proved very useful indeed.

Persuasive skills may prove ineffective in the face of hardened resistance by non-financial managers to courses of action suggested by the Chief Accountant. Often in such circumstances the referral of the matter or issue in question upwards, inviting the intervention of a higher authority, usually a financial director or managing director, was not uncommon. Even the likely threat of intervention may be sufficient in certain circumstances.

I had no difficulty in getting the Production Manager to call a halt to the production of tinned sausage rolls. The shadow of my boss, the Financial Director, in the background had something to do with it.

In 20 to 30 per cent of the time my recommendations are not enthusiastically received. I would then refer the problem to the Managing Director who, if convinced by the soundness of my arguments, would exercise his influence.

The bulk of solid resistance was likely to come from marketing or sales personnel.

181

Sales and Marketing people show a reluctance to accept financial discipline. A good example is the over-optimism with which they put forward proposals for a large capital investment project (selling outlets). We had to deter them. We have a finance oriented parent company who would endorse recommendations which are financially sound.

The Sales Manager did not take kindly to the suggestion that cash should accompany an order where a customer resides overseas. This was brought about by cash flow considerations. He felt this was a harsh imposition and would adversely affect volume of sales, so he was not prepared to go along with it. The only alternative open to me then was to place my recommendation in the hands of my boss, the Financial Director. He won't find it easy either and it will become a real bargaining session.

There can be no denying that this relationship, akin to the classical staff/line relationship, is studded with innumerable behavioural intricacies. In addition to the observations cited above, further variations in the strength of the Chief Accountant's influence were found to be relevant, though occupying a position of lesser importance. They tend to indicate the pragmatism brought to bear on issues by the Chief Accountant in his liaisons with non-financial managers in other functions. From bargaining sessions acceptable compromises surface. Some felt that real influence rested on the quality of the reports or memoranda produced, and in turn were dependent on the quantity and substance of one's 'homework'. An abortive attempt at getting a recommendation accepted could produce benefits by giving rise to the revision and improvement of the original recommendation. In another situation flexibility of approach was heightened by the sudden realisation that the original recommendation lacked cognizance of key commercial considerations. However, when the respondent feels especially knowledgeable in the area in which he is giving advice, e.g., price commission work, he would take a firm stand on his interpretation of the 'grey areas', allegedly 'with the company's interest at heart.' The respondent's influence can be considerably enhanced where he has a 'special' relationship with the general manager. Finally, his authority to act and secure the implementation of his recommendations is more likely to be influential in issues connected with accounting procedures rather than strategic questions affecting other functional areas.

DECISION STYLE IN RELATION TO SIZE

Size constitutes two variables in the research instrument, that is size of company and size of finance function. As illustrated in Figure 5.10, size of finance function moves in sympathy with size of company. When decision style is related to both the size of the company and finance function the statistical pattern that emerges appears in Table 5.10. The overall pattern conveys in each case that restrictive styles tend to be associated with the smaller company, and permissive styles tend to be associated with the larger company. More specifically, the statistically significant results suggest that the Chief Accountant in the smaller company and finance function tends to use the restrictive style 'A' whilst his counterpart in the larger company and finance function adopts a different perspective by subscribing more to the use of permissive styles 'D' and 'E'. The strongest statistical association subsists between a delegative style and size of company. When discussing the impact of size on decision style most of the respondents considered it more meaningful to attribute the major determining influence to size of company rather than to size of finance function. Apparently it is inevitable for an accounting manager to be more preoccupied with detail and to direct operations with a generally lower calibre subordinate staff in the smaller company. On the other hand, the larger company had the distinction of possessing more easily identifiable standardised accounting activities invariably controlled by higher calibre section heads. This appeared to have the

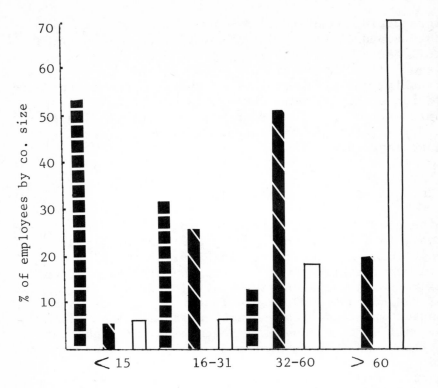

Size of finance function

Key:

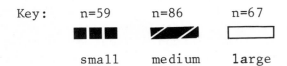

| n=59 | n=86 | n=67 |
| small | medium | large |

Figure 5.10 Size of finance function by company size

effect of fostering close working relationships between section heads and the Chief Accountant where
delegative behaviour was also evident. Representative
comments extracted from the observational data are as
follows:

In the small company you are immersed in detailed
technicalities, worrying about the pennies and
very pedantic. In the large company, though he

184

Table 5.10

Correlation between decision style
and both company and finance function size

n=212

Decision style	Size	
	Company	Finance function
A	-0.13^{b}	-0.15^{b}
B	-0.10	-0.05
C	0.08	0.06
D	0.12^{a}	0.12^{a}
E	0.17^{c}	0.15^{b}

a = $p < 0.05$
b = $p < 0.025$
c = $p < 0.01$

may be out of touch with many aspects of general company policy, the Chief Accountant has the benefit of more specialised sections where delegation is possible. As a result he is generally distant from the areas of operation.

In the smaller organisation one would take more decisions on one's own, primarily because of the calibre of subordinates, and one would also be very much involved in the day to day decision making. The larger organisation offers a greater challenge to qualified people; as a result one has a different breed of subordinate, and this must influence your management style.

You don't have the protection of the 'middle management belt' in the small company so you are likely

to be more directing in your style and use less
consultation than you would do in the large company where the implementation of decisions is a
longer process due to technical complexity.

Respondents tended to distinguish between an increase
in size organically induced and that brought about by
acquisition strategy. In the former case it would
require a very large increase in company size to
activate a variation in management style. In the
latter case structural variation could be a natural
consequence, arising fairly quickly, with the effect
of modifying management style.

Wait until the new divisional manager (subordinate) proves himself before granting him autonomy.

Though a certain degree of independence would be
granted to the head of the finance function in
the new subsidiary company, formal systems of
control to measure performance would be set up.

An iron fist and velvet glove approach is necessary in one's dealings with the Financial Director
of a newly acquired small subsidiary company. I
have let it be known quite firmly what is expected
in terms of reporting, and one will continue to
take a close interest as long as is necessary to
assess acceptable standards of efficiency. So
far I am appalled by his pathetic attempt at preparing a budget. His working papers numbered only
a few sheets. This man must be re-educated.

A result forcefully reinforced by the observational
data is that subordinate involvement and delegative
behaviour on the part of the superior occur to a
marked extent in the large company. In order to illuminate a possible reason for such a phenomenon,
reference to an analysis of perceived skill discrepancy by company size is called for. This appears in
Table 5.10.1. The Chief Accountant in the large
company tends to view his subordinate more favourably,
over all items listed, than his counterpart in the

Table 5.10.1

Discrepancy between desirable and actual
qualities or skills related to company size

n=212

| Type of quality or skill | Discrepancy index | | |
| | Size of company | | |
	Small	Medium	Large
1. Rapid decision ability	40	67	36
2. Verbal ability	95	102	65*
3. Technical ability	81	73	62*
4. Forcefulness	60	92	59
5. Perseverence	54	53	49
6. Sensitive	50	89	48
7. Intelligent	34	40	23*
8. Imaginative	78	83	61*
9. Responsible	64	60	37*
10. Self-confident	63	74	54*
11. Calm under pressure	62	61	40*
12. Tactful	80	99	61*
13. Considerate of other's views	48	66	33*
14. Willingness to pass on information	44	68	36
15. Ready to accept new ideas	65	71	45*

Note:

The Kruskal-Wallis One-Way Analysis of Variance
statistic was calculated with a view to testing
the H_o that the mean index scores for the three

company sizes were equal. The value obtained for this statistic was 15.14. The Chi-Square value at p $<$ 0.001, 2 df, is 13.82. Since 15.14 is greater than 13.82 we can reject the H_O and conclude there is a difference between index scores for the different company sizes. From this result and the inspection of Table 5.10.1, we find it easy to accept that the index scores for the large company are smaller overall. The differentiation is very pronounced in the types marked with an asterisk. A low index number denotes a favourable impression of the subordinate.

medium or small company. Our attention is drawn to those items marked with an asterisk in Table 5.10.1 because they appear to emphasise the skills perhaps most responsible for the favourable impression. This finding is likely to support the view, expressed earlier, that the large company offers an environment conducive to the needs of relatively high calibre staff and manages to attract this type of staff. As a consequence, subordinate involvement in decisions through joint decision making or delegation is therefore not surprising.

Size of company is then an influential variable, having an appreciable impact on decision style. However, when the other independent variables, with the exception of age and functional role, were related to decision style using size classification in the analysis only a few results of interest were noted. Two of them have already been commented on in the discussion on job tenure and specialism. The remaining variable will be discussed in the next section under the heading of level. Therefore the mediating effects of size are present but somewhat limited (see Table 1, Appendix 'C'). Further analysis was conducted, removing the influence of size from the bivariate correlative relationships between the independent and dependent variables specified below. The partialling out of both size of company and finance function in the relationship between decision style and experience variables is shown in Table 5.10.2.

Table 5.10.2

Influence of size on the individual
relationships between decision style
and age and job experience

Decision style	Experience variables n=209 n=212		Size of finance function partialled out		Size of company partialled out	
	Age	Job Experience	Age	Job Experience	Age	Job Experience
A	0.07	0.15[b]	0.07	0.14[b]	0.08	0.15[b]
B	-0.10	-0.07	-0.10	-0.07	-0.10	-0.07
C	-0.04	-0.12[a]	-0.04	-0.11[a]	-0.04	-0.11[a]
D	0.04	-0.01	0.04	-0.01	0.03	-0.01
E	0.02	-0.01	0.02	0.00	0.02	-0.01

a = $p < 0.05$
b = $p < 0.025$

Due to the similarity of the correlations following the
removal of size it is particularly apparent that the
influence of size on the above relationship is minimal.
The very slight tendency for respondents in large companies to stay in the job for a shorter time, which
can be gleaned from Table 5.10.3, does not appear to
have much influence on the result. Conducting an
identical operation, size of company and finance function was partialled out of the relationship between
decision style and span of control. This appears in
Table 5.10.4. The identical set of results achieved
after using the Partial Correlation test tends to suggest that size has little or no impact on the relationship between decision style and span of control.

Table 5.10.3

Relationship between company size and length of time in present position

n=212

Size of company	Number of years			
	<1	1-3	4-6	>6
	%	%.	%	%
Small	20.3	30.5	22.0	27.2
Medium	14.0	33.7	19.8	32.5
Large	15.6	36.3	21.7	26.4

Table 5.10.4

Influence of size on the relationship between decision style and span of control

n=212

Decision style	Size of finance function partialled out	Size of company partialled out
	Span of control	Span of control	Span of control
A	0.16^{c}	0.16^{c}	0.16^{c}
B	-0.04	-0.04	-0.04
C	-0.08	-0.08	-0.08
D	-0.11^{a}	-0.11^{a}	-0.11^{a}
E	-0.02	-0.02	-0.02

a = $p < 0.05$
c = $p < 0.01$

As one respondent remarked, 'no more than a given number will report to you whatever the company size.' One might also add that the size of the company, or for that matter the size of the finance function, is unlikely to upset the conception of a manageable span of control in relation to the requirements of a particular decision. We shall return to size in its association with hierarchical level in the next section, but first it may be worthwhile to depict graphically by size category the decision style, over all decisions, of the Chief Accountant. This can be seen in Figure 5.10.1.

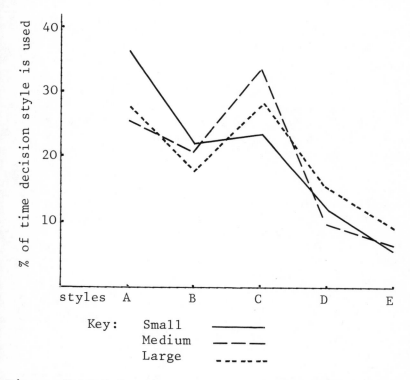

Figure 5.10.1 Profile of Chief Accountant's decision style by size of company

On an overall basis this result suggests that Chief Accountants tend to vary their style between different company sizes, as has been already disclosed in

Table 5.10. Styles which are restrictive and consultative are the more popular, leaving joint
decision making and delegation as the styles lacking
in popularity. Unlike the small company, where the
directive style is very pronounced, the consultative
style receives the greatest emphasis in the medium-
sized company and almost ties with a directive style
in the large-sized company.

DECISION STYLE IN RELATION TO LEVEL
WITHIN THE ORGANISATIONAL HIERARCHY,
AND THE INFLUENCE OF SIZE

The relationship between decision style and organisational level is shown in Table 5.11. In order to
establish the importance of size as a determinant of
this relationship it was decided to partial out both
size of finance function and company separately and
together. From a perusal of Table 5.11 we find that
size cannot be considered an influential agent, as
the statistical magnitude and pattern which emerge
show an infinitesimal difference.

Table 5.11

Correlation between decision style and
organisational level together with the
removal of the influence of size

n=212

Decision style	(a) Size of finance function partialled out	(b) Size of company partialled out	(a) and (b) partialled out
	Level	Level	Level	Level
A	-0.12^a	-0.12^a	-0.11^a	-0.11^a
B	0.05	0.05	0.06	0.06
C	0.01	0.01	0.00	0.00
D	0.10	0.11	0.09	0.10
E	0.03	0.03	0.01	0.02

a = $p < 0.05$

192

The main conclusion to be drawn from the data in Table 5.11 is that there is a likelihood of a directive style prevailing at the lower organisational level. When we turn to the arrangement of the data by size of company in Table 1, Appendix 'C', a fuller picture of the relationship between decision style and level comes into focus. On reading it we discover that in the small firm at the lower level the Chief Account-ant is likely to be directive and at the higher level semi-directive in style. By way of contrast, in the medium and large-sized company at the higher level the Chief Accountant is more likely to use delegation and joint decision-making styles respectively. In reality the true comparison is between levels 1 and 2. This is shown clearly in Table 5.11.1.

Table 5.11.1

Level within the organisation as a function of company size

Company size	Hierarchical level (n=124)	(n=79)	(n=8)	(n=1)
	1	2	3	4
	%	%	%	%
Small (n=59)	66.1	28.8	3.4	1.7
Medium (n=86)	59.3	36.0	4.7	0.0
Large (n=67)	50.7	46.3	3.0	0.0
Aggregate (n=212)	58.5	37.3	3.8	0.5

Though the greater proportion of respondents in each size category perceive themselves as occupying a pos-ition at level 1, it appears a larger number of Chief Accountants in small companies operate at this level.

The question we wish to pose now is to what extent, if at all, does level in the organisation mediate relationships specified below? To begin with, it is proposed to partial out 'level' in the relationship

193

between decision style and the experience variables. This is illustrated in Table 5.11.2.

Table 5.11.2

Influence of hierarchical level on the individual relationships between decision style and age and job experience

Decision style	n=209	n=212	Level partialled out	
	Age	Job experience	Age	Job experience
A	0.07	0.15^b	0.06	0.14^b
B	-0.10	-0.07	-0.10	-0.06
C	-0.04	-0.12^a	-0.04	-0.12^a
D	0.04	-0.01	0.05	-0.01
E	0.02	-0.01	0.02	-0.01

a = $p < 0.05$
b = $p < 0.025$

It is clear that the position occupied in the organisational hierarchy does not appear to assume any importance so far as the relationship between decision style and the experience variables is concerned. The same appears to be true when the relationship between decision style and perceived skill discrepancy is considered. The elimination of level leaves the original statistical pattern almost intact in Table 5.11.3. Next the effects of level, and level and size of company combined, on the relationship between decision style and span of control were examined. Yet again no appreciable transformation of the data, of any real significance, can be observed in Table 5.11.4.

Table 5.11.3

Influence of hierarchical level on the
relationship between decision style
and the discrepancy between actual and
desirable qualities or skills

n=212

Decision style	Skill discrepancy	Level partialled out Skill discrepancy
A	0.05	0.05
B	0.12^a	0.12^a
C	-0.00	-0.00
D	-0.18^c	-0.17^c
E	-0.07	-0.07

a = $p < 0.05$
c = $p < 0.01$

Table 5.11.4

Influence of hierarchical level and company
size on the relationship between decision
style and span of control

n=212

Decision style	Span of control	Level partialled out Span of control	Level and company size partialled out Span of control
A	0.16^c	0.17^c	0.17^c
B	-0.04	-0.04	-0.04
C	-0.08	-0.08	-0.08
D	-0.11^a	-0.12^a	-0.12^a
E	-0.02	-0.02	-0.02

a = $p < 0.05$
b = $p < 0.025$
c = $p < 0.01$

Finally, the removal of hierarchical level from the relationship between decision style and company size produced consequences similar to those recorded above. The identical statistical pattern remaining after partialling out hierarchical level is visible in Table 5.11.5.

Table 5.11.5

Influence of hierarchical level
on the relationship between
decision style and company size

n=212

Decision style	Company size	Level partialled out Company size
A	-0.13^b	-0.13^b
B	-0.10	-0.10
C	0.08	0.08
D	0.12^a	0.12^a
E	0.17^c	0.17^c

a = $p < 0.05$
b = $p < 0.025$
c = $p < 0.01$

The absence of a mediating role for hierarchical level may be attributable, in part at least, to the fact that the overwhelming majority of respondents occupied positions on two high organisational levels - 1 and 2 - which are perhaps closely related. The situation might be quite different if, for example, first-line supervision were accommodated in the analysis.

6 Discussion

The hypotheses have been formulated and are specified in Chapter 4. They will now be subjected to empirical test by invoking the relevant data derived from the research study. In addition ancillary data, frequently extending a perspective on a particular issue, will be acknowledged. The relationship between the individual findings and the pertinent literature will also be explored.

THE DECISION STYLE OF THE CHIEF ACCOUNTANT

In an earlier study the author concluded that financial and management accountants, unlike non-financial managers, experienced more of a restrictive leadership style (McKenna, 1972). It is highly likely that many of those exercising the restrictive style were of the rank of Chief Accountant. Hastings (1968) conducted an exhaustive study of the chartered accountant in industry, and when discussing the accountant's attachment to the value 'caution' he maintained that the accountant who supervises the processes involved in the operation of accounting systems 'shows a particular tendency to check the work of subordinates and in particular to limit the discretion of subordinates who are not qualified accountants.' Commenting on the ingredients of the accountant's personality profile, Barden (1970) had this to say: 'accountants as a group are likely to be practical, realistic, resolute and are inclined to make decisions and take action on their own.' We shall now introduce the first hypothesis which is rather general in nature.

Hypothesis I. The Chief Accountant displays a tendency to manage in a directive fashion.

If we examine Figure 5 (p.143) where the Chief Accountant's decision style profile is depicted we find that

the directive style is narrowly endorsed as the most
frequently used style, but we must also recognise that
a consultative style assumes almost equal prominence.
In fact the overall picture in Figure 5 projects the
view that restrictive and permissive styles receive
equal endorsement. Therefore we have to admit that
hypothesis I is only partially true and needs revision
before it can be accepted. As we shall see later the
decision style profile is influenced by the size of
the company. The type of decision is also influential
in the determination of style.

DECISION STYLE IN RELATION TO DIFFERENT
TYPES OF DECISIONS

The hypotheses dealing with programmed and non-
programmed decisions will be examined first. They
appear in the following form:

> Hypothesis II. Programmed decision situations
> lend themselves to both directive and delegative
> styles of decision-making behaviour.

> Hypothesis III. Non-programmed decision situa-
> tions lend themselves to consultative or partici-
> pative styles of decision-making behaviour.

We can confidently accept both hypotheses as the relevant findings, illustrated in Table 5.1 (p.144),
suggest that directive and delegative decision styles
are commonly used for programmed decisions, but consultation and joint decision making are evidently considered more appropriate when the Chief Accountant is
confronted by non-programmed decisions. We have
already reported the tremendous emphasis placed on
the Chief Accountant's need to be aware of happenings
in programmed decision situations. Elaborate systems
of control and periodic personal checks were not uncommon. These mechanisms of control could be fostered
by the process of professionalisation, and by cultural
forces in the organisation supporting a restrictive
approach. Participation in these circumstances is

198

likely to be dysfunctional, failing to promote the proper motivational disposition (Leavitt, 1962). In the smaller company a directive style was more pronounced, allegedly because of the relatively low calibre of staff, but it assumed a flavour of informality. Whatever the size of the company, delegation as a style does not appear to bestow the high level of autonomy generally believed to be enjoyed by the subordinate. The omnipresence of performance monitoring devices and the referral of exceptional items for the attention of his boss tends to undermine autonomy and promote a state of subordinate dependency. This may explain why this style is a natural ally of a directive style in programmed decision conditions. In different conditions, and perhaps in other functions, delegation may revert to its more conventional form and recover the lost autonomy. Even in the finance function delegated authority connected with very simple tasks, and consequently straightforward decisions, would obviously confer on the subordinate a high degree of autonomy. This type of decision was not accommodated in the research instrument.

The scene changes considerably when we examine the impact of non-programmed decisions. Here we find the Chief Accountant is prepared to permit a high level of subordinate influence in his decisions, periodically inviting lateral influence from other functional personnel as well. As Strauss (1968) points out, a participative style is only suitable where novel problems are frequently encountered for which there are no simple answers. However, we have seen how constraining influences may disturb this balance of influence. These are manifest in a variety of ways: in the secretive nature of the work; the superior believes he is vested with greater knowledge relevant to the decision; the calibre of subordinates is suspected; the company environment militates against it; and the superior uses participation where he recognises the subordinate's influence is minimal but believes the exercise is worthwhile as a developmental experience for the subordinate.

There is a dearth of empirical evidence relating to the above relationships in the literature and much comment appears at a general level of analysis. For example, Hickson (1966) maintains that subordinate influence is negligible in programmed decisions but is marked in non-programmed decisions. Fiedler (1972) tends to share this view when commenting on the influence of the leader. He maintains that tasks which are explicit or programmed give the leader more influence than he acquires in nebulous or unstructured tasks. These observations are generally in line with the main theme running through the findings. However, Dill (1958) takes an opposite view to that of Hickson and Fiedler, but by implication acknowledges that programmed decisions could lead to the superior adopting a delegative style. This view adds credibility to the finding that delegation as a decision style is appropriate in programmed decision situations. Relying on data from empirical observation, Walter (1966) is convinced that subordinate influence is very pronounced in non-programmed decisions, because he believes a superior would, where possible, use the specialised skill and knowledge of the immediate decision environment possessed by the subordinate. He arrived at a less clear-cut position when he subjected to empirical test the hypothesis that superior influence would be greatest in programmed decision situations, a conclusion which challenges the views of Hickson and Fiedler. What Walter did find bears a close resemblance to the result obtained by the author, whereby a directive and delegative decision style prevailed in programmed decision situations. In the case of delegation, the referral of exceptional items for the attention of the superior came through strongly in Walter's observations. When the centralisation hypothesis fared very poorly, he concluded that sometimes subordinates brought to the notice of the superior an issue requiring action and then proceeded to tackle the problem, having first received the superior's authorisation to do so. Conversely, the superior brings to the notice of the subordinate a problem requiring attention with a directive to deal with the matter. In other circumstances a recommendation emanating from the subordinate suggesting a particular course of action may not be heeded because of the emphasis placed by the superior on priorities regarding the use of resources at that particular time.

We shall now examine the hypothesised relationships between task and personnel decisions and decision style.

Hypothesis IV. Task decision situations are more likely to be associated with a directive and delegative style of decision-making behaviour.

Hypothesis V. Personnel decision situations are more likely to be associated with a consultative or participative style of decision-making behaviour.

Faced with the data in Table 5.1 (p.144) and the supporting evidence we can safely accept hypotheses IV and V. The weight of programmed decisions must be felt in the task decision category, but it is interesting to observe that, whereas programmed decisions invited a directive and a delegative style, task decisions in addition called forth a semi directive style – incidentally this produced the strongest statistical relationship. No doubt the influence of non-programmed task decisions was felt here in counterbalancing the effects of programmed activity. As one would expect personnel decisions, being non-programmed and affecting indirect subordinates, generated much interaction and discussion with direct subordinates, often culminating in joint decision making. Heller and Yukl (1969) contend that at the lower levels of management superiors are likely to share more power with subordinates when task decisions, rather than maintenance (personnel) decisions, are under consideration. But a finding of theirs, more relevant to the present study, is that senior managers were more likely to allow greater subordinate influence in decisions affecting indirect rather than direct subordinates. We can only assume that this view is also applicable to decision situations of a personnel nature impinging on the work life of the indirect subordinate.

DECISION STYLE IN RELATION TO EXPERIENCE VARIABLES

Litchfield (1956) maintains that an executive new to his job and feeling uncertain about situations confronting him is likely to seek elaborate counsel, but the self-contained manager prefers to deliberate alone, with the implication that he involves his subordinates to a minimum extent in the decision-making process. Perhaps self-containment in this sense is a function of time spent in the job. This seems an appropriate moment to introduce hypothesis VI.

> Hypothesis VI. The more experienced - age and time spent in job - the Chief Accountant the greater the likelihood of he using a moderately directive style of decision-making behaviour.

A glance at Table 5.2 (p.154) immediately conveys to us that the hypothesis in its present form must be rejected because of the absence of a significant statistical association between decision style and the experience variables - age and job experience combined. On a closer examination of Table 5.2 we find, in accordance with Litchfield's assertion, that job experience is the independent variable that really matters. The finding suggests that the Chief Accountant is more likely to be directive with the passing of time in the job, whilst when he occupies the job for a relatively short time he tends to be consultative. Apparently in the small company there is a greater likelihood of he using joint decision making as a style when new to the job (see Table 1, Appendix 'C').

The supporting evidence tends to support the view that when one is a relatively recent job occupant there is a tendency to engage in consultation with subordinates. This might arise because one wished to discover the rationale behind various conventions and practices in the department, to remove uncertainty and allay anxiety, and gain the respect of the subordinate. As one absorbs the meaning and relevance of techniques and develops awareness of critical operations, which is a function of increasing time spent in the job, a movement to a directive style is not inconceivable. As a result of increasing job familiarity, some Chief Accountants manage to secure an improvement in procedures which has the effect of facilitating delegation. Perhaps this is what Heller and Yukl (1969) had in mind when they forwarded the view that senior managers tended to use more delegation as their stay in the job increased. Closer to the main finding discussed above, the same authors feel that the longer the time spent by first and second line supervisors in their job, the greater the tendency to experience a shift from a permissive to a directive leadership style. The amended hypothesis should now read as follows: the Chief Accountant new to the job is more likely to be consultative in his approach, but with increased time spent in the job he is more likely to be directive.

DECISION STYLE IN RELATION TO SPECIALISATION
AND SPECIALISM

We have already noted that specialised accounting sub-systems are well established in the finance function. It does not follow that each sub-system is managed or controlled by a section head who is well qualified in his narrow specialism (see Table 5, Appendix 'C'). The two hypotheses connected with both specialisation and specialism in their individual relationships with decision style will now be introduced.

Hypothesis VII. A high level of specialisation is likely to be associated with a directive style of decision-making behaviour.

Hypothesis VIII. A high level of specialism is likely to lead to the use of a less centralised style of decision-making behaviour.

On reading Table 5.3 (p.157) we soon become aware of
the relationship between specialisation and decision
style. We find a directive style associated with a
high level of specialisation, and a consultative style
associated with a low level of specialisation. In
circumstances of high specialisation the prevalence
of formalisation is conspicuous. It does appear that
the Chief Accountant is active, receiving signals from
his monitoring devices and other sources of information. He experiences a burning need to establish what
is going on, he wants to know the justification for
particular courses of action and frequently he offers
guidance. His interfering mode of operation applies
irrespective of whether he is knowledgeable or ignor-
ant of operations within his realm of interest. He
feels particularly threatened by a section head whose
expertise he has not fully grasped or understood. He
is likely to justify a directive style on the grounds
that the interdependent nature of specialist activities in his department dictates a firm co-ordinating
role for him, or that subordinate expectations demand
such a style in any case. Turning to the hypothesised
relationship, there appears to be no reason why we
should not accept hypothesis VII.

It is not difficult to amass support for this finding. Worthy (1950) postulates that the 'over-complex,
over-functionalised organisation structure' requires
a directive leadership approach. Shaw and Blum (1966)
associate a directive style with highly structured
tasks in conditions of peak efficiency. Likewise
Fiedler (1967) found an empirical association between
a directive style and high task structure when other
situational variables were also high. Korten (1968)
associates a directive style with high job structuring brought about by stressful conditions. According
to Bass et al. (1975) a tight organisational structure is a natural concomitant of a directive style,
whilst a non-bureaucratic organisational environment
bears a relationship to a participative leadership
style. This is a view not too dissimilar to that of
Hage and Aiken (1967). A dissentient view is that
participation is slightly lower in the less bureau-

cratic small organisation (Payne et al., 1971).

Reverting to Table 5.3 (p.157) we discover that no statistically significant relationship subsists between decision style and specialism. Therefore we are forced to reject hypothesis VIII, though we might accept it if it applied to medium-sized companies only. Viewing this variable in isolation, we recognise that the level of qualification of the section head is not very high (see Table 5, Appendix 'C'). If it was, we might expect to find a relationship between specialism and a consultative style. Somewhat unexpectedly this materialises in the case of the Chief Accountant in the medium-sized company only. But we come across a reverse situation when attention is focussed on the small company. Here the Chief Accountant often assumes responsibility for and direction of a number of sections, so it is not surprising to find a relationship between a directive style and high specialism (see Table 1, Appendix 'C'). When Hage and Aiken (1967) were commenting on the unique predicament of the professional in the organisation they probably had not our typical section head in mind because they were of the opinion that he demands autonomy, and when competent he is consulted by decision makers.

When specialism is merged with specialisation and related to decision style the previous relationship subsisting between decision style and specialisation reappears. It is meaningful therefore to speak of a directive style in conditions of high specialisation and specialism on the one hand, and a consultative style in conditions of low specialisation and specialism on the other. Already we have dealt with an explanation of the former; in the latter case a plausible explanation to account for the result is that the Chief Accountant needs to be very much involved, through exhaustive consultation, in a situation symbolised by low quality section supervision and a low level of formalisation. Finally, the mediating effect of specialisation on the relationship between decision style and non-programmed decisions should be

acknowledged. The end result appears to be an attempt
to structure ill-structured decision situations when
high specialisation prevails by the use of a directive
style.

DECISION STYLE IN RELATION TO PERCEIVED
QUALITIES OR SKILLS IN SUBORDINATE

In an empirical study of senior managers in twelve
large companies in the USA Heller (1971) found large
differentials of skill associated with autocratic
leadership styles and small differentials associated
with more power-sharing. This result was obtained
after asking respondents whether their jobs required
more or less of selected skills than their subordinates' jobs. In the present study the respondent was
asked to perceive actual and desirable qualities or
skills in his subordinate. Therefore there is a
difference in approach between the two studies. Now
is an opportune moment to introduce hypothesis IX.

Hypothesis IX. When the Chief Accountant perceives a larger discrepancy between actual and
desirable skills or qualities in the subordinate
he is more likely to use a directive decision
style. The opposite is true when he perceives a
smaller discrepancy.

When we examine the statistical pattern in Table 5.4
(p.163) we find that a large skill discrepancy invites
the introduction of a semi-directive style. A small
discrepancy produces a different effect by invoking a
joint decision-making approach. Though the direction
of this pattern is maintained when types of decisions
are considered, nevertheless differentiations do arise.
In conditions of high skill discrepancy in ill-
structured decision situations the Chief Accountant
assumes a more intense directive posture. Where he
perceives a small skill discrepancy in programmed
decision situations he is encouraged to contemplate
seriously, and put into effect, delegation as a
style. The total picture presented above appears to

bear a similarity to that portrayed by Heller.
Hypothesis IX can now be accepted in its present
form.

When individual qualities or skills were related to
decision style, certain items — set out below —
occupied a key role in influencing the choice of
decision style.

Technical ability (knowledge, skill and current
information related to industrial accountancy)

Possession of self-confidence without being too
arrogant

Ability to react calmly to pressure of work

Tactful in a delicate situation

Willingness to pass on information to others

To these we could add:

Knowledge of the problem in hand

Communicating clearly in writing

Effective cross-functional liaison

The remaining qualities or skills considered important are listed in Figure 5.4 (p.168). The skills
referred to appear to be of critical significance in
an industrial accountancy environment, and therefore
one could argue it is meaningful to suggest that the
Chief Accountant reflects or dwells on the adequacy
of subordinates' characteristics prior to their involvement in the decision process. The crucial importance attached to subordinate skills or qualities as
determinants of decision style has been recognised
already and the evidence available appears to be sympathetic to that derived from the present study. Yukl
(1971) believes that where the subordinate suffers a
deficiency in knowledge or skill relevant to a partic-

ular decision, and the superior possesses the appropriate talents, a centralised style is justified.
A stable group that has the skill and experience to
take decisions would probably find a democratic style
most suitable (Uris, 1963). Trust and confidence in
the subordinate was one of the key mediating variables
in the relationship between leadership style and
satisfaction noted by Ritchie and Miles (1970).
Recent evidence also supports the importance of personality related factors residing in the subordinate
(Weed, Mitchell and Moffitt, 1976; Durand and Nord,
1976). In addition Weed et al. would recognise the
mediating influence of task ambiguity.

DECISION STYLE IN RELATION TO STATUS,
POWER AND INFLUENCE

Some of the ingredients of this variable are evident
in other studies. Fiedler (1967) considers position
power as one of the three important situational
variables in his contingency model. Pelz (1963)
views influence with the boss as a critical variable
in the leadership situation. For the purposes of the
present study a hybrid variable was formulated and
related to decision style. We shall now acknowledge
the relevant hypothesis.

> Hypothesis X. Chief Accountants enjoy a high
> level of organisational status, power and influ-
> ence and this is likely to be so irrespective of
> the style of decision-making behaviour adopted.

Faced with the data in Table 2, Appendix 'C', there is
no doubt that the Chief Accountant enjoys a high level
of organisational power and influence. However, no
direct relationship between this variable and decision style emerges in Table 5.5 (p.169). The observational data points to a tenuous relationship between
the dependent and independent variable but only after
recognising the interventionist role of 'respect'. A
high level of respect is likely to surface where
institutional forces bestow on the leader the power

to act and influence events, though the manner in which this is achieved will mirror the true nature of the respect gained. In these conditions apparently the Chief Accountant feels relaxed, open, and confident in his disposition, with the strong likelihood of he projecting a permissive-oriented style. The converse situation of low respect could breed symptoms manifest in withdrawal, inhibition, suspicion and irascibility, and lead to a restrictive-oriented style. With a certain degree of caution we may proceed to accept hypothesis X.

DECISION STYLE IN RELATION TO MANAGERIAL BEHAVIOUR CHARACTERISTICS

The managerial behaviour characteristics - employee orientation and task orientation - bear a close resemblance to the leadership behaviour dimensions - initiating structure and consideration - of the Ohio State school. Some would argue that initiating structure is complementary to the directive end of the decision style continuum, and consideration to the permissive end. This would preclude the possibility of being considerate in approach whilst being concerned about accomplishing an exacting work target and ensuring the means and necessary motivation to bring it about. One is therefore inclined to the view expressed by Yukl (1971) that though task-oriented behaviour is implicit in initiating structure, this is not tantamount to denying the subordinate the chance to use his influence in the decisions of his superior. So one can be directive in managing subordinates towards achieving organisational goals and at the same time establishing highly supportive relations with them (Weissenberg and Kavanagh, 1972). From an analysis of his empirical data, Kavanagh (1975) concludes that the role of the leader does, and is expected to, integrate the approaches of initiating structure and consideration. A perusal of Table 3, Appendix 'C', shows that an almost equal emphasis is given by Chief Accountants to both task and employee-oriented aspects of their decision-making behaviour; this completely

substantiates the view of Kavanagh. Yukl is also of
the opinion that there is some relationship between
consideration and a measure of decision centralisation.
We shall now direct our attention to an examination of
hypothesis XI.

> Hypothesis XI. Employee-oriented behaviour,
> rather than task-oriented behaviour, is associated
> with decision style.

On reading the data set out in Table 5.6 (p.171) we
soon find the only statistically significant relationship pertaining to the association between delegation and employee orientation. The next best
relationship, though marginally short of significance
on a parametric test, and significant on a non-
parametric test, (see Table 6, Appendix 'D') lies
between a directive style and employee orientation.
Can we then assume that the leader who delegates,
granting his subordinate a fair degree of autonomy,
professes genuine concern at the individual and group
level for the human relations aspects of the job?
This appears to be what the data is suggesting, and
this view is somewhat reinforced when the other weaker
relationship tells us that when the Chief Accountant
is directive in style he is less considerate in his
dealings with subordinates. When respondents were
given the opportunity to express their own views on
desirable managerial behaviour characteristics overwhelming emphasis was placed on those attributes which
could be classified as employee-oriented in character.
They stressed the importance of encouraging self-
evaluation and direction; promoting autonomy and
innovation; encouraging self-development and giving
impetus to group integration and harmony. Due to the
high level of standardisation and formalisation in
the finance function, perhaps there was a lesser need
to stress task-oriented behaviour. It should be borne
in mind that relatively weak non-significant statistical associations were found to exist between decision
style and task-oriented behaviour. Hypothesis XI may
now be accepted.

DECISION STYLE IN RELATION TO LPS, AND
LPS AND MANAGERIAL CHARACTERISTICS TOGETHER

We have used the LPS as a measure of the Chief Accountant's opinion of his least preferred subordinate,
and unlike Fiedler's LPC it is not intended to denote
the style or motivational disposition of the leader.
As an instrument it is practically similar to that
used by Fiedler and the score derived from its use
may be more akin to his group atmosphere score than
to the LPC score. However, it has been suggested that
there is a similarity between the scales used to measure LPC and the group-centred dimension of leader
member relations (McMahon, 1972). We shall now
introduce hypothesis XII.

> Hypothesis XII. A directive style is likely to
> be associated with a low LPS and a permissive
> style with a high LPS.

An examination of Table 5.7 (p.174) results in the
view that the high LPS leader, who can be described
as warm, friendly and open, is more likely to engage
in permissive behaviour of a delegative nature. His
counterpart who receives a low LPS rating, and is
antithetical in behavioural disposition, is more
likely to resort to the use of a directive style.
The statistical pattern seems convincing because of
the association that exists between negative values
and directive styles and positive values and permissive styles. We can now accept hypothesis XII.

The existence of a significant relationship between
perceived skill discrepancy - a semi-personality
variable - which we have already encountered, together
with the relationship between LPS and decision style
recognised above, lends credence to the postulation
that personality-based factors are influential in the
leadership situation. The relationship which surfaced
after relating decision style to LPS is far more conclusive than that achieved when task and employee-
oriented behaviour were related to decision style.
The interactive nature of employee and task-oriented

behaviour could have been instrumental in preventing a more definitive relationship emerging, though employee orientation did have a satisfactory relationship with decision style.

Merging LPS and employee orientation and relating the combined variable to decision style (see Table 5.7, p.174) we achieve a result which totally endorses the individual relationships the independent variables have already secured with decision style. This suggests persuasively that the human relations oriented leader relies impressively on a permissive (delegative) style. Though marginally falling short of significance, the negative relationship between the combined variable and decision style is inclined to suggest that a directive style is associated with a lesser concern for the human relations aspects of the job.

Throughout the foregoing discussion high and low LPS have automatically been considered synonymous with a permissive and restrictive-oriented leadership style respectively. This is a view not totally subscribed to in the literature. Weissenberg and Gruenfeld (1966) challenge the view that the LPC is a good predictor of leadership behavioural characteristics and allege that a low LPC can be placed in an intermediate position between the extreme ends of initiating structure and consideration. Sample and Wilson (1965) cannot lend support to the notion that the low LPC leader is generally socially distant and unfriendly. They found that the low LPC leader became more human relations oriented during the performance phase of an assignment. The high LPC leader also reversed his orientation during the performance stage. More recent evidence vehemently attacks the validity of the LPC as a predictor of leadership behaviour (Graen et al., 1971; Stinson and Tracy, 1974). We now know that Fiedler (1972) himself is prepared to concede that the LPC is not a fixed, invariate style. Both high and low LPC leaders may vary their behaviour in different circumstances. Fiedler quotes the example of the high LPC leader who, finding himself in a favourable situation, may become more preoccupied with the task and plays 'the role of the responsible, efficient and even officious leader.' This appears to be precisely the behavioural pattern of high LPS respondents, as far as one can tell from the data which appears in Table 5.7.1 (p.175). Though there is a striking similarity between the LPC and LPS, it seems worthwhile repeating that the LPS was used as a measure designed to establish the degree of psychological closeness between the Chief Accountant and his subordinates, and not as a measure of leadership style.

DECISION STYLE IN RELATION TO SPAN OF CONTROL

Span of control is a structural variable which has captured the attention of classical theorists, who were primarily concerned with its optimum size (Urwick, 1935), and present day empiricists (Woodward, 1965; Child, 1973) whose concern extends to how contextual variables - technology and size - affect it. Here the concern is more localised; in effect we are concerned with its impact on the leadership process. This relationship is hypothesised in hypothesis XIII.

Hypothesis XIII. When the span of control of the Chief Accountant is wider a directive decision style is more likely to be used, whereas a permissive decision style is more applicable when the span of control is narrower.

When we turn to Table 5.8 (p.176) we immediately discern that a large span of control is likely to invite a directive style, whilst a small span of control attracts a permissive style in the form of joint decision making. This seems eminently credible should we accept the validity of pertinent viewpoints expressed by three contributors. Hemphill (1950) could be referring to the size of the span of control when he makes the point that as the size of organisational groups increases, direction of group activities which is leader-centred is associated with members expressing attitudes of greater tolerance for this type of leadership. The other contributors maintain that larger groups require a longer time to reach consensus with less opportunity for members to participate, and as a result members experience less satisfaction from interactions (Entwisle and Walton, 1961). Heller and Yukl (1969) provide empirical endorsement of the above finding when they allege that subordinate-centred styles of leadership - consultation and participation - were almost dispensed with by senior managers when the span of control tended to be large. They also concluded that delegation was an acceptable alternative style in these circumstances. Running against this stream of opinion is an empirical observation emanating from Blankenship and Miles (1968). They contend that the greater number of managers, with thirteen or more subordinates reporting to them, maintained that they frequently depended on their subordinates for ideas and initiation of decisions. With a narrower span of control managers were less dependent on subordinates. These relationships were, however, mediated by organisational level.

Going back to the question of a large span of control, it is extremely difficult to envisage a situation whereby a manager, having at least thirteen subordinates reporting to him directly, can engage in meaningful consultation or participation with each individual subordinate. Of course he could meet them as a group and exchange views on that basis, but if many of them are engaged in dissimilar tasks this would present real difficulties in trying to establish fruitful discussions. These meetings would then be almost tantamount to personalised reporting systems and would inevitably be reinforced by more impersonal methods of control.

A further glance at Table 5.8 (p.176) could suddenly make one realise that the intervention of type of decision in the analysis produces a very interesting result. One discovers that the best prediction of the relationship between decision style and span of control materialises when non-programmed decisions, including personnel decisions, are considered. The force of this finding is felt in the suggestion that when a task decision situation is ill-structured, or the decision is a personnel one, the Chief Accountant is likely to indulge in a permissive style - joint decision making or consultation - but only if the span of control is narrow. Where the span of control is wide and the problems confronted are ill-defined, he takes a different view of the question of subordinate involvement. Now he appears to become more directive in his approach, probably realising that power-sharing would be fraught with difficulty because of the numerous interactions, based on consultation or participation, that would be required. Apparently programmed decision situations which are normally well prescribed in a procedural sense are unlikely to tax the leader's span of attention to the same extent as non-programmed decision situations when the span of control is relatively wide - as is evident in the area of production management when certain forms of standardisation are prevalent. This conclusion sounds plausible in the light of a lack of a significant relationship between decision style and span of control in the context of programmed decisions. A similar line of reasoning could be applicable to task decisions on the understanding that programmed decision situations make their presence felt in this decision category.

There is reason to believe that the wide span of control can be instrumental in engendering a remote, detached style with less time available for subordinate consultation, and a high incidence of formalisation of access to the superior. However, two minority points of view aligned themselves with the assertions that a large span of control is therapeutic by nurturing good working relationships with subordinates, and that the calibre of subordinate could be a critical factor in determining the manageability of a wide span of control. Worthy (1950) would go along with these sentiments when he suggests that the wide span of control makes close supervision impossible and devolution of authority and responsibility possible, subject to a fair measure of self-confidence and personal capacity on the part of subordinates. Other constraining influences could hinge on task similarity and supervisory competence.

The reaction to the narrow span of control appears to be quite different. The narrow span of control is likely to foster an informality of approach, greater subordinate involvement in problem-centred activity and the release of the superior from a somewhat arduous co-ordinating role, allowing him to concentrate more on matters of policy. Entwisle and Walton (1961) recognise that a positive disadvantage of the narrow span of control is the likelihood of close supervision and the stifling of initiative. It was therefore interesting to find Chief Accountants emphasise the need to be aware of this danger. We can only hope that awareness of the problem of unnecessary interference is the first concrete step in action directed at preventing it. Finally, we can accept hypothesis XIII. Though hypothesis XIII may be generally true we must add forcefully that the type of decision encountered mediates the relationship between decision style and span of control.

DECISION STYLE IN RELATION TO THE FUNCTIONAL
ROLE OF THE CHIEF ACCOUNTANT

The tendency is to identify the finance function as a staff specialism, although Fisch (1961) is of the opinion that an area of specialisation such as finance is so vitally important to organisational success that it is unwise to treat it as a staff function. If he had his way he would bestow on the financial controller more authority than he has at present to initiate changes in order to remedy deficiencies in other functions. So he is not too happy about the advisory role of someone of the status of a Chief Accountant. The distinction between staff and line managers is not as marked as one might expect. An extreme position is taken by Logan (1966) who maintains it is an obsolete concept. Heller (1971) recognises the distinction but concedes that confusion surrounds its meaning. In his research he found some managers keen to accept the label 'line' because to them it meant more authority; in another instance seniority rather than function was associated with 'line'. In the midst of the confusion many managers chose a combination of both. Thompson (1961) and Porter and Henry (1964b) also recognise the distinction and ascribe different personality charac- teristics to line and staff personnel.

In the research instrument the staff/line distinc- tion in the classical sense is not intended. Being aware of the staff status of finance, one anticipated that some Chief Accountants would act solely in an advisory capacity, whilst others would possess direct authority to implement their recommendations. Others still would find it difficult to be categorical about their role. The person exercising executive authority would probably occupy a position nearest to that of line rather than staff. In Table 5.9 (p.179) we see the role embracing direct authority receiving the greatest single percentage weight of 42 per cent, but the majority of Chief Accountants perform either an advisory role or are unable to classify their role in accordance with the descriptions of role given. Influ- enced by Heller's speculation that line rather than staff managers would be more directive in approach, the following hypothesis was formulated.

Hypothesis XIV. The Chief Accountant whose functional role embraces the use of direct author- ity to implement his recommendations is likely to have a penchant for a directive decision style.

When we examine Table 5.9.1 (p.180) we discern no statistically significant relationship between decision style and functional role, so therefore we are unable to accept hypothesis XIV.

Dalton (1950) speaks of the delicacy of the staff/ line relationship whereby the staff specialist has got to reach a tacit agreement with line managers so as to foster a workable relationship, otherwise there is the danger of line personnel seeking to jeopardise propo- sals with which they disagree. If we lend credence to

217

a significant body of opinion critical of the accountant's staff role we would almost automatically accept
that he adopts an autocratic exterior and fails abys-
mally to establish the workable relationship which
Dalton speaks of. The role of accountants in budgeting comes under strong attack. The way they operate
budgetary control systems is punitive rather than
supportive (Argyris, 1953). Dysfunctional behavioural
consequences are the direct result of the imposition
of rigid budgets (Hopwood, 1973). It is a policing
mechanism based on inaccurate information (Beresford
Dew and Gee, 1973). According to Fletcher (1972),
managers complained about the accountants' obstructive
tactics and the way they divulged information to superiors about budget performance. However, the accountants did not get it all their own way, for the managers
played games with them when purchases they wanted to
make were being justified.

Outside the narrow sphere of budgeting the accountant has also come under fire. He is alleged to assess
inadequately the needs of management for information
(Tricker, 1967; Robson, 1965); he is also accused of
not furnishing the right sort of information, nor of
presenting it in a form which aids rapid comprehension
(Young, 1973; Beresford Dew and Gee, 1973). Though
struggles or friction are inherent in the staff/line
relationship (Dalton, 1950), a specific reference to
ill-feeling between accountants and managers comes
from Woodward (1965).

Since success and failure of company operations are
normally presented in financial terms, and the accountant through his analysis and presentations highlights
areas of economic weakness, it is not surprising that
on occasions he brings upon himself the wrath of other
functional managers. Perhaps he overplays his policing
role, engaging sometimes in selective perception by
not recognising factors not easily lending themselves
to quantification, or ignoring factors having future
value or relevance.

It is so easy to indulge in platitudes about ideal

staff/line relationships, free of friction, where the line manager recognises the advice of the staff man as both valid and genuine and experiences little difficulty in accepting it. It is conceivable that Teuling's (1971b) interpretation of the role of the effective staff man is nearer the truth. He maintains he has to be somewhat independent, able to manipulate situations informally and generally machiavellian in approach. Bearing in mind the feelings harboured by those who find fault with both his attitudes and the quality of his advisory services, how does the Chief Accountant perceive his own role? Where his formal recommendations are resisted he is likely to exercise persuasion, and failing that he is likely to activate political processes with the aim of securing some advantage. There are situations when his advice is ignored. The novelty of this event is likely to prompt him to search for the rationale behind such obstinacy, perhaps culminating in a compromise set of proposals or a clearer understanding of the contentious issue. He does not find it difficult to accept bargaining as a necessity on some occasions and considers it a legitimate pursuit at his level in the organisation. In the face of hardened resistance he is likely to invite a higher authority to intervene and mediate or, if necessary, own the problem. In this context he considers the main culprits to be marketing or sales managers whose lack of good financial sense is conspicuous.

Turning to the minority view, we find the Chief Accountant considers himself a pragmatic creature, who believes his bargaining strength can be enhanced by exacting homework. He is prepared to concede that failing to have a recommendation accepted at the first attempt is not disastrous. Because key commercial considerations could come to light, which he did not consider initially, thereby improving the quality and acceptability of the second submission. Where he is very knowledgeable on a particular issue he is less likely to give away ground or retreat in instances conventionally accepted as 'grey areas'. Should he possess a special relationship with, for example, the

Chief Executive, this helps him enormously as far as getting recommendations accepted. His influence is more widely felt in accounting procedural, rather than policy, matters. The above profile is compatible with Teuling's interpretation. Whether the quality of his advice is suspect, or his manner authoritarian, remains uncertain. A concluding remark based on observations from an empirical study conducted by Henning and Moseley (1970), and compatible with a lot of what has been said about the functional role of the Chief Accountant, seems to be in order.

> The profile of the controller is that of an executive with substantial authority in some functions and more limited authority in others; with varying degrees of authority in different decisions within a function, many times as making unilateral decisions and often sharing in the making of decisions; perceiving himself as having more authority than he is seen to have by his superior and peers. He occupies a role with great opportunity, yet is both ill-defined and fraught with potential conflict.

DECISION STYLE IN RELATION TO SIZE

Size of company seems to be a key variable determining or influencing a variety of structural properties of organisation as well as behavioural patterns. Both Pugh et al. (1969) and Child (1973) see it as a critical contextual factor influencing structural design. Worthy (1950) draws a distinction between large and small organisations in terms of job stimulation and interpersonal contact, and comes down firmly on the side of the small organisation where the incidence of minute specialisation and the use of impersonal control mechanisms is that much less; and the prospect of higher job satisfaction that much greater. Tallachi (1960) pursues a not too dissimilar theme by attributing to the large organisation a well established division of labour and status differentials - unlikely to be found in the small organisation - and suggests that the ensuing impersonality is likely to promote job dissatisfaction. He expects to find more informality and greater job satisfaction in the small organisation. This looks almost too idyllic, more so because later one hopes to establish that subordinates experience more direction and less autonomy in the small organisation. Dale (1952) believes that as we progress from the medium to the large company the span of control increases. Entwisle and Walton (1961) feel that increasing size has no great impact on the size of the span of control. The author concurs with the latter view. When increasing size of span of control was related to increasing company size no material variation was detected. This relationship is shown in Table 4, Appendix 'C'.

A few attempts have been made to relate leadership style to size (Blankenship and Miles, 1968; Wofford, 1971). The manager whose style is oriented towards personal security and group maintenance is likely to be most effective in the large complex organisation (Wofford, 1971). The bulk of opinion focusses on a discussion of the impact of size of organisation, but what influence does size of department have in this respect? Porter and Lawler (1965) believe that the evidence on the relationship between size of sub-unit and the relevant variables is more convincing than that which is said to materialise when company size is substituted for sub-unit size. However, in the present study size of company appears to be the stronger predictive variable. But this must not detract from the realisation that sub-unit size, in this case size of finance function, is an influential variable. Hypothesis XV shall now be introduced.

Hypothesis XV. The larger the size of the company and finance function the greater is the likelihood of a permissive-oriented decision style prevailing.

On reviewing the data in Table 5.10 (p.185) one can conclude that the likelihood of a directive style making its presence felt in the smaller company is greater, whilst the reverse situation tends to apply

221

in the larger company where permissive styles - joint decision making and delegation - are more likely to reign. The same is true of the relationship between size of finance function and decision style. Hypothesis XV can therefore be accepted.

A feature of the large company appears to be the well developed accounting sub-systems which certainly create a favourable environment for delegation to be practised. Also the prospect of finding better qualified staff eager to accept challenge, and more willing and able to assume responsibility, is not unique. Further the decision processes are more complex and lengthy and this is likely to force the Chief Accountant to rely on subordinates to a greater extent. In a sense all this could have the effect of facilitating and actually encouraging the Chief Accountant to share decisions with subordinates and feel confident in delegating responsibilities. His job as a consequence may be more meaningful. Porter (1963a) found that managers in large companies had jobs which are more interesting, competitive and challenging. A very interesting finding manifests itself in Table 5.10.1 (p.187). With hardly any qualification the message is clear. The Chief Accountant in the large company has a very favourable impression of the calibre of his subordinate; to use a permissive style therefore seems to be a natural consequence.

Size of company also influences the decision style profile of the Chief Accountant. This is highlighted in Figure 5.10.1 (p.191) where the directive and consultative styles vie for the greatest popularity, and the popularity of joint decision making and delegation is conspicuous by its absence. The use of a directive style is very pronounced in the smaller company. The greatest emphasis is given to a consultative style in the medium-sized company. As established elsewhere, this is the only situation where a high level of specialism is related to a permissive style (i.e., consultation) and confirms hypothesis VIII. In the large company the directive and consultative style tie for the distinction of the most widely used style. We can now proceed cautiously to accept hypothesis XIX.

Hypothesis XIX. Overall the Chief Accountant's decision style is likely to be influenced by the size of the company.

Though company size does not permeate a number of the relationships the independent variables have with decision style to any marked degree, it does have a selective impact as a mediating variable. In a global sense its mediation influence, and that of finance function size, is negligible in the relationships between decision style and (i) experience variables, (ii) span of control (see Tables 5.10.2; 5.10.4, pp. 189-90). Therefore we cannot accept hypotheses XVI and XVII presented below.

Hypothesis XVI. Size of company and finance function mediates the relationship between decision style and the experience variables.

Hypothesis XVII. Size of company and finance function mediates the relationship between decision style and span of control.

Its localised effect is felt in the following instances. As a result of increasing job tenure in the small company a shift from a consultative style to joint decision making is experienced. A high level of specialism, mostly attributable to the intervention and influence of the Chief Accountant, is compatible with a directive style in the small company. The influence of high specialism in the medium-sized company has been noted above. Also its mediating effect is noticed in the relationship between decision style and hierarchical level. This will be discussed in the next section. Finally, there is reason to believe that we should distinguish between organic growth in size of the company, which is internally generated, and that due to acquisition strategy. Apparently the latter is more likely to bring about a variation in decision style.

DECISION STYLE IN RELATION TO LEVEL
WITHIN THE ORGANISATIONAL HIERARCHY,
RECOGNISING THE INFLUENCE OF SIZE

Acknowledgement of hierarchical level as an independent variable of some importance scarcely escapes our notice. In distinguishing between different levels on the basis of personality characteristics Porter and Henry (1964a) arrive at a general conclusion which says that the 'organisation man' is more likely to inhabit the lower rather than the higher stratum of the hierarchy. Likewise Porter and Ghiselli (1957) differentiate between top and middle managers on the basis of identifiable personality traits. Apparently greater higher-need gratification is a feature of management positions at the higher organisational level (Porter 1962). Subordinate managers were found to suffer perceptual displacement towards a higher degree of influence in their superiors' decisions (Heller, 1971). Martin (1959) maintains that decision complexity is a function of hierarchical level. Weissenberg and Kavanagh (1972) believe that level within the organisation mediates the independence of both Consideration and Initiating Structure.

Having established the influential nature of hierarchical level, we shall now turn to the hypothesised relationship between level within the organisation and decision style.

> Hypothesis XX. The higher the organisational level the greater is the likelihood of the Chief Accountant exercising a permissive oriented style.

The data set out in the second column from the left hand side of Table 5.11 (p.192) indicates that at the lower hierarchical level the likelihood of a restrictive style is prevalent. The positive association between level and joint decision making, though marginally short of significance, reinforces the significant result by reversing the above trend when the Chief Accountant occupies a higher level position. We may now cautiously accept hypothesis XX. Empirical

224

endorsement of the above finding is available. Blankenship and Miles (1968) report that higher level managers were more likely to involve their subordinates in decisions, whilst those lower in the hierarchy felt a lesser need to rely on subordinates. Heller and Yukl (1969) associate a less centralised decision style with a higher level within the organisation. When Jago and Vroom (1977) relied on the perceptions of direct rather than indirect subordinates of the leader, they found that there was a greater propensity to use participative methods at higher organisational levels.

A very interesting result is discernible when the localised impact of company size is examined in Table 1, Appendix 'C'. Here we find that a high level within the small organisation brings in its wake a semi-directive style. As we move vertically downwards the style becomes directive. So it can be maintained that the lower level attracts the more directive style, but in any case both positions are associated with restrictive styles. This pattern changes when we consider the medium and large-sized company. Permissive styles - delegation and joint decision making respectively - are associated with a higher level organisational position in these companies.

Hypothesis XVIII was formulated following consideration of Fisch's (1963) speculative assertion that the relationship between level and span of control was mediated by company size. It was felt that size might produce a similar effect in the relationship between level and decision style.

> Hypothesis XVIII. Size of company and finance function individually and combined mediate the relationship between decision style and hierarchical level.

On a re-examination of Table 5.11 (p.192) we see that partialling out size of company and finance function on an individual and collective basis of the relationship between decision style and hierarchical level

produces no concrete effect. Therefore we cannot
accept hypothesis XVIII.

   Our attention shall now be directed to the mediating effects of level itself. Porter (1963b) found
hierarchical level as a factor which modified the
relationship between size and motivation. Of particular relevance to the present study is the view
of Blankenship and Miles (1968) who contend that the
relationship between size and decision-making
behaviour is modified by hierarchical level. This
appears to be an opportune moment to introduce hypothesis XXIII.

   Hypothesis XXIII. Hierarchical level mediates
   the relationship between decision style and
   company size.

The immediate reaction on reading Table 5.11.5
(p.196) is that hierarchical level produces no mediating effect whatsoever. Therefore one feels unable
to accept hypothesis XXIII. None of the following
hypotheses can be accepted due to the lack of any
evidence to suggest that hierarchical level has a
mediating role. In hypothesis XXIV blending hierarchical level and company size to create an independent mediating variable met with a fate already
encountered above.

   Hypothesis XXI. Hierarchical level mediates the
   relationship between decision style and the
   experience variables.

   Hypothesis XXII. Hierarchical level mediates the
   relationship between skill discrepancy and decision style.

   Hypothesis XXIV. Hierarchical level mediates the
   relationship between decision style and span of
   control. It produces a similar effect when combined with company size.

How can we relationalise the failure of hierarchical

level as a mediating influence? In the first instance
we could argue that there is rather limited evidence
available pointing in this direction. Secondly, the
evidence that is available is not overwhelmingly convincing; it often appears to be inserted as an after-
thought. Finally, the comparison of levels within
the organisation in the present research study is
confined to virtually two senior levels, so the comparative analysis of levels is not as meaningful as
it might be with an additional level of supervision
included.

7 Conclusion

Managerial leadership or decision-making behaviour is a well charted and explored area. In chapter 2 a commentary and analysis of significant strands of opinion and research evidence were undertaken in order to illuminate the striking complexity of this area of study. At different stages in its development we have witnessed different perspectives on the subject. A personality trait approach gave way to a preoccupation with leadership style, with the inevitable normative prescription as to what constitutes the best or optimum style. In recent years the relevance of style as an explanatory concept still remains but there is a growing body of opinion which suggests that it is only meaningful to discuss style in the context of situational variables. The present study was designed with a view to making a contribution to the development of situational leadership theory.

JUSTIFICATION FOR A SITUATIONAL PERSPECTIVE

In recent times democratic leadership or participative management has captured the imagination and interest particularly of educators and those responsible for management training. In the related area of job redesign, job enrichment has been enthusiastically received. Both share a common theoretical foundation discernible in the proposition that man strives to self-actualise. The views of proponents of this school of thought are well known to students of management or managerial psychology; Herzberg's dual-factor theory, McGregor's theory Y, Argyris's mature individual and Likert's leadership system 4. All bear witness to the superiority of a leadership style or motivational system which appeals to the higher level human needs. These theoretical propositions advocate the implication of the total personality in the task and are without doubt immensely humane with widespread

228

appeal. Their foundation - the force for growth theory of personality - appears rather shaky and has been the subject of a well-articulated attack. Nevertheless impressive claims are made on behalf of participative management pointing to its superiority on the basis of morale and productivity. Though heavily endorsed by the findings of survey investigations, the superiority of participative leadership is by no means conclusive; in fact it is seriously challenged by evidence emanating from experimental studies. Speculations derived from the personality-based evidence tend to suggest a restrictive style is responsible for promoting disadvantageous conditions for the subordinate, but equally there is the recognition that in certain circumstances it may be compatible with the personality disposition of the superior.

A number of participative management experiments or studies have been criticised for their lack of consideration of crucial factors which ought to be recognised. Also there is a belief that the participative process produces some dysfunctional consequences - e.g., it promotes anxiety; the frequent interaction may impede problem-solving activity. Finally, the universality of the findings related to participative management is seriously undermined when the impact of cultural variation is recognised. It is then understandable why researchers have turned to an examination of situational and structural forces in the immediate environment of the decision process in order to seek a better explanation of leadership phenomena. Developments in situational leadership theory are gathering momentum in North America but there are few signs of any activity in this direction in Britain. It is true to say that situational theory is still very much at the embryonic stage offering tremendous scope for further exploration. It is hoped that during its development personality-based factors will be kept firmly in focus.

THE PRESENT STUDY

A distinctive feature of the research study conducted by the author is the selection of an occupational group - accountants - whose leadership style and situational environment have been subjected to close and careful analysis for the first time. In addition the dissection of decisions into programmed and non-programmed categories, and then related to leadership style, has not been operationalised hitherto. Apart from personnel decisions, the decision types are specifically finance in orientation, so the leadership pattern that emerges is far more meaningful and authentic than that derived from a set of decisions common to a number of functional areas. The same applies to the measures of specialisation and specialism, but particularly to specialisation. The specialisation dimension incorporates typical accounting sub-systems. The specialism dimension is somewhat crude but along with specialisation is capable of further development. Decision type is also open to further development and refinement. Regrettably there appears to be a tendency in this type of study to select and examine situational factors allegedly common to a variety of occupational groups, whilst those factors appropriate to a particular group are ignored or receive cursory attention. This might be attributable to the manner in which the sample is composed; in many instances it cuts across different functional groupings. However, one must acknowledge that the leadership process itself is often differentiated by occupational group to highlight the different leadership style profiles.

A welcome departure in the gauging of leadership style is the adoption of a continuum of subordinate influence in the leadership process. This seems preferable to the emphasis on a bi-polar measure with the accent on extreme positions - autocratic/democratic. A useful leadership continuum has been put forward by Tannenbaum and Schmidt (1958), but the power/influence continuum postulated by Heller (1971) had particular appeal to the author because of its acknowledgement of delegation as a legitimate component of the leadership process. One now recognises that delegation cannot be considered unequivocal. For the sake of clarity it can be viewed as containing two interpretations. On the one hand, it extends to the recipient of delegated authority a tremendous amount of autonomy and as a consequence has a distinct permissive leadership connotation to it. On the other hand, authority is delegated but is done so within rather rigid procedural boundaries or guidelines where inbuilt control mechanisms are alert, transmitting to the superior a variety of data on significant organisational happenings or events. In this sense delegation cannot be regarded as the custodian of real autonomy. It is almost tantamount to a direction to operate within specified procedural guidelines, subject to the referral of major items of interest to the superior for his assessment, comment or decision. The above distinction surfaces visibly from the research evidence and it comes as no surprise to find delegation sharing a leadership platform with restrictive styles in the context of programmed decisions.

Another interesting feature of the power/influence continuum measure is that respondents are informed prior to completing it that no one style has preference or superiority over another. However in the research study we must be prepared to accept the likelihood of the presence of a cultural counter-force vitiating the strength of this instruction by suggesting that it is acceptable, and even desirable, to consult or involve subordinates in the decision-making process. Perceptual distortion is a real likelihood in this instance, perhaps reinforced by personal aspiration pointing in the direction of participative management. We must also admit that in some circumstances a manager embraces a participative style as a conscious act with all the outward manifestations of real participation, but in essence it is not legitimate since he has already reached an irreversible decision prior to subordinate involvement.

A further point worthy of note, which has not been acknowledged in previous research, is the influential mediating role of decision style - particularly the programmed/non-programmed dichotomy - in the relation-ships between decision style and two important inde-pendent variables - span of control and perceived skill discrepancy. The relevance of personality-based factors must not be allowed to go unnoticed. The LPS measure focusses attention on the psychological dis-tance between the superior and his subordinates and has direct relevance to the personality disposition of the superior. By way of contrast, the measure designed to arrive at the perceived skill discrepancy score concentrated on the qualities and skills poss-essed by the subordinates. In both cases significant relationships between decision style and the two independent variables were found. Therefore in any future development of situational leadership theory it is realistic and worthwhile to emphasise personal-ity-related factors residing in both the superior and subordinate.

Measures such as the LPS appear to have greater substance and relevance when it comes to depicting the behavioural disposition - autocratic/democratic - of the leader. It is difficult to concede, as is often suggested, that task-oriented behaviour is synonymous with a restrictive style. After all Likert's employee-centred supervisor paid a fair amount of attention to planning and scheduling. But it appears employee-oriented behaviour is compatible with a permissive style. It seems there is nothing to prevent the leader, who is psychologically close to his subordinates, from concentrating his talents and abilities on task-related matters. This was found to be the case in the present study.

On reading the relevant literature one gets the impression that the accountant as a functional manager is directive in his leadership style. Evidence de-rived from the present study does not altogether support this view. When the Chief Accountant is presented with a representative set of decisions he places almost equal emphasis on restrictive and per-missive styles. A direct comparison of the single

232

most widely used directive and permissive style reveals a minute advantage accruing to the directive style.

There can be no denying the important role played by what are essentially structural features of organisation. Size assumes a position of particular importance in its direct relationship with the dependent variable, and it retains its position of relevance, but to a minor extent, as a mediating variable. There is a dearth of evidence indicating a direct relationship between size and leadership style. The mediating role of size in the relationship between decision style and a situational variable appears not to have been previously recognised. Hierarchical level is likewise a determinant of leadership style but one would place greater confidence in this result if more levels were examined. In effect the comparison was between level 1 and 2, because a tiny proportion of respondents occupied positions lower than level 2. It has to be acknowledged that the incidence of programmed activity with its constraining influence is that much greater at the lower levels. At the higher level it would appear these constraints on the manager's freedom are less prevalent in a procedural sense, but perhaps this is offset by the constricting influence of political and social forces.

Span of control also enjoys a direct significant relationship with leadership style. Proponents of participative management would undoubtedly find it convenient to ignore its importance. But it must be recognised that a wide span of control normally precludes the possibility of true participation of subordinates in superiors' decisions. Finally, a resurrection of interest in the staff role of a key operator is perhaps overdue. Finance as a discipline has acquired a position of strategic importance for the economic welfare of the organisation, particularly in present circumstances. It could be argued that the traditional concept of staff/line is due for an explosion, if it has not already happened. We have seen how fluid and flexible it has become from the viewpoint of the functional role of the Chief Accountant.

SUMMARY OF FINDINGS

With a recognition of the limitations of the research method used the time has arrived to summarise the main findings of the study.

1. The Chief Accountant, in a universal sense, places equal emphasis on restrictive and permissive decision styles and cannot be regarded as having a significant leaning towards the adoption of a directive style. Though a directive style - 'A' - is fractionally the more popular, it is followed closely by a consultative style. The least popular styles are joint decision making and delegation.

2. The Chief Accountant resorts to the use of both directive and delegative decision styles when confronted with programmed decision situations. He modifies his style when faced with non-programmed decisions. Here he considers the use of consultative and joint decision-making styles more appropriate. Delegation in the above sense is likely to be constrained as a style by procedural considerations and subject to a fair measure of personal or impersonal control.

3. Task decision situations, which are likely to be influenced by programmed decisions, invite both a directive and a delegative style. Personnel decision situations, possessing non-programmed decision ingredients, align themselves with consultative and joint decision-making styles.

4. When relatively new to the job the Chief Accountant is likely to adopt a consultative decision style, but with the passing of time he is prone to gravitate towards a directive style. In the smaller company when relatively recent in the job he embraces a participative style which embodies

234

joint decision making.

5. In conditions of a high level of specialisation a
   directive style prevails. The opposite is true
   with a low level of specialisation where a consultative style is used. Though specialism does
   not have a significant individual relationship
   with decision style, however, a selective relationship emerges when the localised effect of
   size is considered. By combining specialisation
   and specialism and relating them to decision
   style we find a directive style is appropriate
   in conditions of high specialisation and specialism, whilst a consultative style applies in conditions of low specialisation and specialism.
   Specialisation produces a mediating effect in the
   relationship between decision style and non-
   programmed decisions.

6. A large discrepancy between perceived actual and
   desirable qualities or skills in the subordinate
   of the Chief Accountant invites the introduction
   of a semi-directive decision style. A small discrepancy produces a different effect by opening
   the way for the introduction of a joint decision-
   making style. However, the extent to which a
   decision is programmed has a bearing on the style
   used. The Chief Accountant assumes more of a
   directive posture in non-programmed decision situations when he perceives a large skill discrepancy. He is encouraged to use delegation as a
   style when he perceives a small skill discrepancy
   in programmed decision situations.

7. The Chief Accountant enjoys a high degree of
   status, power and influence. No significant relationship materialises between this variable and
   decision style. As a result of the intervention
   of 'vertical respect', a tenuous relationship
   with decision style may ensue.

8. A permissive style - delegation - is linked to
   employee-oriented behaviour; conversely a restric-

tive style reflects a lower degree of concern for employee-oriented behaviour.

9. The Chief Accountant who appears to have a warm, friendly and open relationship with his subordinates - high LPS - firmly embraces a permissive decision style of a delegative nature. Those found lacking in this disposition - low LPS - are likely to use a directive style. The high LPS leader, not unduly worried about the quality of human relations, may feel a need to emphasise the task-related components of his job.

10. A wide span of control, where the number of immediate subordinates is large, calls for the application of a directive decision style. A permissive style, manifest in joint decision making, is compatible with a narrow span of control. The best prediction of the relationship between decision style and span of control arises when non-programmed, including personnel, decisions are considered.

11. No significant relationship subsists between decision style and the functional role of the Chief Accountant. His functional role appears to be ill-defined and devoid of the therapeutic human relations approach which is often alleged to beset the staff man's role. Instead reliance is placed on a mixture of behavioural tactics - directives, persuasion, bargaining - frequently culminating in compromise.

12. In the larger company permissive decision styles - joint decision making and delegation - are more likely to be found. The reverse is the case in the smaller company with the emphasis on a directive style. An identical pattern emerges in the relationship between size of finance function and decision style. When the decision style profile of the Chief Accountant is viewed from the angle of company size the following relationships can be seen. The use of a directive style is very pro-

nounced in the small company and the use of a
consultative style in the medium and large-sized
company is very noticeable. In the larger company
the Chief Accountant views the calibre of his subordinates very favourably indeed and it seems
natural as a consequence for him to use a permissive decision style. In general, size of company
has a selective mediating effect.

13. A restrictive decision style is likely to reign in
the lower echelons of the organisation but a permissive style is evident at the higher levels.
However, in the small company this pattern is
not maintained because a directive style prevails
at the upper and lower levels, but with greater
intensity at the lower level.

PRACTICAL IMPLICATIONS

The evidence derived from the research certainly poses
a serious challenge to the view that a particular
leadership style is suitable irrespective of the
prevailing organisational circumstances. What is
suggested is that managers must develop awareness of
the need to introduce flexibility into their management style so that they are able to adapt to differing
situational and structural demands within their organisation. For example, a participative style may be
suitable when faced with non-programmed decisions but
unsuitable in the context of programmed decisions.
Equally if the manager establishes that his subordinates suffer a significant deficiency in skill relevant
to the problem in hand, the only sensible course of
action open to him in the immediate situation may be
to adopt a directive style. Of course this could signal a need for training. In the domain of organisational design widening the span of control of a manager at a time when the organisation is committed to
the adoption and implementation of a participative
management scheme would not appear to be a wise course
of action. Likewise stepping-up standardisation and
formalisation of work activities (i.e., specialisation)

may not be conducive to the successful operation of a participative management scheme. Experiences at the Volvo works in Sweden bear out this point by the implied recognition of an inherent incompatibility between acute specialisation and a commitment to job enrichment.

In the arena of management training we must recognise that an undue emphasis on the interpersonal behaviour aspect of the leader's role may not produce the anticipated desirable effects. Therefore we have to consider alternative strategies. Perhaps organisational engineering should become a more important input component to management training programmes. Due to time constraints this would leave less time available for the coverage of the interpersonal aspects of the programme such as process consultation and sensitivity training. In the field of management education perhaps we should become more adventurous and be prepared to cross disciplinary boundaries where we feel justified in doing so. Efforts along these lines are actively pursued at the present time, but the sub-discipline of organisational behaviour – primarily a combined sociological and psychological approach to the study of behaviour in organisations – is still at the formative stages of development. In the light of the impact of the immediate organisational environment on leadership processes in the present study perhaps its development ought to be accelerated. Finally, in a climate characterised by a growing awareness among professional accountancy bodies of the need to consider the educational value and relevance of studying the behavioural aspects of accounting, a situational perspective of the leadership role of a key financial executive could be considered a valuable contribution.

FUTURE RESEARCH

As a first priority it seems worthwhile to continue with the development of the decision categorisation process and the measure of specialisation. In order to make a better assessment of the importance of hierarchical level as a structural variable at least three levels ought to be chosen for analysis. An interesting development would be the continuation of the line of enquiry pursued in the present study in other occupational areas where situational features – e.g., decision type, specialisation – are peculiar to the areas surveyed, and subsequently to carry out comparative analysis. I believe it is paramount to establish localised determinants of leadership behaviour before searching for globalised ones. Delegation as a concept needs to be operationalised in a more sophisticated and rigorous fashion in order to differentiate between real autonomy and situations where autonomy is more apparent than real. Efforts should be directed at devising measures to assess the impact of the relevant environment on the decision-making process. One cannot deny its importance but so far its measurement has presented insurmountable difficulties. Finally, an equally intractable problem, we should seriously consider tackling the question of devising a performance measure for a service function, such as finance. Only then can we speak of leadership effectiveness in an economic sense for managers in service functions.

Appendix A

<u>Confidential</u>

For the attention: Financial Controller
                          or
                     Chief Accountant

> Department of Business Studies
>   and Finance,
> Birmingham Polytechnic,
> Aston Street,
> Birmingham. B4 7HA.
> (Tel: 021 359 6851)

Dear Sir,

Senior Accountants in industry and commerce are an influential body of people primarily engaged in the interpretation of accounting and financial data, and offering a valuable service to all levels of management. It is generally acknowledged that not enough is known about the various aspects of their jobs.

The aim of this project, which forms the basis of a research programme at the Department of Psychology, University of Surrey, is to gather information about the management style of the Financial Controller or Chief Accountant in relation to a number of other important considerations.

The information you provide will be treated in the strictest confidence and will no doubt be of value in increasing our knowledge of this important area of investigation. You are not required to disclose the name of your company, and a copy of the synopsis of the findings will be sent to you on request.

Thank you for your assistance.

Yours faithfully,

Eugene F. McKenna, MSc, DIA, ACIS
Senior Lecturer

The format of the questionnaire which appears below
has been modified but its contents remain unaltered.

Questionnaire No.

You are asked to give a carefully considered answer
to each question on the questionnaire. There are
four main types of questions viz: First, standard
biographical questions. Second, questions requiring
you to ring the number opposite the answer which
reflects your view. Third, a question requiring you
to give an answer in the form of a percentage number.
Finally, a question requiring you to place an X
against the appropriate answer. (A couple of questions
offer you the opportunity to introduce additional observations).

Please send the completed questionnaire to:

Eugene F. McKenna, Esq.,
Senior Lecturer in Organisational Behaviour,
Department of Business Studies and Finance,
Birmingham Polytechnic,
Aston Street,
Birmingham. B4 7HA.

1. Biographical questions

i. Name............................

Telephone No. (office)............

ii. Year of birth........................

iii. What age did you leave school?.......

iv. Did you proceed to full time further education?.........

   If yes, what type of full time further education did you receive?............................

v. List degrees and other qualifications held (use designatory letters where appropriate)

   ....

vi. In what industry do you work?
   (Examples of industrial classification: Chemical and allied; engineering and electrical goods; textiles; publishing)

   ....

vii. Area of work....................
   (Example: Finance)

viii. Job title (brief description of job)..........

   ....

ix. Length of time in present position (no. of years) Ring the number opposite the appropriate range.

Less than 1	1
1 - 3	2
4 - 6	3
over 6	4

2. This question sets out different approaches to decision making (A, B, C, D, E), listed below, and various types of decisions found in the finance area. First, you are asked to examine carefully the different approaches to decision making, each of which can be equally effective.

   Second, if you have the authority in your present position to make the final decision, or at least to make a formal recommendation that will usually be accepted, then for each relevant decision, listed overleaf, indicate the decision making approach (from A, B, C, D, E) you normally adopt. If one or more of the decisions are not relevant, place 'Not applicable' opposite the appropriate item.

(Were you to choose more than one of the approaches for a particular decision, then split 100% between them. It is more than likely you will put 100% next to one approach from A, B, C, D, E).

A. Own decision without detailed explanation.

These are decisions made by you without previous discussion or consultation with subordinates and no special meeting or memorandum is used to explain the decision. (This method includes decisions made after consulting with managers at the same level or with superiors).

B. Own decision with detailed explanation.

The same as above, but afterwards you explain the problem and the reasons for your choice in a memo or in a special meeting.

C. Prior consultation with subordinate.

Before the decision is taken, you explain the problem to your subordinate and ask for his advice and help. You then make the decision by yourself. Your final choice may, or may not, reflect your subordinate's influence.

D. Joint decision making with subordinate.

You and your subordinate(s) together analyse the problem and come to a decision. The subordinate(s) usually has as much influence over the final choice as you. Where there are more than two in the discussion, the decision of the majority is accepted more often than not.

E. Delegation of decision to subordinate.

You ask your subordinate to make the decisions

244

regarding a particular subject. You may or may not request him to report his decisions to you. You seldom veto his decisions.

Type of decision	Decision making approach				
	A %	B %	C %	D %	E %

The decision to examine a historical accounting procedure with a view to a major modification. (1)

The decision to promote members of staff in your department who are not your direct subordinates (2)

The decision to recommend taking legal action on arrears in a customer's account where the amount involved is large and long overdue. (3)

The decision to fix the level of cash surplus to be budgeted for in the draft cash budget (to cover unforeseen contingencies). (4)

The decision to establish guidelines to be used in deciding whether variances, arising from comparing actual with planned performance, are worth investigating. (5)

The decision to examine the 'age' of debtors. (6)

The decision to set up or review a standard or marginal

245

	Decision making approach				
Type of decision	A %	B %	C %	D %	E %

costing system which could
result in a far better breakdown of product costs. (7)

The decision to encourage the
resignation or transfer of a
member of your staff who does
not report to you directly. (8)

The decision to re-categorise
the costs of products so as
to show more clearly the
profit margin being made on
each type of product. (9)

The decision to suggest the
best alternative source of
funds for the financing of a
project which has already
been agreed. (10)

The decision to define the
expected life of a new fixed
asset for depreciation
purposes. (11)

The decision to revise a
department's budget forecast
as a result of information
received during the year. (12)

The decision to increase or
decrease the number of employees in your department. (13)

The decision to set aside
provisions against bad debts. (14)

3. Departments within organisations can differ in the manner in which work activities are special- ised and controlled by individuals or section heads with different levels of expertise.

For each job area listed below, please indicate the extent to which it is established in your department, and the type of staff responsible for managing or operating it. Where an activity is performed by accounting staff of equal rank, choose the individual with whom you have most contact.

Ring the appropriate number opposite each item which most closely describes your view. If one or more of these job areas are not relevant, place 'Not applicable' opposite the appropriate item.

Job area	Extent to which job area is established	Operated or managed by someone who is:
	5.Very well 4.Fairly well 3.Adequately 2.Not so well 1.Poorly	4.Fully qualified 3.Senior unqualified 2.Partly qualified 1.Junior unquali- fied

Credit control

Debtor's ledger
and control

Sales analysis

Monitoring the
cash flow

Creditor's ledger
and control

Capital expendi-
ture proposals

Job area	Extent to which job area is established	Operated or managed by someone who is:
	5.Very well 4.Fairly well 3.Adequately 2.Not so well 1.Poorly	4.Fully qualified 3.Senior unqualified 2.Partly qualified 1.Junior unquali- fied
Allocation of expenditure into 'Capital' and 'Revenue' items		
Short-range budget planning and profit forecasting		
Long-range budget planning and profit forecasting		
Preparation of final accounts		
Standard or marginal costing		
Periodic management reports		
Product or job or process costing		

4. (i) Many senior managers would like to work with
        subordinates who possess a combination of
        qualities and skills which they believe enhance

the subordinates' ability to do a job well.

You are asked to consider carefully the qualities or skills, listed below, in relation to questions (a) and (b) posed below. If you have more than one direct subordinate, focus your attention on the subordinate with whom you most frequently come in contact.

The questions represented by (a) and (b) read as follows:

(a) How much of this quality or skill would you consider desirable in a person occupying your subordinate's position? (=Desirable)

Min. 1   7 Max.

(b) How much of this quality or skill does your subordinate have? (=Actual)

Min. 1   7 Max.

(Low numbers represent low or minimum amounts and high numbers high or maximum amounts).

Please ring the number which most closely describes your view.

Type of quality or skill	Rating of quality or skill			
	Desirable		Actual	
	Min. 1	Max. 7	Min. 1	Max. 7
Ability to make rapid decisions				
Verbal ability (to speak fluently to staff at all levels)				

249

Type of quality or skill	Rating of quality or skill			
	Desirable		Actual	
	Min. 1	Max. 7	Min. 1	Max. 7
Technical ability (knowledge, skill and current information related to industrial accountancy)				
Forceful in putting forward ideas and plans for action				
Perseverence in the face of adversity				
Sensitive to people's needs				
High level of intelligence				
Imaginative in approach to a work problem				
Ability to readily accept responsibility for the consequences of actions or decisions				
Possession of self-confidence without being too arrogant				
Ability to react calmly to pressure of work				
Tactful in a delicate situation				

Type of quality or skill	Rating of quality or skill			
	Desirable		Actual	
	Min. 1	Max. 7	Min. 1	Max. 7
Willingness to consider the other person's point of view				
Willingness to pass on information to others				
Readiness to accept new ideas				

4. (ii) Are there any other qualities or skills important to you but not listed above? If yes, please list and rate.

5. Below are listed certain characteristics which highlight organisational relationships. Please ring the number opposite the answer which best describes the situation as you see it.

    (a) My position offers me considerable latitude to deal with major personnel issues (e.g., reward, discipline, etc.) on my own.   Yes 1

    No 0

    (b) The status attached to my position is easily recognisable by subordinates.   Yes 1

    No 0

(c) The authority to assign, super-
    vise, and assess jobs underneath   Yes   1
    me is a normal feature of my
    position.   No   0

(d) By reason of my present position
    I possess a great deal of know-   Yes   1
    ledge about the technical nature
    of subordinates' jobs.   No   0

(e) Frequently my superior consults   Yes* 1
    me on matters connected with
    major decisions.   No   0

*If Yes, proceed to (f)

(f) Invariably the advice I offer   Yes   1
    carries a lot of weight with
    my superior.   No   0

6. Below are listed statements highlighting charac-
    teristics which are sometimes associated with the
    behaviour of managers.

    To what extent do you perceive these character-
    istics as a manifestation of your own style of
    management? Ring the number attached to the
        item which best describes your view.

                        5.To a high degree
                        4.To a fair degree
                        3.To a reasonable
                          extent
                        2.To a limited extent
                        1.Hardly at all

    i. I believe I am respon-
       sible for promoting a
       feeling of personal
       worth and importance
       in my subordinate(s).

5.To a high degree
4.To a fair degree
3.To a reasonable
   extent
2.To a limited extent
1.Hardly at all

ii. I believe I am responsible
    for encouraging my subor-
    dinates to develop close,
    mutually satisfying work
    relationships.

iii. I believe I am responsible
     for stimulating an enthu-
     siasm to achieve an im-
     pressive level of perfor-
     mance.

iv. I believe I am responsible
    for facilitating the
    attainment of work targets
    or objectives because of
    my administrative and
    technical competence.

7. Are there any other characteristics not listed
   above which you feel ought to be emphasised?
   If yes, please specify.

   ....

   ....

   ....

8. People differ in the manner in which they think
   about those with whom they work. Listed overleaf
   are pairs of words which are opposite in meaning.

   Please give your immediate first reaction to each
   pair of words and describe the subordinate whom

you prefer the least by placing an X in one of
the eight spaces on the line between each pair
of words. Each space represents the extent to
which an adjective fits the person you are
describing.

Pleasant	. . . .	Unpleasant
Friendly	. . . .	Unfriendly
Rejecting	. . . .	Accepting
Helpful	. . . .	Frustrating
Unenthusiastic	. . . .	Enthusiastic
Tense	. . . .	Relaxed
Distant	. . . .	Close
Cold	. . . .	Warm
Cooperative	. . . .	Uncooperative
Supportive	. . . .	Hostile
Boring	. . . .	Interesting
Quarrelsome	. . . .	Harmonious
Self-assured	. . . .	Hesitant
Efficient	. . . .	Inefficient
Gloomy	. . . .	Cheerful
Open	. . . .	Guarded

9. At what level in the formal organisation structure
    is the position you now occupy? To help you lo-
    cate your particular level take as an aid the
    following guideline:

    Top managers of a company or division are desig-
    nated 'Level 1'. Managers one step removed from
    them on the organisation chart are considered to
    be at 'Level 2'; those two steps away constitute
    'Level 3', and so on.

    Please ring the appropriate level number.

Level	1
Level	2
Level	3
Level	4

10. Please indicate the number of subordinates you are directly responsible for supervising by ringing the number opposite the appropriate range.

Less than 3	1
3 - 6	2
7 - 10	3
Over 10	4

11. Approximate size of finance function (No. of employees). Ring the number opposite the appropriate range.

Less than 15	1
16 - 31	2
32 - 60	3
Over 60	4

12. Approximate size of company (No. of employees). Ring the number opposite the appropriate range.

Under 500	1
500 - 2000	2
Over 2000	3

13. Please ring the number opposite the statement which best describes your role within the company.

(a) As the representative, or acting for the representative, of the finance

function I act in a purely advisory role
to other functions (e.g., production,
marketing) without possessing direct
authority to implement my recommendations.　1

(b) As the representative, or acting for
the representative, of the finance
function I possess direct authority
to implement my recommendations of
an accounting and finance nature in
other functions (e.g., production,
marketing).　2

(c) Neither (a) or (b) reflect the real
situation as I see it.　3

Thank you for your cooperation.

I would very much appreciate any further comment on
the topics covered in this questionnaire.

Appendix B

SAMPLE CHARACTERISTICS

Table 1

Age distribution of respondents

| Age distribution | Percentage number of respondents | |
	Total sample *n=209	Interview sample +n=32
	%	%
< 30	7.2	3.1
30 - 40	43.1	62.5
41 - 50	34.9	28.1
> 51	14.8	6.3

* The age range is 23 to 64 and the median average age is 40

+ The age range is 29 to 61 and the median average age is 37

Table 2

Age respondents left school

Sample type	Median average age
Total sample n=209	$16\frac{1}{2}$
Interview sample n=32	17

Table 3

Number of respondents who received further
education and possess various qualifications

Education/ qualifications	Percentage number of respondents	
	Total sample n=209	Interview sample n=32
	%	%
Further education	13.9	18.7
Recognised profess- ional qualifications	84.2	87.5
Degrees	11.0	15.6
Diplomas	4.3	9.3

Table 4

Respondents with recognised professional
qualifications analysed by professional title

Professional title	Percentage number of respondents	
	Total sample *n=176	Interview sample +n=28
	%	%
Chartered accountant	63.7	60.7
Cost and management accountant	27.8	21.4
Certified accountant	11.4	14.2
Chartered secretary	6.8	7.1

* 16 respondents bore two professional titles and
1 respondent bore three

+ 1 respondent bore two professional titles

Therefore the total percentage figure exceeds
100 per cent in both cases

Table 5

Distribution of respondents by type of industry

Standard industrial classification	Percentage number of respondents	
	Total sample n=212	Interview sample n=32
	%	%
Mining and quarrying	0.9	
Food, drink, tobacco	9.9	12.5
Coal and petroleum	0.9	
Chemical and allied	7.5	6.2
Metal manufacture	3.3	6.2
Mechanical engineering	10.4	9.4
Instrument engineering	2.4	3.1
Electrical engineering	9.4	12.5
Vehicles	2.4	
Metal goods not specified elsewhere	3.8	6.3
Textiles	4.2	
Leather goods and furs	0.6	
Clothing and footwear	2.8	3.1
Bricks, pottery, glass cement	2.8	3.1
Timber, furniture	2.4	
Paper, printing, publishing	8.9	9.4
Other manufacturing industry	5.7	6.3
Construction	4.2	9.4
Service and distribution	16.0	9.4
Miscellaneous	1.5	3.1

Table 6
Area of work of respondents

Area of work	Percentage number of respondents	
	Total sample n=212	Interview sample n=32
	%	%
Finance	63.2	75.0
Finance and secretarial	19.8	15.6
Finance and administration	17.0	9.4

Table 7
Job titles of respondents

Title classification	Percentage number of respondents	
	Total sample n=209	Interview sample n=32
	%	%
Chief Accountant	22.9	31.3
Chief Accountant and Company Secretary	14.4	9.4
Chief Accountant and Director	2.9	9.4
Financial Controller	20.1	21.8
Financial Controller and Company Secretary	2.4	9.4
Financial Director	15.3	3.1
Financial Director and Company Secretary	6.2	9.4
Miscellaneous, e.g., Director of Accounting Financial Planning Manager Company Secretary and Administrative Manager Group Accountant	15.8	6.2

260

Table 8

Time spent by respondents in present position

Number of years	Percentage number of respondents	
	Total sample n=212	Interview sample n=32
	%	%
< 1	15.6	18.8
1 - 3	36.3	46.9
4 - 6	21.7	21.8
> 6	26.4	12.5

Appendix C

Table 1

Mediating effect of company size on a number
of direct relationships between
the dependent and independent variables

	Decision styles														
	A			B			C			D			E		
Independent variables	S	M	L	S	M	L	S	M	L	S	M	L	S	M	L
Job tenure	0.27^b	0.03	0.21^a	-0.10	-0.03	-0.11	-0.06	-0.09	-0.29^c	-0.36^d	0.16	0.10	0.10	-0.06	0.00
Specialisation	0.20	0.18^a	0.11	0.01	0.05	-0.16	-0.23^a	-0.05	-0.14	-0.01	-0.15	-0.09	-0.17	-0.21^b	0.06
Specialism	0.36^d	0.00	-0.07	-0.24^a	-0.06	0.01	-0.29^b	0.19^a	0.04	0.02	-0.10	0.06	-0.02	-0.17	-0.00
Quality or skill discrepancy	0.15	-0.04	-0.00	-0.05	0.10	0.30^c	0.04	-0.00	0.01	-0.28^b	-0.08	-0.15	0.03	0.04	-0.19
Status, power, influence	0.05	-0.18^a	0.19	-0.00	0.15	-0.01	-0.11	0.05	-0.14	-0.05	0.13	-0.02	0.14	-0.18^a	-0.13
Managerial characteristics	0.02	-0.14	-0.07	0.07	0.12	0.02	-0.16	0.00	-0.05	0.07	-0.02	0.04	-0.03	0.14	0.12
LPS	-0.08	-0.09	-0.19	-0.21	0.22^b	-0.06	0.23^a	-0.04	0.11	0.04	-0.03	0.06	0.25^a	-0.08	0.22^a
Level	-0.24^a	0.02	-0.12	0.33^d	-0.16	0.03	-0.05	0.03	0.01	-0.01	0.01	0.29^c	0.09	0.18^a	-0.16
Span of control	0.24^a	0.16	0.13	-0.07	-0.06	0.02	-0.14	-0.04	-0.12	-0.17	-0.12	-0.06	-0.03	-0.00	-0.03
Size of finance function	-0.20	-0.09	0.07	-0.08	0.30^d	-0.21^a	0.15	-0.06	-0.09	0.18	-0.04	0.05	0.20	-0.19^a	0.16

Note: S = Small
       M = Medium
       L = Large

a = p < 0.05
b = p < 0.025
c = p < 0.01
d = p < 0.001

Table 2

Endorsement of status, power and influence

n=212

Organisational characteristics	Percentage score
	%
Position possesses considerable power	75.9
Status attached to position is conspicuous	98.1
Supervisory authority is evident	98.6
Awareness of technical features of subordinates' jobs	81.1
*Influence with superior	91.0
*If influential, advice carries a lot of weight	85.8

Table 3

Index of managerial behaviour characteristics

n=212

Type of characteristic	Index
Employee orientation:	
1. Promote feelings of personal worth	80
2. Encourage subordinates to develop close and satisfying work relationships	80
Aggregate (1 + 2)	80
Task orientation:	
3. Concerned about meeting performance standards	85
4. Arranging the right work conditions to meet work targets	83
Aggregate (3 + 4)	84

Table 4

Span of control as a
function of company size

n=212

Company size	Span of control			
	< 3	3-6	7-10	> 10
	%	%	%	%
Small	6.8	59.3	13.6	20.3
Medium	7.0	55.8	8.1	29.1
Large	6.0	58.2	14.9	20.9
Aggregate	6.6	57.5	11.8	24.1

Table 5

Index of specialisation and specialism

n=211

Job area	Specialisation index	Specialism index
Credit control	87	58
Debtor's ledger and control	87	55
Sales analysis	82	50
Monitoring the cash flow	85	70
Creditor's ledger and control	84	54
Capital expenditure proposals	75	66
Allocation of expenditure into 'capital' and 'revenue' items	86	64
Short-range budget planning and profit forecasting	86	74
Long-range budget planning and profit forecasting	69	70
Preparation of final accounts	94	74
Standard or marginal costing	58	49
Periodic management reports	89	72
Product or job or process costing	60	49

Appendix D

A COMPARISON OF RESULTS ACHIEVED BY USING
(a) PEARSON'S PRODUCT MOMENT CORRELATION
COEFFICIENT (b) KENDALL'S TAU RANK ORDER
CORRELATION COEFFICIENT

Table 1

Correlation between decision style
and experience variables

Decision style	Experience variables			
	n=212 Job experience		n=209 Age	
	Pearson	Kendall	Pearson	Kendall
A	0.15^b	0.13^c	0.07	0.03
B	−0.07	−0.06	−0.10	$−0.08^a$
C	$−0.12^a$	$−0.10^b$	−0.04	−0.04
D	−0.01	−0.03	0.04	0.05
E	−0.01	−0.06	0.02	−0.03

a = $p < 0.05$
b = $p < 0.025$
c = $p < 0.01$

Table 2

Correlation between decision style
and specialisation and specialism

n=211

Decision style	Specialisation		Specialism	
	Pearson	Kendall	Pearson	Kendall
A	0.15^b	0.07	0.04	-0.02
B	-0.02	-0.04	-0.10	-0.08^a
C	-0.11^a	-0.08^a	0.06	0.05
D	-0.03	-0.03	0.01	0.00
E	-0.07	-0.05	-0.04	-0.01

a = $p < 0.05$
b = $p < 0.025$

Table 3

Correlation between decision style,
with regard to decision type,
and specialisation

Specialisation

n=211

Decision style

Type of decision	A		B		C		D		E	
	Pearson	Kendall	Pearson	Kendall	Pearson	Kendall	Pearson	Kendall	Pearson	Kendall
Non-programmed	0.15[b]	0.08[a]	-0.11[a]	-0.07	-0.07	-0.06	0.01	-0.01	-0.01	-0.06
Programmed	0.05	0.04	0.02	0.00	-0.08	-0.07	-0.02	-0.03	-0.01	0.00

a = $p < 0.05$
b = $p < 0.025$

Table 4

Correlation between decision style, analysed by decision type and aggregate decisions, and perceived qualities or skills in subordinate

n=212

Perceived skill discrepancy

Decision style

Decision type	A		B		C		D		E	
	Pearson	Kendall	Pearson	Kendall	Pearson	Kendall	Pearson	Kendall	Pearson	Kendall
Programmed	-0.03	-0.03	0.11[a]	0.05	0.02	0.06	-0.02	-0.05	-0.11[a]	-0.06
Non-programmed	0.11[a]	0.07	0.07	0.03	-0.01	0.01	-0.19[c]	-0.11[c]	-0.01	0.00
Personnel	0.13[b]	0.09[b]	0.03	0.03	-0.00	0.01	-0.14[b]	-0.09[b]	0.01	-0.06
Task	0.01	0.02	0.12[a]	0.06	0.00	0.03	-0.13[b]	-0.10[b]	-0.08	-0.01
Aggregate	0.05	0.04	0.12[a]	0.13[c]	0.00	0.03	-0.18[c]	-0.12[c]	-0.07	-0.03

a = p $<$ 0.05
b = p $<$ 0.025
c = p $<$ 0.01

269

Table 5

Correlation between decision style
and status, power and influence

n=212

Decision style	Status, power, influence	
	Pearson	Kendall
A	0.02	0.03
B	0.04	0.06
C	-0.04	-0.04
D	0.02	0.01
E	-0.08	-0.08[a]

a = $p < 0.05$

Table 6

Correlation between decision style and
managerial behaviour characteristics

n=212

| Decision style | Managerial behaviour characteristics | | | | | |
| | i and ii Employee orientation | | iii and iv Task orientation | | i, ii, iii, iv | |
	Pearson	Kendall	Pearson	Kendall	Pearson	Kendall
A	-0.10	-0.08[a]	-0.01	-0.00	-0.07	-0.05
B	0.08	0.05	0.04	-0.00	0.07	0.04
C	-0.06	-0.05	-0.03	-0.04	-0.06	-0.04
D	0.06	0.02	-0.01	-0.00	0.03	0.01
E	0.12[a]	0.05	0.05	0.06	0.09	0.06

a = p $<$ 0.05

Table 7

Correlation between decision style
and LPS

n=212

Decision style	LPS	
	Pearson	Kendall
A	-0.12^{a}	-0.06
B	-0.01	-0.01
C	0.06	0.03
D	0.03	0.04
E	0.13^{b}	0.07

a = $p < 0.05$
b = $p < 0.025$

Table 8

Correlation between LPS and
managerial behaviour characteristics

n=212

Opinion of least preferred sub-ordinate	Managerial behaviour characteristics			
	Task orientation		Employee orientation	
	Pearson	Kendall	Pearson	Kendall
LPS	0.19^{c}	0.11^{c}	0.08	0.05

c = $p < 0.01$

272

Table 9

Correlation between decision style, with regard to
decision type, and span of control

n=212

Span of control

Decisions

Decision style	Aggregate		Programmed		Non-programmed		Personnel		Task	
	Pear-son	Ken-dall	Pear-son	Ken-dall	Pear-son	Ken-dall	Pear-son	Ken-dall	Pear-son	Ken-dall
A	0.16^c	0.11^c	0.04	0.03	0.21^d	0.15^d	0.35^d	0.26^d	0.07	0.05
B	-0.04	-0.02	-0.06	-0.05	-0.01	0.01	-0.03	-0.02	-0.03	-0.01
C	-0.08	-0.08^a	-0.01	-0.03	-0.09	-0.06	-0.11^a	-0.09^b	-0.05	-0.05
D	-0.11^a	-0.10^b	0.05	0.01	-0.14^b	-0.12^c	-0.17^c	-0.14^c	-0.02	-0.06
E	-0.02	-0.01	-0.01	-0.01	-0.01	0.03	-0.05	-0.02	0.01	0.01

a = p $<$ 0.05
b = p $<$ 0.025
c = p $<$ 0.01
d = p $<$ 0.001

273

Table 10

Correlation between decision style
and both company and finance
function size

n=212

Decision style	Size			
	Company		Finance function	
	Pearson	Kendall	Pearson	Kendall
A	-0.13^b	-0.10^b	-0.15^b	-0.12^c
B	-0.10	-0.06	-0.05	-0.01
C	0.08	0.06	0.06	0.04
D	0.12^a	0.09^b	0.12^a	0.10^b
E	0.17^c	0.13^c	0.15^b	0.11^c

a = p $<$ 0.05
b = p $<$ 0.025
c = p $<$ 0.01

Table 11

Correlation between decision style
and organisational level

n=212

Decision style	Level	
	Pearson	Kendall
A	-0.12^a	-0.09^b
B	0.05	0.00
C	0.01	0.01
D	0.10	0.04
E	0.03	0.05

a = p $<$ 0.05
b = p $<$ 0.025

274

Appendix E

For the attention: Financial Controller
                    or
                    Chief Accountant

> Department of Business Studies
>   and Finance,
> Birmingham Polytechnic,
> Aston Street,
> Birmingham. B4 7HA.
> (Tel: 021 359 6851)

> July 1975

Dear Sir,

You may recall receiving a questionnaire towards the end of June which posed a number of questions about the nature and context of the job of the Financial Controller or Chief Accountant. Perhaps for one reason or another you felt unable to participate in the study at the time.

However, if you are still interested in the survey, I sincerely seek your cooperation and participation by sending the completed questionnaire to me as soon as possible. As a teacher of undergraduate students planning to pursue a career in accountancy, I believe the information you provide, which will be treated in the strictest confidence, will have real educational value and ultimately I hope some practical ramifications.

> Yours faithfully,

> Eugene F. McKenna

275

Appendix F

Name: ....

Title: ....

Company:........................

1. What differences do you see between the job of the Financial Controller and that of the Chief Accountant?

2. Is it likely with an increase in the number of years spent in one job, such as yours, for one to change or modify the approach to making decisions or managing subordinates?

3. Could you briefly describe your style of management (as explained in Questionnaire) when a decision for which you bear ultimate responsibility is

    1) Clearcut or routine   e.g., taking action on customers' arrears

2) Complex or uncertain,   e.g., setting guidelines
   or non routine   for investigation of
                                   variances, promoting
                                   staff.

4. When a section is highly specialised (e.g., credit
   control, budgeting) and is headed by a member of
   your staff who is well qualified in that area, how
   do you go about managing in such circumstances?

5. Would you adopt a similar style of management
   towards a section not highly specialised with a
   less qualified person in charge?

   If no, why not?

6. What sort of qualities or skills do you look for in a subordinate before you are prepared to involve him, through consultation, participation, or delegation, in decisions for which you bear responsibility?

7. Some people maintain that if a job in a company offers one enough power, influence with and respect from both a superior and subordinate, then this could have a favourable influence on ones choice of management style.

   If the above description fits your job, how does it affect your management style?

   If it does not, how do you see your job and briefly describe your management style?

8. Have you ever had the experience of your style of management changing as the number of subordinates reporting to you increased or decreased.

   If so, in what way did it change?

   If you had such an experience and your style remained constant, to what do you attribute this uniformity of style?

9. Can you envisage a situation where a variation in the size of the finance function or the size of the company leads to a change in the style of management of the Financial Controller or Chief Accountant?

   If yes, how can you explain it?

   If no, why should the style remain the same in such circumstances?

10. How restricted is your authority in your present position when it comes to getting production, personnel or marketing managers to do what you think is financially desirable?

Bibliography

Aiken, M. and Hage, J., Organisational Alienation: a comparative analysis, <u>American Sociological Review</u>, 31, 1966, pp.497-507.

Andrews, F.M. and Farris, G.F., Supervisory Practices and Innovation in Scientific Teams, <u>Personnel Psychology</u>, vol.20, no.4, 1967, pp.497-515.

Argyle, M, Gardner, G. and Cioffi, F., Supervisory Methods related to Productivity, Absenteeism and Labour Turnover, <u>Human Relations</u>, XI, 1958, pp.23-40.

Argyris, C., Human Problems with Budgets, <u>Harvard Business Review</u>, January-February, 1953, pp.97-110.

Argyris, C., The Individual and Organisations: An Empirical Test, <u>Administrative Science Quarterly</u>, 4(2), 1959, pp.145-67, 1959.

Argyris, C., <u>Integrating the Individual and the Organisation</u>, Wiley, New York 1964.

Argyris, C., Personality and Organisation Theory Revisited, <u>Administrative Science Quarterly</u>, vol.18, no.2, 1973, pp.141-67.

Barden, V., Yes, the Accountants are Different (Report of a Study at the Ashridge Management College), <u>Accountancy Age</u>, 16 October 1970, p.15.

Barnowe, J.T., Leadership and Performance Outcomes in Research Organisations: The Supervisor of Scientists as a Source of Assistance, <u>Organisational Behaviour and Human Performance</u>, vol.14, no.2, 1975, pp.264-80.

Bass, B.M., Authoritarianism or Acquiesence, <u>Journal of Abnormal and Social Psychology</u>, 51, 1955, pp.616-23.

Bass, B.M., <u>Leadership, Psychology and Organisational Behaviour</u>, Harper, New York 1960.

Bass, B.M., Some Effects on a Group of Whether and When the Head Reveals his Opinion, <u>Organisational Behaviour and Human Performance</u>, vol.2, no.4, 1967, pp.375-82.

Bass, B.M. and Leavitt, H., Some Experiments in Planning and Operating, Management Science, no.4, 1963, pp.574-85.

Bass, B.M., Valenzi, E.R., Farrow, D.L. and Soloman, R.J., Management Styles Associated with Organisational, Task, Personal and Interpersonal Contingencies, Journal of Applied Psychology, vol.60, no.6, 1975, pp.720-9.

Baumgartel, H., Leadership Style as a Variable in Research Administration, Administrative Science Quarterly, 2, 1957, pp.344-60.

Bavelas, A., Leadership: Man and Function, Administrative Science Quarterly, 4, 1960, pp.491-8.

Bavelas, A. and Strauss, G., Group Dynamics and Intergroup Relations, in W.G. Bennis et al. (eds), The Planning of Change, pp.587-91, Holt, New York 1961.

Bennis, W., Changing Organisations, McGraw-Hill, New York 1966.

Beresford Dew, R. and Gee, K.P., Management Control and Information, Macmillan, London 1973.

Blake, R. and Mouton, J., Group Dynamics: Key to Decision-Making, Gulf Publishing Co., Houston 1961.

Blake R. and Mouton, J., The Managerial Grid, Gulf Publishing Co., Houston 1964.

Blankenship, L.V. and Miles, R.E., Organisation Structure and Managerial Decision Behaviour, Administrative Science Quarterly, 13, 1968, pp.106-20.

Blau, P.M. and Scott, W.G., Formal Organisations: A Comparative Approach, Routledge and Kegan Paul, London 1963.

Bobbitt, H.R. Jr., Breinholt, R.H., Doktor, R.H. and McNaul, J.P., Organisational Behaviour: Understanding and Prediction , Prentice-Hall, Englewood Cliffs 1974.

Bowers, D.G. and Seashore, S.E., Predicting Organisational Effectiveness with a Four-Factor Theory of Leadership, Administrative Science Quarterly, vol.11, no.11, 1966, pp.238-63.

Brayfield, A.H. and Crockett, W.H., Employee Attitudes and Employee Performance, Psychological Bulletin, vol.52, no.5, 1955, pp.396-424.

Brown, M.L., The Use of a Postcard Query in Mail Surveys, Public Opinion Quarterly, vol.29, 1965 pp.636-7.

Brummet, R.L., Pyle, W.C. and Flamholtz, E.G., Human Resource Measurement - A Challenge for Accountants, The Accounting Review, xliii, 1968, pp.217-24.

Burns, T., The Direction of Activity and Communication in a Departmental Executive Group: A Quantitative Study in a British Engineering Factory with a Self-recording Technique, Human Relations, 7, 1954, pp.73-97.

Burns, T. and Stalker, M., The Management of Innovation, Tavistock, London 1961.

Cannel, C.F. and Fowler, F.J., Comparison of a Self-enumerative Procedure and a Personal Interview: A validity study, Public Opinion Quarterly, 27, 1963, pp.250-64.

Caplan, E.H., Management Accounting and Behavioural Science, Addison-Wesley, Reading 1971.

Cartwright, A. and Ward, A.W.M., Variations in General Practitioners' Response to Postal Questionnaires, British Journal of Preventative and Social Medicine, 22, 1968, pp.199-205.

Chandler, A., Strategy and Structure, Doubleday, New York 1966.

Child, J., Organisation Structure, Environment and Performance: The Role of Strategic Choice, Sociology, vol.6, no.1, 1972, pp.1-22.

Child, J., Predicting and Understanding Organisation Structure, Administrative Science Quarterly, vol.18, no.2, 1973, pp.168-85.

Child, I.L. and Whiting, J.W.M., Determinants of Level of Aspiration: Evidence from Everyday Life, in Brand (ed.), The Study of Personality, Wiley, New York 1954.

Coch, L. and French, J.R.P., Overcoming Resistance to Change, Human Relations, 1, 1948, pp.512-32.

Cotgrove, S. and Box, S., Science, Industry and Society: Studies in the Sociology of Science, Allen and Unwin, London 1970.

Craft, J.A. and Birnberg, J.G., Human Resource Accounting: Perspective and Prospects, Industrial Relations, vol.15, no.1, 1976, pp.2-12.

Cumming, E., Dean, L.R. and Newell, D., What is Morale? A Case History of a Validity Problem, Human Organisation, vol.17, no.2, 1958, pp.3-8.

Cyert, R.M., Dill, W.R. and March, J.G., The Role of Expectations in Business Decision Making, in L.A. Welsch and R.M. Cyert (eds), Management Decision Making, Penguin, London 1970(a).

Cyert, R.M., Simon, H.A. and Trow, D.B., Observation of a Business Decision, in L.A. Welsch and R.M. Cyert (eds), Management Decision Making, Penguin, London 1970(b).

Dahl, R.A., The Concept of Power, Behavioural Science, 2, 1957, pp.201-18.

Dale, E., Planning and Developing the Company Organisation Structure, American Management Association Research Report, no.20, New York 1952.

Dalton, M., Conflicts between Staff and Line Managerial Officers, American Sociological Review, vol.15, no.3, 1950, pp.342-51.

Dauten, C.A., The Necessary Ingredients of a Theory of Business Finance, The Journal of Finance, vol.X, no.2, 1955, pp.107-20.

Davis, K., Management Communication and the Grapevine, Harvard Business Review, 31(5), 1953, pp.43-9.

Day, R.C. and Hamblin, R.L., Some Effects of Close and Punitive Styles of Supervision, American Journal of Sociology, LXIX, 1964, pp.499-510.

Dill, W.R., Environment as an Influence on Managerial Autonomy, Administrative Science Quarterly, 2, 1958, pp.409-43.

Drucker, P., The Practice of Management, Harper, New York 1954.

Dufty, N.F. and Taylor, P.M., The Implementation of a Decision, in L.A. Welsch and R.M. Cyert (eds), Management Decision Making, Penguin, London 1970.

Dunbar, R.L.M., Budgeting for Control, Administrative Science Quarterly, vol. 16, 1971, pp.88-96.

Durand, D.E. and Nord, W.R., Perceived Leader Behaviour as a Function of Personality Characteristics of Supervisors and Subordinates, Academy of Management Journal, 19, 1976, pp.427-38.

Elgin, R., Management Accounting in Practice, Business, November 1965, pp.76-80.

Emery, F.E. and Trist, E.L., The Causal Texture of
  Organisational Environments, Human Relations, 18,
  1965, pp.21-31.
Englander, M.E., A Psychological Analysis of Vocation-
  al Choice - Teaching, Journal of Counseling Psychol-
  ogy, vol.7, no.4, 1960, pp.257-64.
Entwisle, D.R. and Walton, J., Observations on the
  Span of Control, Administrative Science Quarterly,
  vol.5, no.4, 1961, pp.522-33.
Etzioni, A., A Comparative Analysis of Complex Organ-
  isations, Free Press, New York 1961.
Ferber, R., The Problem of Bias in Mail Returns: A
  Solution, Public Opinion Quarterly, 12, 1948,
  pp.669-76.
Ferris, A.L., A Note on Stimulating Response to
  Questionnaires, American Sociological Review, 16,
  1951, pp.247-9.
Fiedler, F., A Theory of Leadership Effectiveness,
  McGraw-Hill, New York 1967.
Fiedler, F., Validation and Extension of the Contingen-
  cy Model of Leadership Effectiveness: A review of
  empirical findings, Psychological Bulletin, 76,
  1971(a), pp.128-48.
Fiedler, F., Note on the Methodology of the Graen,
  Alvares and Orris studies testing the Contingency
  Model, Journal of Applied Psychology, 55, 1971(b),
  pp.202-4.
Fiedler, F., Personality, Motivational Systems and
  the Behaviour of High and Low LPC Persons, Human
  Relations, 25, 1972(a), pp.391-412.
Fiedler, F., The Effects of Leadership Training and
  Experience: A Contingency Model Interpretation,
  Administrative Science Quarterly, vol.17, 1972(b),
  pp.453-70.
Firnberg, D., Can the Accountant Survive? Accountancy,
  vol.83, no.954, February 1973, pp.24-7.
Fisch, G.G., Line/Staff is Obsolete, Harvard Business
  Review, 39(5), 1961, pp.67-79.
Fisch, G.G., Stretching the Span of Management,
  Harvard Business Review, 41(5), 1963, pp.74-85.
Fleishman, E.A., The Measurement of Leadership Atti-
  tudes in Industry, Journal of Applied Psychology,
  vol.37, no.3, 1953, pp.153-8.

Fleishman, E.A. and Harris, E.F., Patterns of Leadership Behaviour Related to Employee Grievances and Turnover, Personnel Psychology, 15, 1962, pp.43-56.

Fleishman, E.A., Harris, E.F. and Burtt, H.E., Leadership and Supervision in Industry, Columbus: Bureau of Educational Research, The Ohio State University, 1955.

Fletcher, C., Managers' Stress at Work, (Unpublished PhD Thesis), University of Aston in Birmingham, 1972.

French, J.R.P., Israel, J. and As, D., An Experiment on Participation in a Norwegian Factory, Human Relations, 13, 1960, pp.3-19.

French, J.R.P. and Snyder, R., Leadership and Interpersonal Power, in D. Cartwright (ed.), Studies in Social Power, pp.118-49, Ann Arbor: University of Michigan, Institute for Social Research, 1959.

Fromm, E., Fear of Freedom, Routledge and Kegan Paul, London 1942.

Galbraith, J. and Cummings, L.L., An Empirical Investigation of the Motivational Determinants of Task Performance: Interactive effects between instrumentality-valence and motivation ability, Organisational Behaviour and Human Performance, 2, 1967, pp.237-57.

Gibson, J., Management by Objectives, Management Accounting, May 1970, pp.173-7.

Gomberg, W., The Trouble with Democratic Management, Trans-Action, vol.3, 5, 1966, pp.30-5.

Gordon, G. and Becker, S., Organisational Size and Managerial Succession: A re-examination, American Journal of Sociology, 70, 1964, pp.215-23.

Gouldner, A.W., Organisational Analysis, in R.K. Merton et al. (eds), Sociology Today, Mayflower, London 1959.

Graen, G., Alvares, K., Orris, J.B. and Martella, J.A., Contingency Model of Leadership Effectiveness - antecedent and evidential results, Psychological Bulletin, 74, 1970, pp.285-96.

Graen, G., Orris, J.B. and Alvares, K.M., Contingency Model of Leadership Effectiveness: some experimental results, Journal of Applied Psychology, 55, 1971, pp.196-201.

Graham, W.K., Description of Leader Behaviour and Evaluation of Leaders as a Function of LPC, Personnel Psychology, 21, 1968, pp.457-64.

Gray, P.G., A sample Survey with both a Postal and an Interview Stage, Applied Statistics, 6, 1957, pp.139-53.

Greenwood, J.M. and McNamara, W.J., Leadership Styles of Structure and Consideration and Managerial Effectiveness, Personnel Psychology, 22, 1969, pp.141-52.

Grusky, O., Corporate Size, Bureaucratisation and Managerial Succession, American Journal of Sociology, 67, 1961, pp.261-9.

Gullahorn, J. and Gullahorn, J., An Investigation of the Effects of Three Factors on Response to Mail Questionnaires, Public Opinion Quarterly, 27, 1963, pp.294-6.

Hage, J. and Aiken, M., Relationship of Centralisation to other Structural Properties, Administrative Science Quarterly, vol.12, 1967, pp.77-92.

Haire, M., Ghiselli, E.E. and Porter, L.W., Cultural Patterns in the Role of the Manager, Industrial Relations, 2, 1963, pp.95-117.

Hall, R.H., Professionalisation and Bureaucratisation, American Sociological Review, 33, no.1, 1968, pp.92-104.

Halpin, A.W. and Winer, J., A Factorial Study of the Leader Behaviour Description, in Leader Behaviour: Its description and measurement, in R.M. Stogdill and A.E. Coons (eds), Research Monograph no.88, pp.39-51, Bureau of Business Research, Ohio State University, Columbus Ohio 1957.

Hamblin, R.L., Leadership and Crises, Sociometry, 22, 1958, pp.322-35.

Hartmann, H., Managers and Entrepreneurs: A useful distinction, Administrative Science Quarterly, 1959, pp.429-51.

Hastings, A., The Chartered Accountant in Industry, A Study of Values, (Unpublished PhD Thesis), University of Birmingham, 1968.

Hekimian, J.J. and Jones, C.H., Put People on your Balance Sheet, Harvard Business Review, 45(1), January-February 1967, pp.105-13.

Heller, F.A., Managerial Decision-making: A Study of Leadership Styles and Power-sharing among Senior Managers, Tavistock, London 1971.

Heller, F.A. and Porter, L.W., Perceptions of Managerial Needs and Skills in two National Samples, Occupational Psychology, vol.40, no.1 and 2, 1966, pp.1-13.

Heller, F.A. and Yukl, G., Participation, Managerial Decision-making and Situational Variables, Organisational Behaviour and Human Performance, vol.4, no.3, 1969, pp.227-41.

Hemphill, J.K., Relation between the Size of the Group and the Behaviour of 'Superior' Leaders, Journal of Social Psychology, 32, 1950, pp.11-32.

Hemphill, J.K., Job Descriptions for Executives, Harvard Business Review, XXXVII, 1959, pp.56-67.

Hemphill, J.K., Why People Attempt to Lead, in L. Petrullo and B. Bass (eds), Leadership and Interpersonal Behaviour, pp.201-15, Holt, Rinehart and Winston, New York 1961.

Henning, D.A. and Moseley, R.L., Authority Role of a Functional Manager: The Controller, Administrative Science Quarterly, vol.15, no.4, 1970, pp.482-9.

Herzberg, F., Work and the Nature of Man, Staples Press, London 1966.

Hickson, D.J., A Convergence in Organisation Theory, Administrative Science Quarterly, vol.2, no.2, 1966, pp.224-37.

Hill, W.A., Leadership Style: Rigid or Flexible? Organisational Behaviour and Human Performance, 9, 1973, pp.35-47.

Hofstede, G.H., The Game of Budget Control, Tavistock, London 1968.

Hollander, E.P. and Julian, J.W., Studies in Leader Legitimacy, Influence and Innovation, in Berkowitz (ed.), Advances in Experimental Social Psychology, vol.5, pp.33-69, Academic Press, New York 1970.

Hopwood, A., An Accounting System and Managerial Behaviour, Saxon House, Farnborough 1973.

Horne, J.H. and Lupton, T., The Work Activities of Middle Managers, Journal of Management Studies, 2, 1965, pp.14-33.

House, R.J., A Path Goal Theory of Leader Effectiveness, Administrative Science Quarterly, 16, 1971,
pp.321-38.

Hughes, P.J. and Barclay, S.J., Wharton - Life at an
American Graduate Business School, Accountancy,
March 1967, pp.172-4.

Hunt, J.G., Fiedler's Leadership Contingency Model:
An empirical test in three organisations, Organisational Behaviour and Human Performance, 2, 1967,
pp.290-308.

Hyman, R., The Nature of Psychological Inquiry,
Prentice-Hall, Englewood Cliffs 1964.

Irvine, M., Why Hunch may help the Right Decision,
The Financial Times, 16 April 1974, p.11.

Jago, A.G. and Vroom, V.H., Hierarchical Level and
Leadership Style, Organisational Behaviour and
Human Performance, 18, 1977, pp.131-45.

Janowitz, M., Changing Patterns of Organisational
Authority: the military establishment, Administrative Science Quarterly, 3, 1959, pp.473-93.

Kanuk, L. and Berenson, C., Mail Surveys and Response
Rates: A literature review, Journal of Marketing
Research, vol.XII, 1975, pp.440-53.

Katz, D. and Kahn, R., Leadership Practices in Relation
to Productivity and Morale, in D. Cartwright and
A. Zander (eds), Group Dynamics - Research and
Theory, Harper, New York 1960.

Katz, D. and Kahn, R., The Social Psychology of Organisations, Wiley, New York 1966.

Katz, D., Maccoby, N., Gurin, G. and Floor, L.G.,
Productivity, Supervision and Morale among Railroad
Workers, Ann Arbor, Institute for Social Research,
1951.

Kavanagh, M.J., Leader Behaviour as a Function of
Subordinate Competence and Task Complexity,
Administrative Science Quarterly, 17, 1972,
pp.591-600.

Kavanagh, M.J., Expected Supervisory Behaviour, Interpersonal Trust and Environmental Preferences. Some
Relationships based on a Dyadic Model of Leadership,
Organisational Behaviour and Human Performance, no.1,
vol.13, 1975, pp.17-30.

Kawash, M.B. and Aleamoni, L.M., Effect of Personal Signature on the Initial Rate of Return of a Mailed Questionnaire, Journal of Applied Psychology, 55, 1971, pp.589-92.

Kemsley, W.F.F., Some Technical Aspects of a Postal Survey into Professional Earnings, Applied Statistics, 11, 1962, pp.93-105.

Kernan, J.B., Are Bulk-Rate Occupants really Unresponsive? Public Opinion Quarterly, 35, 1971, pp.420-24.

Kerr, S., Schriesheim, C.A., Murphy, C.J. and Stogdill, R.M., Toward a Contingency Theory of Leadership based upon Consideration and Initiating Structure Literature, Organisational Behaviour and Human Performance, 12, 1974, pp.62-82.

Kimball, A.E., Increasing the Rate of Return in Mail Surveys, Journal of Marketing, 25, 1961, pp.63-5.

Korten, D.C., Situational Determinants of Leadership Structure, in D. Cartwright and A. Zander (eds), Group Dynamics - Research and Theory, Tavistock, London 1968.

Lancashire, R. and Cohen, B., Final Report on the First of Two Studies of Vocational Guidance undertaken for the Clement Wilson Foundation Ltd. National Institute of Industrial Psychology, April 1970.

Lansley, P., Sadler, P.J. and Webb, T.D., Organisation Structure, Management Style and Company Performance, OMEGA, vol.2, no.4, 1974, pp.467-85.

Lawrence, P.R. and Lorsch, J.W., Organisation and Environment: Managing Differentiation and Integration, Harvard Business School, Boston 1967.

Lazarus, R.S., Personality, Prentice-Hall, Englewood Cliffs 1971.

Leavitt, H.J., Unhuman Organisation, Harvard Business Review, July-August 1962, pp.90-8.

Leavitt, H.J., Applied Organisational Change in Industry: Structural, Technological and Humanistic Approaches, in J.G. March (ed.), Handbook of Organisations, pp.1152-3, Rand McNally, Chicago 1965.

Lee, R.W., Top Managements Challenge to the Accountant, Management Accounting, April 1968, pp.153-6.

Levesque, J.R., The Changing Role of the Chief Financial Officer, C.A. Magazine, vol.108, no.2, 1976, pp.40-4.

Levinson, D.J., Role, Personality and Social Structure in the Organisation Setting, Journal of Abnormal and Social Psychology, vol.58, no.2, 1959, pp.170-80.

Lewin, K., Group Decision and Social Change in E.E. Maccoby et al. (eds), Readings in Social Psychology, third edition, pp.197-211, Holt, New York 1968.

Likert, R., New Patterns of Management, McGraw-Hill, New York 1961.

Likert, R., The Human Organisation, McGraw-Hill, New York 1967.

Linsky, A.S., A Factorial Experiment in Inducing Responses to a Mail Questionnaire, Sociology and Social Research, vol.49, 1965, pp.183-9.

Linsky, A.S., Stimulating Responses to Mail Questionnaires: A Review, Public Opinion Quarterly, vol.XXXIX, no.1, 1975, pp.82-101.

Lippit, R. and White, R., An Experimental Study of Leadership and Group Life, in E.E. Maccoby et al. (eds), Readings in Social Psychology, Holt, New York 1958.

Lippit, R. and White, R., Leader Behaviour and Member Reaction in three Social Climates in D. Cartwright and A. Zander (eds), Group Dynamics - Research and Theory, Tavistock, London 1968.

Litchfield, E.H., Notes on a General Theory of Administration, Administrative Science Quarterly, vol.1, no.1, 1956, pp.3-29.

Litzinger, W.D., Entrepreneurial Prototype in Bank Management: A comparative study of Branch Bank Managers, Academy of Management Journal, vol.6, no.1, 1963, pp.36-45.

Locke, E.A., Toward a Theory of Task Motivation and Incentives, Organisational Behaviour and Human Performance, 3, 1968, pp.157-89.

Logan, H.H., Line and Staff: An Obsolete Concept, Personnel, 43, 1966, pp.26-33.

Lowe, E.A., Accounting Education and the Needs of Management, The Accountants Journal, October 1964, pp. 385-7.

Lowe, E.A. and Shaw, R.W., An Analysis of Managerial
    Biasing: Evidence from a Company's Budgeting Pro-
    cess, Journal of Management Studies, V, October
    1968, pp.304-15.
Lowin, A., Participative Decision Making: A model,
    literature critique and prescription for research,
    Organisational Behaviour and Human Performance, 3,
    no.1, 1968, pp.68-106.
Lowin, A. and Craig, J.R., The Influence of Level of
    Performance on Managerial Style: An experimental
    object-lesson in the ambiguity of correlational
    data, Organisational Behaviour and Human Perfor-
    mance, 3, 1968, pp.440-58.
McCurdy, H.G. and Eber, H.W., Democratic versus
    Authoritarian: A further investigation of group
    problem-solving, Journal of Personality, XXII,
    1953, pp.258-69.
McDonagh, E.C. and Rosenblum, A.L., A Comparison of
    Mailed Questionnaires and Subsequent Structured
    Interviews, Public Opinion Quarterly, vol.29,
    1965, pp.131-36.
McGee, H.M., Measurement of Authoritarianism and its
    Relation to Teacher Classroom Behaviour, Genetic
    Psychological Monograph, LII, 1955, pp.89-146.
McGregor, D., The Human Side of Enterprise, McGraw-
    Hill, New York 1960.
McGregor D., The Professional Manager, McGraw-Hill,
    New York 1967.
Machlup, F., Marginal Analysis and Empirical Research,
    The American Economic Review, vol.XXXV, no.4, 1946,
    pp.519-54.
McKenna, E.F., Leadership Styles in Industry,
    (Unpublished MSc Thesis), University of Lancaster,
    1972.
McMahon, J.T., The Contingency Theory: Logic and
    Method Revisited, Personnel Psychology, 25, 1972,
    pp.697-710.
McMurry, R.N., The Case for Benevolent Autocracy,
    Harvard Business Review, vol.36, no.1, 1958,
    pp.82-90.
McRae, T., The Behavioural Critique of Accounting,
    Accounting and Business Research, no.2, Spring 1971,
    pp.83-92.

Mahoney, T.A., Jerdee, T.H. and Carroll, S.J., The Job(s) of Management, Industrial Relations, IV, 1965, pp.97-110.

Maier, N.R.F., Psychology in Industry, Houghton Mifflin, Boston 1965.

March, J.C. and Simon, H.A., Organisations, Wiley, New York 1958.

Martin, N.H., The Levels of Management and their Mental Demands, in L.W. Warner and N.H. Martin (eds), Industrial Man - Businessmen and Business Organisations, pp.276-94, Harper, New York 1959.

Maslow, A.H., Motivation and Personality, Harper, New York 1954.

Maslow, A.H., Eupsychian Management, Dorsey, Homewood 1965.

Mechanic, D., Sources of Power of Lower Participants in Complex Organisations, Administrative Science Quarterly, 7, 1962, pp.349-64.

Merton, R.K., The Unanticipated Consequences of Purposive Sociological Action, American Sociological Review, 1, 1936, pp.894-904.

Merton, R.K., Social Theory and Social Structure, Free Press, Chicago 1949.

Merton, R.K., Gray, A.P., Hockey, B. and Selvin, H.C., Reader in Bureaucracy, Free Press, Glencoe 1957.

Michels, R., Political Parties, Free Press, Chicago 1949.

Miles, R.E., Conflicting Elements in Managerial Ideologies, Industrial Relations, 4, 1964, pp.77-91.

Miles, R.E., Human Relations or Human Resources? Harvard Business Review, 43, 1965, pp.148-63.

Miller, S., Experimental Design and Statistics, Methuen, London 1975.

Millerson, G., The Qualifying Associations: A Study in Professionalisation, Routledge and Kegan Paul, London 1964.

Misnmi, J. and Seki, F., Effects of Achievement Motivation on the Effectiveness of Leadership Patterns, Administrative Science Quarterly, 16, 1971, pp.51-9.

Mitchell, T.R., Biglan, A., Oncken, G.R. and Fiedler, F., The Contingency Model: Criticisms and Suggestions, Academy of Management Journal, vol.13, no.3, 1970, pp.253-67.

Morse, N.C. and Reimer, E., The Experimental Change
of a Major Organisational Variable, Journal of
Abnormal and Social Psychology, LI, 1956,
pp.120-9.

Moser, C.A. and Kalton, C., Survey Methods in Social
Investigation, Heinemann, London 1971.

Mulder, M., Power Equalisation through Participation,
Administrative Science Quarterly, vol.16, no.1,
1971, pp.31-8.

Mulder, M. and Stemerding, A., Threat, Attraction to
Group and Strong Leadership: A Laboratory Experiment in a Natural Setting, Human Relations, 16,
1963, pp.317-34.

Nealey, S.M. and Fiedler, F.E., Leadership Functions
of Middle Managers, Psychological Bulletin, vol.70,
no.5, 1968, pp.313-29.

Obradovic, J., Workers Participation: Who Participates?
Industrial Relations, vol.14, no.1, 1975, pp.32-44.

Ognibene, P., Traits Affecting Questionnaire Response,
Journal of Advertising Research, 10, 1970, pp.18-20.

Oppenheim, A.N., Questionnaire Design and Attitude
Measurement, Heinemann, London 1972.

Osgood, C.E., Suci, G.J. and Tannenbaum, P.H., The
Measurement of Meaning, University of Illinois
Press, Urbana, Ill, 1957.

Parsons, Talcott, Suggestions for a Sociological
Approach to the Theory of Organisations - I and II,
Administrative Science Quarterly, 1, 1956, pp.63-85;
224-39.

Payne, R.L., Pheysey, D.C. and Pugh, D.S., Organisation Structure, Organisational Climate and Group
Structure: An Exploratory Study of their Relationships in Two Manufacturing Companies, Occupational
Psychology, 45, 1971, pp.45-55.

Pellegrin, R. and Coates, C., Executive and Supervisors - Contrasting Definitions of Career Success,
Administrative Science Quarterly, 1, 1957,
pp.506-17.

Pelz, D.C., Influence: A Key to effective Leadership
in the First-line Supervisor, in R.A. Sutermeister
(ed.), People and Productivity, McGraw-Hill, 1963.

Pelz, D.C. and Andrews, F.M., Scientists in Organisations: Productive Climates for Research and
Development, Wiley, New York 1966.

Perrin, J.R., The Graduate Entrant, Accountancy,
vol.LXXXII, no.938, October 1971, pp.554-62.

Plog, S.C., Explanations for a High Return Rate on a
Mail Questionnaire, Public Opinion Quarterly, vol.27,
no.2, 1963, pp.297-8.

Porter, L.W., A Study of Perceived Job Satisfaction
in Bottom and Middle Management Jobs, Journal of
Applied Psychology, 45, 1961, pp.1-10.

Porter, L.W., Job Attitudes in Management I, Perceived Deficiencies in Need Fulfilment as a
Function of Job Level, Journal of Applied Psychology, 46, 1962, pp.375-84.

Porter, L.W., Where is the Organisation Man? Harvard
Business Review, 41(6), 1963(a), pp.53-61.

Porter, L.W., Job Attitudes in Management IV, Per-
ceived Deficiencies in Need Fulfilment as a
Function of Size of Company, Journal of Applied
Psychology, 47, 1963(b), pp.386-97.

Porter, L.W., Job Attitudes in Management IV, Per-
ceived Deficiencies in Need Fulfilment as a
Function of Line vs Staff Type Job, Journal of
Applied Psychology, 47, 1963(c), pp.267-75.

Porter, L.W. and Ghiselli, E.E., The Self-perceptions
of Top and Middle Management Personnel, Personnel
Psychology, 10, 1957, pp.397-406.

Porter, L.W. and Henry, M.M., Job Attitudes in Management V, Perceptions of the Importance of Certain
Personality Traits as a Function of Job Level,
Journal of Applied Psychology, vol.48, no.1,
1964(a), pp.31-6.

Porter, L.W. and Henry, M.M., Job Attitudes in Management VI, Perceptions of the Importance of Certain
Personality Traits as a Function of Line vs Staff
Type of Job, Journal of Applied Psychology, vol.48,
no.5, 1964(b), pp.305-9.

Porter, L.W. and Lawler, III, E.E., Properties of
Organisation Structure in Relation to Job Attitudes
and Job Behaviour, Psychological Bulletin, vol.64,
no.1, 1965, pp.23-51.

Pugh, D.S., Hickson, D.J., Hinings, C.R. and Turner, C., Dimensions of Organisation Structure, Administrative Science Quarterly, vol.13, no.1, 1968, pp.65-105.

Pugh, D.S., Hickson, D.J., Hinings, C.R. and Turner, C., The Context of Organisation Structures, Administrative Science Quarterly, vol.14, no.1, 1969, pp.91-114.

Rhode, J.G., Lawler, III, E.E. and Sundem, G.L., Human Resource Accounting: A Critical Assessment, Industrial Relations, vol.15, no.1, 1976, pp.13-25.

Rice, R.W. and Chemers, M.N., Personality and Situational Determinants of Leaders' Behaviour, Journal of Applied Psychology, 60, 1975, pp.20-7.

Ritchie, J.B. and Miles, R.E., An Analysis of Quantity and Quality of Participation as Mediating Variables in the Participative Decision-Making Process, Personnel Psychology, vol.23, no.2, 1970, pp.347-60.

Robson, A.P., Eliminating Weakness in Management Accounting, Management Accounting, June 1965, pp.200-5.

Roeher, G.A., Effective Techniques in Increasing Response to Mailed Questionnaires, Public Opinion Quarterly, 27, no.2, 1963, pp.299-302.

Rogers, C.R., Client-Centred Therapy, Houghton Mifflin, Boston 1951.

Rosen, N., Anonymity and Attitude Measurement, Public Opinion Quarterly, 24, 1960, pp.675-80.

Rosen, H., Desirable Attributes of Work: Four levels of Management describe their Job Environments, Journal of Applied Psychology, 45, 1961, pp.156-60.

Rubin, I.M. and Goldman, M., An Open System Model of Leadership Performance, Organisational Behaviour and Human Performance, 3, 1968, pp.143-156.

Sales, S.M., Supervisory Style and Productivity: Review and Theory, Personnel Psychology, vol.19, no.3, 1966, p.275.

Sample, J.A. and Wilson, T.R., Leader Behaviour, Group Productivity and Rating of Least Preferred Co-worker, Journal of Personality and Social Psychology, 1, 1965, pp.266-70.

Santocki, J., Management Audit - A Survey and Critical Appraisal, (Unpublished MPhil Thesis), CNAA, 1975.

Schiff, M. and Lewin, A.Y., Impact of People on
   Budgets, The Accounting Review, XLV, April 1970,
   pp.259-68.
Scott, C., Research on Mail Surveys, Journal of the
   Royal Statistical Society, XXIV, Series A, 1961,
   pp.143-205.
Scott, W.R., Professionals in Bureaucracies - Areas of
   Conflict, in H.M. Vollmer and D.L. Mills (eds),
   Professionalisation, pp.265-75, Prentice-Hall,
   Englewood Cliffs 1966.
Selznick, P., Foundations of the Theory of Organisa-
   tions, American Sociological Review, vol.13, 1948,
   pp.23-35.
Shaw, M.E., A Comparison of Two Types of Leadership
   in various Communication Nets, Journal of Abnormal
   and Social Psychology, L, 1955, pp.127-34.
Shaw, M.E. and Blum, J.M., Effects of Leadership
   Style upon Group Performance as a Function of Task
   Structure, Journal of Personality and Social
   Psychology, 3, 1966, pp.238-42.
Siegel, S., Non-parametric Statistics for the Behav-
   ioural Sciences, McGraw-Hill, New York 1956.
Silverman, D., Formal Organisations or Industrial
   Sociology, Sociology, vol.2, 1968, pp.221-38.
Simon, H.A., The New Science of Management Decision,
   in L.A. Welsch and R.M. Cyert (eds), Management
   Decision-Making, pp.13-29, Penguin, London 1970.
Slater, P. and Bennis, W., Democracy is Inevitable,
   Harvard Business Review, vol.42, no.2, 1964,
   pp.51-9.
Smith, P.B., Groups within Organisations, Harper and
   Row, London 1973.
Solomons, D. and Berridge, T.M., Prospectus for a
   Profession, The Report of the Long Range Enquiry
   into Education and Training for the Accountancy
   Profession, Advisory Board of Accountancy Education,
   1974.
Speak, B.M., Communication Failure in Questioning:
   Errors, Misinterpretations and Personal Frames of
   Reference, Occupational Psychology, vol.41, no.4,
   1967, pp.169-79.

296

Stanton, F., Notes on the Validity of Mail Questionnaire Returns, _Journal of Applied Psychology_, 23,
1939, pp.95-104.

Stedry, A.C. and Kay, E., The Effects of Goal
Difficulty on Performance: A Field Experiment,
Behavioural Science, 11, 1966, pp.459-70.

Steiner, I.D. and Johnson, H.H., Authoritarianism and
Conformity, _Sociometry_, 26, 1963, pp.21-34.

Stinson, J.E. and Tracy, L., Some Disturbing Characteristics of the LPC Score, _Personnel Psychology_,
vol.27, no.3, 1974, pp.477-86.

Stogdill, R.M., Personal Factors associated with
Leadership: A Review of the Literature, _Journal of
Psychology_, 25, 1948, pp.35-71

Stogdill, R.M. and Shartle, C.L., Methods for determining Patterns of Leadership Behaviour in Relation
to Organisation Structure and Objectives, _Journal
of Applied Psychology_, vol.32, no.3, 1948,
pp.286-91.

Stone, L.A. and James, R.L., Interval Scaling of the
Prestige of Selected Secondary Education Teacher
Specialities, _Perceptual and Motor Skills_, 20,
1965, pp.859-60.

Strauss, G., Some Notes on Power Equalisation, in
H. Leavitt (ed.), _The Social Science of Organisa-
tions_, Prentice-Hall, New York 1963.

Strauss, G., Human Relations - 1968 Style, _Industrial
Relations_, vol.7, no.3, 1968, pp.262-76.

Super, D.E., A Theory of Vocational Development,
American Psychologist, 8, 1953, pp.185-90.

Talacchi, S., Organisation Size, Individual Attitudes
and Behaviour: an empirical study, _Administrative
Science Quarterly_, vol.5, no.3, 1960, pp.398-420.

Tannenbaum, A.S., Control in Organisations: Individual
Adjustment and Organisational Performance, _Adminis-
trative Science Quarterly_, vol.7, no.2, 1962,
pp.236-57.

Tannenbaum, A.S. and Allport, F.H., Personality Structure and Group Structure: An Interpretative Study of
their relationship through an Event-structure Hypothesis, _Journal of Abnormal and Social Psychology_,
vol.53, no.3, 1956, pp.272-80.

Tannenbaum, R. and Massarik, F., Participation by
Subordinates in the Managerial Decision-making
Process, in R.A. Sutermeister (ed.), People and
Productivity, McGraw-Hill, New York 1963.

Tannenbaum, R. and Schmidt, W.H., How to Choose a
Leadership Pattern, Harvard Business Review, vol.36,
no.2, 1958, pp.95-101.

Taylor, J., How Geller Convinced Me, Observer Magazine, 6 April 1975, pp.21-8.

Teulings, A., Project Pentagon: Staff-Line Relations
in Large Organisations - Part I, Management Decision,
vol.9, no.2, 1971(a), pp.168-78.

Teulings, A., Project Pentagon: Staff-Line Relations
in Complex Organisations - Part II, Management
Decision, vol.9, no.3, 1971(b), pp.275-85.

Thompson, V.A., Hierarchy, Specialisation and Organisational Conflict, Administrative Science Quarterly,
vol.5, no.4, 1961, pp.485-521.

Thompson, V.A., Bureaucracy and Innovation, Administrative Science Quarterly, 10, 1965, pp.1-20.

Time Magazine, Where are the Leaders? (Special Section), 15 July 1974, pp.23-53.

Tosi, H., A re-examination of Personality as a
Determinant of the Effects of Participation,
Personnel Psychology, 23, 1970, pp.91-9.

Tricker, L., The Accountant in Management, Batsford,
London 1967.

Trueblood, R.M., Education for a Changing Profession,
Journal of Accounting Research, vol.1, Spring 1963,
pp.86-94.

Uris, A., How Good a Leader are You? in R.A. Sutermeister (ed.), People and Productivity, McGraw-Hill,
New York 1963.

Urwick, L., Executive Decentralisation with Functional
Co-ordination, The Management Review, December 1935,
pp.355-68.

Vatter, W.J., Education and Professional Training in
E.S. Lynn (ed.), The Journal of Accountancy,
January 1964, pp.88-91.

Vincent, C.E., Socio-economic Status and Familial
Variables in Mail Questionnaire Responses, American
Journal of Sociology, 69, 1964, pp.647-53.

Vroom, V.H., Some Personality Determinants of the
Effect of Participation, Prentice-Hall, Englewood
Cliffs 1960.

Vroom, V.H., Can Leaders Learn to Lead? Organizational
Dynamics, vol.4, no.3, 1976, pp.17-28.

Vroom, V.H., Grant, L.D. and Cotton, T.S., The Consequences of Social Interaction in Group Problem
Solving, Organisational Behaviour and Human Performance, 4, 1969, pp.77-95.

Wallace, D., A Case for and against Mail Questionnaires, Public Opinion Quarterly, 18, 1954,
pp.40-52.

Wallace, M.E., Behavioural Considerations in Budgeting, Management Accounting (USA), 47, 1966, pp.3-8.

Walter, B., Internal Control Relations in Administrative Hierarchies, Administrative Science Quarterly,
vol.II, 1966, pp.179-206.

Warner, M., Whither Yugoslav Self-management, Industrial Relations Journal, 6, Part I, 1975, pp.65-72.

Watson, J.J., Improving the Response Rate in Mail
Research, Journal of Advertising Research, 5, 1965,
pp.45-50.

Wax, R.H., Reciprocity as a Field Technique, Human
Organisation, XI, 1952, pp.34-7.

Weber, M., Essays in Sociology, H.H. Gerth and C.W.
Mills (eds), Oxford University Press, New York
1946.

Weed, S.E., Mitchell, T.R. and Moffitt, W., Leadership
Style, Subordinate Personality and Task Type as
Predictors of Performance and Satisfaction with
Supervision, Journal of Applied Psychology, 61,
1976, pp.58-66.

Weissenberg, P., Introduction to Organisational
Behaviour, Intext, Pennsylvania 1971.

Weissenberg, P. and Gruenfeld, L., Relationships among
Leadership Dimensions and Cognitive Style, Journal
of Applied Psychology, vol.50, no.5, 1966,
pp.392-5.

Weissenberg, P. and Kavanagh, M.J., The Independence
of Initiating Structure and Consideration: A review
of the evidence, Personnel Psychology, 25, 1972,
pp.119-30.

Weschler, I., Kahane, M. and Tannenbaum, R., Assessing
Organisation Effectiveness, Leadership and Organisa-
tion, McGraw-Hill, New York 1952.
Weston, J., The Finance Function, Journal of Finance,
vol.9, September 1954, pp.265-82.
Whyte, W.F., Incentives for Productivity: The Bundy
Tubing Company Case, Applied Anthropology, 7, 1948,
pp.1-16.
Whyte, W.F., Toward an Integrated Approach for Re-
search in Organisational Behaviour, in P. Weissen-
berg (ed.), Introduction to Organisational Behaviour,
Intext, Pennsylvania 1971.
Wilson, C., Management Services. The Way Ahead,
Management Accounting, 46, 1965, pp.274-8.
Wispe, L.G. and Lloyd, K.E., Some Situational and
Psychological Determinants of the Desire for
Structured Interpersonal Relations, Journal of
Abnormal and Social Psychology, 51, 1955, pp.57-60.
Wofford, J.C., Managerial Behaviour, Situational
Factors and Productivity and Morale, Administrative
Science Quarterly, vol.16, no.1, 1971, pp.10-17.
Woodward, J., Industrial Organisation - Theory and
Practice, Oxford University Press, London 1965.
Woodward, J., Industrial Organisation - Behaviour and
Control, Oxford University Press, London 1970.
Worthy, J.C., Organisational Structure and Employee
Morale, American Sociological Review, 15, 1950,
pp.169-79.
Young, D.M., Tailoring Information Systems to Managers'
Decision-making, Accountancy, vol.83, no.954, Feb-
ruary 1973, pp.18-23.
Younger, W.F., Heart and Head must Work Together, The
Times, 2 December 1974, p.18.
Yukl, G., Toward a Behavioural Theory of Leadership,
Organisational Behaviour and Human Performance, 6,
1971, pp.414-40.
Yunker, G.W. and Hunt, J.G., An Empirical Comparison
of the Michigan Four-Factor and the Ohio State
LBDQ Leadership Scales, Organisational Behaviour
and Human Performance, 17, 1976, pp.45-65.

Index

Power centralisation and complexity, 95
Productivity criterion, 117-18
Pugh, D.S. et al. 2, 72, 76, 90, 95, 220

Questionnaire, advantages and limitations of 102-3; anonymity of respondents 110-11; contents of 112-17, 109, 241-56; despatch of 120; reminder letter 275

Research, findings 234-7; future 238-9; hypotheses 140-2, 197, 198, 201, 202, 203, 206, 208, 210, 211, 213, 217, 218, 219, 221, 223, 224-26; interview 104-5, 130-31, pilot survey 107-8; practical implications 237-8; methods 101-6; reasons for 1; response 121-9; sample 119-20; sample characteristics 257-61; sponsorship 109; statistical analysis 132-39
Rhode, J.G. et al. 11
Rice, R.W. and Chemers, M.N. 57
Ritchie, J.B. and Miles, R.E. 2, 39, 208
Robson, A.P. 89, 218
Roeher, G.A. 111
Rogers, C.R. 44
Rosen, N. 80, 111
Rubin, I.M. and Goldman, M. 55

Sales, S.M. 26, 32, 38
Sample, J.A. and Wilson, T.R. 54, 212
Santocki, J. 128
Schiff, M. and Lewin, A.Y. 41
Scott, C. 109, 110, 112, 121
Scott, W.R. 8
Selznick, P. 71
Shaw, M.E. 37
Shaw, M.E. and Blum, J.M. 3, 204
Siegel, S. 138
Silverman, D. 72
Simon, H.A. 65
Situational perspective, advantages of 228; justification for 230-33
Size, 81-2; and morale 83; and skill discrepancy 187
Slater, P. and Bennis, W. 31
Smith, P.B. 53, 56
Solomons, D. and Berridge, T.M. 6
Span of control 90; optimum size 91-2
Speak, B.M. 102
Staff/line 84; friction 85
Stanton, F. 109
Stedry, A.C. and Kay, E. 40
Steiner, I.D. and Johnson, H.H. 25
Stinson, J.E. and Tracy, L. 56, 212
Stogdill, R.M. 20, 21
Stogdill, R.M. and Shartle, C.L. 97

Stone, L.A. and James, R.L. 139
Strauss, G. 44, 60, 93, 199
Super, D.E. 7

Talacchi, S. 81, 220
Tannenbaum, A.S. 24, 25
Tannenbaum, A.S. and Allport, F.H. 78
Tannenbaum, R. and Massarik, F. 27, 47
Tannenbaum, R. and Schmidt, W.H. 23, 25, 26, 61, 230
Taylor, J. 63
Teulings, A. 58, 86, 87, 219
Thompson, V.A. 23, 27, 50, 78, 85, 93, 96, 217
Time Magazine 20
Tosi, H. 25
Tricker, I. 6, 9, 13, 89, 218
Trueblood, R.M. 4

Uris, A. 23, 47, 208
Urwick, L. 73, 90, 213

Vatter, W.J. 4
Vincent, C.E. 129
Vroom, V.H. 1, 24, 61
Vroom, V.H. et al. 41

Wallace, D. 129
Wallace, M.E. 40, 88
Walter, B. 59, 68, 106, 200
Warner, M. 46
Watson, J.J. 121
Wax, R.H. 131
Weber, M. 70

Weed, S.E. et al. 208
Weissenberg, P. 19
Weissenberg, P. and Gruenfeld, L. 51, 212
Weissenberg, P. and Kavanagh, M.J. 30, 98, 209, 224
Weschler, T. et al. 34
Weston, J. 12, 114
Whyte, W.F. 36, 94, 104
Wilson, C. 9
Wispe, L.G. and Lloyd, K.E. 24, 25, 49
Wofford, J.C. 58, 94, 99, 221
Woodward, J. 2, 74, 76, 85, 90, 97, 119, 213, 218
Worthy, J.C. 81, 92, 94, 204, 215, 220

Young, D.M. 89, 218
Younger, W.H. 20
Yukl, G. 2, 21, 42, 47, 49, 61, 207, 209
Yunger, G.W. and Hunt, J.G. 29